8 ℉

policy analysis and education series

DALE MANN, GENERAL EDITOR

OTHER TITLES IN THE POLICY ANALYSIS AND EDUCATION SERIES

Policy Decision Making in Education
An Introduction to Calculation and Control
Dale Mann

Impact and Response
Federal Aid and State Education Agencies
Mike M. Milstein

Delivering Educational Service
Urban Schools and Schooling Policy
David Goodwin

IMPLEMENTATION, CHANGE, and the FEDERAL BUREAUCRACY

SCHOOL DESEGREGATION POLICY in H.E.W., 1964-1968

BERYL A. RADIN

TEACHERS COLLEGE PRESS
Teachers College, Columbia University
New York and London

Copyright © 1977 by Teachers College, Columbia University
Library of Congress Catalog Card Number: 76-58320

Library of Congress Cataloging in Publication Data:

Radin, Beryl.
    Implementation, change, and the Federal
bureaucracy.

    (Policy analysis and education series)
    Based on the author's thesis, University of
California, Berkeley, 1973, issued under title:
Implementing change in the Federal bureaucracy.
    Bibliography: p.
    1. Segregation in education—Law and legislation
—United States. 2. United States. Dept. of
Health, Education, and Welfare. I. Title. II. Se-
ries.
KF4155.R29   344'.73'0798   76-58320

ISBN 0-8077-2522-6

Manufactured in the United States of America
Designed by **Angela Foote**

GENERAL EDITOR'S FOREWORD

The study of public policy is an audacious business. Our most compelling policy concerns are likely to be extremely complex, ambiguous, and intractable. Understanding the process of their resolution commits an analyst to a process that shares many of the characteristics of the subject being studied. In school desegregation policy, for example, any sensible observor would expect to find the multiple inputs of agencies, bureaus, departments, interest groups, legislators, clients, constituents, and so on. Actually, naming each of those actor groups is a case of misplaced concreteness, since virtually every group itself comprises actions, cliques, and fiefs. Although all the groups may be nominally concerned with the same policy—or at least with an area for potential government action that has a similar label—they will disagree on the gravity of the problem and especially on the means and the effects of its redress. "Policy" is what gets squeezed out of all those interactions, over time, and across a number of arenas.

Those difficulties are compounded when the topic for analysis is race *and* education. Professor Radin's book does an admirable job of clarifying the struggles around recent attempts by the Office of Education and by the Department of Health, Education, and Welfare to deal with Federal responsibilities for local school desegregation. Should, for example, the Federal government have withheld funds intended to improve the learning opportunities of poor children until districts complied with the desegregation guidelines—both are aimed at improving the learning opportunities of poor children. Or should the priorities between curricular improvement and desegregation have been reversed? Which might have contributed the most, the quickest? Efforts that at the Federal level may have required attention to abstractions like organizational structure and process on the local level are translated into busing, into boundaries for school attendance, into questions of tracking, discipline, and the employment of adults. One of the strengths of this book is Radin's ability to identify the policy significance in such mundane matters as organizational responsibility. Why should we care that one part of HEW's alphabet soup has responsibility for school desegregation but not another? Radin's analysis demonstrates that, as responsibility for school compliance matters shifted up the bureaucratic chain of command, it became much more difficult for districts to get consideration for educational, not legal, ramifications. And as responsibility moved up the hierarchy, everyone's compliance efforts became more visible and more vulnerable to political influence.

Astronomers and quantum physicists both use lenses in their science, but it makes a big difference which lens is used for which purposes. Implementing desegregation has been (continues to be) administrative politics, judicial politics, bureaucratic politics, and presidential politics. Radin's analysis moves among those varied worlds and applies a variety of concepts to those topics. Structural, legal, and constituency/clientele concerns are used in the analysis. And, in a departure from most policy analysis, Radin treats the officials whose conduct she is studying, not as anonymous *personae*, but with full identification of who did what to whom, when, why, and with what consequences. Some of the officials discussed in this book knew education but not schooling, others knew administration but not politics, others politics but not schooling, others law but not politics. Some treated desegregation as a crusade, others saw it as a process of mechanical enforcement, mechanically applied. It all made a difference for what happened—at every level from the kids all the way up to the President.

Race and schooling are two of this country's enduring problems. And decentralization, or the attempt to move government closer to the people, is an enduring solution. On all three grounds, this is a relevant and useful analysis for anyone who would understand federal policy implementation or for anyone who would like to improve federal policy implementation. The last of this book's virtues is that, after describing what was done, and after commenting on it critically, Professor Radin accepts the policy analyst's responsibility to set out some improvements for a situation that remains a concern for all of us.

Dale Mann

New York, New York
January 1977

PREFACE

Every study is autobiographical to some degree or another. Often the autobiographical elements are obvious—as when one writes about an experience in which direct and public participation provided the "stuff" of the study. Other works reflect concerns that are less public and more personal, exposing value commitments and posing questions framed in response to a private pursuit of truth, knowledge, or right. The pages that follow have both public and private elements to them.

The substance of this study of attempts to implement change in the federal bureaucracy is set in the Office of Education (OE) within the U. S. Department of Health, Education, and Welfare (HEW) and in the Office for Civil Rights (OCR) in the Office of the Secretary of HEW. I was not working in either place during the period under study (nor at any time, for that matter). During the early part of the period studied, as a staff member of the U.S. Commission on Civil Rights, I was involved with the general civil rights area and concerned about attempts to implement Title VI in HEW—particularly in education. I had come to the Civil Rights Commission after spending several years involved with activist civil rights projects in CORE while earning a living by working for a trade union.

    This study has roots in conscious recollection of personal experiences
and in the questions raised as a result of these experiences. In the spring
of 1965, during the Civil Rights Commission regional meeting on Title VI
in Atlanta, I remember attending a small session in which Washington
HEW officials were attempting to explain civil rights policies to HEW
regional staff members. At the time, I was hardly sympathetic to these
regional staff members; I tended to be intolerant of Southern officials who
found reasons and ways to question or minimize their responsibilities to
implement the law. My memory of that meeting is very clear. I can still
see the Office of Education Regional Representative from the Office of the
Commissioner—an old man, speaking with a thick, Southern accent—
questioning a fast-talking Northerner, David Seeley, director of the OE
civil rights operation. During these conversations, it seemed clear to me
that the regional official was not very sympathetic to the civil rights issue.
At the same time, I was concerned when the regional staff member told
Seeley that he had been asked for information about school desegregation
requirements by both state and local education people and was unable to
answer their requests because he had not received any information about
these requirements from Washington. It seemed to me that the regional
official was asking a valid question—and one that did not receive a satisfactory answer. The memory of that exchange really led me to explore the
questions of organization structure found in Part II of this study.

    Part III—the analysis of the role of the law in the enforcement
attempts—was based on a more prolonged personal experience. During
my tenure at the Civil Rights Commission, I was continually conscious of
the federal government's dependence on attorneys, especially the
bureaucracy's deference to lawyers in the civil rights area. I recognize
that at least a part of my own criticisms of lawyers was in reaction to the
fact that lawyers ran the Civil Rights Commission; I probably would have
been as critical of anyone in those authority positions. But beyond the
Commission, I remember debates on political questions that were
answered in legal terms by members of HEW's Office of General Counsel
or by staff within the Justice Department. In Part III I have attempted
both to evaluate my first perception of the problem as one of lawyers *qua*
lawyers, and to concentrate on the problems that were raised as a result of
the choices made within the repertoire of legal possibilities.

    Part IV of the study—the analysis of the constituency—reflects a
series of personal contacts and concerns. Some of these concerns were
developed during the period I was at the Commission, some before then,
and some after that time. Although I had no affiliation with CORE once I
came to the Civil Rights Commission, I continued to identify with the

civil rights activists; I found the Leadership Conference on Civil Rights less than sympathetic to concerns I felt strongly about. At the same time, I had a number of friends who were active in the Leadership Conference, especially in trade union representation roles. On the agency side, I was directly involved with the Civil Rights Commission's outreach activities and thus in a position personally to see the failure of OE and HEW staff to develop sustained contacts with potential constituent groups.

These past experiences formed particular areas of concern within this study of the implementation of school desegregation policies in HEW. The subsequent research, done in 1971-72, provided me with information that mandated a quite different analysis from what I could have made in 1966 or 1967, however. My purpose in undertaking this study has been to probe my own dissatisfaction with the answers that I (and others) gave to questions raised by the experience of agencies with Title VI.

Extensive document searches in OE and HEW files deposited in the National Record Center provided information that conflicted with my earlier opinions. I interviewed people in the middle reaches of the implementation policy, especially program staff and people outside the government affected by the civil rights policies. My most fruitful interviews were often with civil rights staff members whom I had not known well before the conversation. "Old friends" tended to assume that I knew more than I actually did, to fall back into old explanations and gripes we had shared, and sometimes to be less than candid for personal reasons.

But my past experiences and contacts gave me entrée to individuals who otherwise might have been reluctant to spend time with me. In most cases, people were very willing to talk, and some often-interviewed individuals were relieved that new kinds of questions were being asked of them.

I constantly battled with myself to keep from telling the old stories in the old familiar ways. I knew that if this study of Title VI implementation should fall into old traps, the lessons to be learned from its analysis would not be very useful. Some of the familiar explanations, however, could not be denied. But it seemed to me that, although one could acknowledge that some people are racists or that the federal/state relationship does constrain federal officials, another series of questions had to be asked that went beyond these pronouncements. I believed that the implementation strategy devised to carry the civil rights legislation to operation deserved more attention than it had been given. To me, the years between 1964 and 1968 represented an opportunity that was too easily lost.

By the time I began formal research on the project, administrative enforcement of school desegregation policy had effectively dissolved.

Administrators holding civil rights job titles continued to call for equal opportunity in education. The effective authority to make this occur was back, once again, in the federal court system, however. The administrative process had a minimal role in the quest. I did not understand how and why this had happened.

Although I knew the questions I wanted to ask, it was necessary for me to find new ways to ask them. Theory became the most useful tool in preventing my backsliding. New ideas brought to familiar facts allowed information to be organized in new ways. I used organization theory, the sociology of law, and the theory of constituency and interest groups to provoke new ideas—to provide a structure for my analysis of the familiar. At the same time, the theoretical literature allowed me to view the civil rights issue in broader categories of concern than I had allowed myself earlier. The civil rights issue is a special case in the American experience, but it is not totally unique. Other groups in the society have attempted to carve out a role for themselves and to cause a redistribution of power and resources held by others. Although the issues involved in the Title VI experience evoked a complicated set of concerns and reactions, it had policy links to other issues. Hopefully, this study will provide new light on the school desegregation issue and, at the same time, will offer insight into a general category of questions about the role of the federal bureaucracy in social change.

A Note on Implementation Studies

The study of implementation of the Economic Development Administration program in Oakland by Pressman and Wildavsky included a bibliographic comment on implementation studies in the social science literature. Although they used a relatively broad definition of implementation of government programs, Pressman and Wildavsky found few examples of significant analytic works dealing with implementation.

There are even fewer studies of the kind I have attempted in this volume. I must acknowledge that this study rests upon a set of assumptions about policy and implementation that are repellant, threatening, or simply ring "untrue" to some individuals concerned with public policy analysis. Thus I have attempted to make my assumptions about implementation as explicit as possible. I introduce this study with the following caveats:

1. I believe that implementation is·a complex process, involving multiple steps. The process begins when legislation leaves a legislative

body, continues when it is handed to top leaders of an administrative organization, permeates through an agency as it is translated into operating policies and procedures, and finally results in activities that might be characterized as the "output" of the implementation cycle.

I believe each step in this process is important and each is characterized by a distinct set of problems, opportunities, and constraints. I have chosen to concentrate this study on the stage at which a legislative mandate is translated into day-to-day administrative policies and procedures. Very little attention has been given to that stage in the sparse policy implementation literature. Although a study that concentrates on this stage in the process cannot resolve all possible questions about implementation, it can raise a series of valid and important issues.

2. The complexity and diversity within the multiple stages of the implementation process are mirrored by a complex cast of characters. Each stage within the process is dependent on a distinct set of actors. The transfer of a policy from Congress to an administrative agency involves the top officials within the agency—for example, the secretary of a department or the top program official. These individuals are frequently political appointees who must balance agency concerns with political survival.

The set of actors on whom I chose to concentrate were less frequently political appointees than they were professionals in the field—often career professionals within the civil service. These middle-level individuals have the technical competence and responsibility to formulate the substantive alternatives for the top decision-makers. The role of these individuals is rarely examined, although the influence they exert in these technical decisions is often of great import to the policy implementation process.

The significance I have ascribed to middle-level officials is a judgment that is not shared by all individuals in the world of policy analysis. Some critics of this weighting agree that middle-level officials do have the discretion to choose among policy alternatives but disagree that these choices are of consequence to the ultimate success or failure of the policy implementation. I find that it is misleading to ignore the influence of middle-level actors; without an understanding of their role and influence, it is frequently difficult to comprehend the process by which goals and objectives of legislation are displaced or modified and the product of the policy is rendered unrecognizable to the architects of the original legislation.

3. Significant policy alternatives are frequently cast in the language of technical administrative determinations. Development of guidelines

for program administration, allocations of resources and determination of budget needs, decisions about organizational structure, legal interpretations, and procedures for monitoring are among the day-to-day administrative decisions that shape the implementation policy. A specific decision to choose one or another policy alternative in any of these areas is not, *per se*, a constraint to the implementation of a policy.

Although one might argue that decisions in these areas are derivative of broader policy questions, frequently decisions cast in technical administrative terms are the only overt expressions of underlying value and ideological conflicts within an agency. Thus it is significant for the policy analyst to examine the specific decision process surrounding "purely" administrative determinations. Policy debate over these issues is both surrogate for and symbolic of larger policy conflict.

Acknowledgments

A number of friends gave me counsel, which I always heard, although I did not always heed it. I would like to thank Eugene Bardach, Robert Bennett, Robert Biller, Elaine Heffernan, Elizabeth Howe, Elliott Medrich, Francis Rourke, Donna Shalala, and Michael Teitz.

But most of all, I must be grateful to American citizens across the country who worry about children . . . and who do something about it.

Beryl A. Radin

Austin, Texas
January 1977

CONTENTS

III THE LAW

IV CONSTITUENCY

V CONCLUSIONS

An elephant belonging to a traveling exhibition had been stabled near a town where no elephant had been seen before. Four curious citizens, hearing of the hidden wonder, went to see if they could get a preview of it. When they arrived at the stable they found that there was no light. The investigation therefore had to be carried out in the dark.

One, touching its trunk, thought that the creature must resemble a hosepipe; the second felt an ear and concluded that it was a fan. The third, feeling a leg, could liken it only to a living pillar; and when the fourth put his hand on its back he was convinced that it was some kind of throne. None could form the complete picture; and of the part which each felt, he could only refer to it in terms of things which he already knew. The result of the expedition was confusion. Each was sure that he was right; none of the other townspeople could understand what had happened, what the investigators had actually experienced.

Indries Shah, *The Sufis* (New York: Anchor Books, 1971), pp. 40-41.

I
INTRODUCTION

1
.
THE POLICY SETTING

Education, Federalism, and Desegregation

For the past few decades, observers of the American policy world have been accustomed to characterizing the system of U.S. federalism as a marble-cake arrangement. When Morton Grodzins shifted the imagery from a layer cake to a marbled version, analysts were comfortable with the picture of asymmetrical relationships that the changed image provoked. Although the roles assumed by the cast of characters were more or less active or passive, depending on the particular policy area, the assumption underlying the marble-cake characterization was one of stability. Divisions of power and functions were "baked" in; the relationships among the federal, state, and local goverments were relatively predictable.

Up to the 1960's, American education policy was accurately characterized as a complex but relatively stable policy system. Relationships had been carved out and policies implicit in the few federal education efforts were respectful of them. The ideology of local control of education was protected by state agencies. As such, it was expected that funds and programs would be filtered through the state before traveling to a local system.

By the mid-1960's, however, program expectations were changing. The federal government, responsive to a plethora of criticisms about American eduction, was attempting to assume a more active role, either playing the part of a "change agent" or underwriting others to play that role. That new role—most dramatically illustrated in the Elementary and Secondary Education Act of 1965 (ESEA)—meant that federal policy would affect school financing, curriculum, classification of students and teachers, and placement of both students and teachers in classrooms. Although justifications for the new policies were varied, all assumed that the federal role required national standards aimed at changing the balance of power in education decision-making. If implemented, Washington decisions would create new situations for state and local education authorities as well as for teachers, students, and parents. New organizational relationships and structures were needed to institutionalize federal policy expectations. Marble-cake federalism, as defined by past education policy actors, gave few answers to the new questions. New paradigms were needed to set the framework in which the emergent relationships could be conceptualized.

School Desegregation and Civil Rights Policies

Few federal policy efforts illustrate the difficulties involved in reaching for new relationships as well as those involving school desegregation. Not only did the efforts to implement this policy confront all the changing relationships shifting in the education policy sphere, but the efforts also brought along the pulsations and pressures of another policy system: namely, civil rights policy. Up to the point of enactment of the Civil Rights Act of 1964, civil rights policy was viewed as a strictly federal matter; as such, it violated the spirit of traditional federalism. Civil rights activists, as well as critics of the educational establishment, tended to view states and localities as a part of the problem. "States rights" arguments were frequently used by those opposed to the establishment of equal rights for all citizens, regardless of race. Decisions by the federal courts in the 1950's and 1960's interpreting the Fourteenth Amendment struck hard at "state action" that inhibited opportunities for American blacks.

When the debate on the civil rights issue extended to the legislative and executive branches of government, it was assumed that action for change would come from the federal level. The volatile, highly emotional debate on civil rights legislation followed a series of upheavals in the American political and social climate; when the Civil Rights Act emerged from Congress in July 1964, it received the support of a Southern president and a bi-partisan legislative branch. Passage of that Act, combined with the action of the U.S. Supreme Court, meant that all three branches of the American federal govenment affirmed a commitment to change patterns of discimination.

The civil rights measure originally sent to Congress in the 1960's reflected a hodge-podge of concerns, many of which had been discussed in Washington liberal circles since the 1957 civil rights legislation had been enacted. That 1957 legislation was a disappointment to advocates of federal activity to assure equal opportunity; Lyndon Johnson, then majority leader of the Senate, orchestrated one of his famous legislative maneauvers to assure that the bill that passed provided no real possibility for federal intervention to assure equal treatment to all regardless of color. The 1957 Civil Rights Act established a Civil Rights Division within the Department of Justice and created an independent Civil Rights Commission to serve a fact-finding role. The Commission had no enforcement authority, and the Justice Department division had very limited jurisdiction over voting and school issues.

By 1964, however, Lyndon Johnson was in a different office and wanted to prove that he no longer spoke as the representative of a Southwestern constituency and was, rather, the president of *all* Americans. The civil rights bill supported by Johnson had been developed by the Kennedy administration as the basis for legislative bargaining—as is often the case, the White House asked for more than it thought it would get from Congress. With the assasination of Kennedy and Johnson's move to the White House, the bill was taken seriously and pushed through Congress with extraordinary skill and fortitude. That legislation was important to Johnson in its symbolic proportions; it showed the nation that the President embraced the goal of equal opportunity and did not accept the back-door treatment of American black citizens. In its broadest proportions, the enactment of the 1964 Civil Rights Act carried the inevitability of change. The unified voice of the federal government defined a sweeping goal. But the path to achieve that goal was mainly uncharted. Congress completed its work of legislative policy formulation and handed the law to the administration for an implementation stage. That stage was filled with unanswered, partially answered, or unasked questions.

The uncertainty that accompanied the implementation of the civil rights policies was not atypical of the period.[1] The troops of the New

Frontier tended to ignore the procedures by which policies are translated into programs. John Kennedy knew how to organize ward politicians, party leaders, and the paraphernalia of electoral politics to get himself into the White House. But once there, it was no accident that he mused about Thomas Jefferson as he invited the best brains of the nation to dinner. John Kennedy had little interest in the procedures by which policy ideas are implemented in a bureaucracy that seems irrational to those outside of it nor in the methods by which proposed legislation may be accepted by a skeptical Congress.

But the Kennedy bright young men were somewhat shorter on political acumen in dealings with Congress than on intellect. It took the tragedy of an assassin's bullet in Dallas to give the Kennedy legislative legacy a realistic political cast—a Lyndon Johnson approach that made the promise to "get America moving again" come alive in the halls of Congress.

The 1964 Civil Rights Act

The 1964 Civil Rights Act was an attempt to franchise citizens who previously had been excluded from full participation within the American society. Some of the franchising moves were aimed at changing social opportunities for black citizens:[2] the right to be treated equally in places of public accommodation and to expect the federal government to intervene legally to assist in the attainment of equal treatment. Still other parts of the Act created new governmental structures or new authority for the federal government to take responsibility for aspects of the civil rights issue. The legislation established a federal Equal Employment Opportunity Commission, patterned after state and local fair employment agencies, as well as the Community Relations Service, a group to provide assistance to persons or communities experiencing civil rights problems. The U.S. Commission on Civil Rights was given broader authority to continue as the gadfly of the executive branch, and the U.S. Office of Education was authorized to provide technical assistance to desegregating schools.

But the section of the 1964 Civil Rights Act that potentially had the most sweeping effect was Title VI—a general prohibition against discrimination in grants, loans, or contracts by all federal agencies. This mandate to eliminate discimination in programs supported by the federal dollar was not limited to activities directly administered by the federal government. Theoretically, at least, the prohibition permeated throughout American society, extending to state and local public programs receiving federal support and to private activities (such as projects in private colleges and universities) that received federal monies for specific programs. The inclusion of Title VI in the 1964 legislation represented an acknowledgment by the Congress that black Americans were systematically excluded from the benefits of the federal tax dollar. The dollar figure was enormous; in 1960, states and localities received 14% of their income from federal grants-in-aid—some $7 billion. The figure was significantly larger in 1964.

Since 1964, most agencies of the federal government have given little more than rhetorical attention to the goal of nondiscrimination stated in Title VI.[3] But in the Department of Health, Education, and Welfare— and especially in the education activities of the Department—serious attempts were made to condition the federal dollar on nondiscrimination requirements.

These serious efforts were made after the enactment of ESEA—the first massive federal outlay of dollars to local school systems. Within that program, aid under Title I (funds to provide assistance to local educational agencies for the education of children of low income families) was substantial. Funds were allocated to states to distribute to school districts on the basis of the number of children from families with incomes under $2,000 per year times 50% of each state's average expenditure per school child. Because race and low income are often related, the Title I formula for distribution of funds provided states with high black populations with a large potential source of funds. Southern states received sizeable amounts of money through Title I. In fiscal 1967, for example, Title I allocations accounted for about half of the federal expenditure in states like South Carolina and Georgia.[4]

The "Right" of School Desegregation

Through Title VI of the Civil Rights Act, beneficiaries of educational programs supported by the federal government had the *right* to expect that federal programs and programs subsidized by federal monies would be administered in a nondiscriminatory fashion. But defining that right was another matter. In the context of Title VI, that right was the right to *desegregation.* But that use simply begged the question: what is a desegregated school system? The range of definitions is broad and often confusing.

According to one definition, a desegregated school district is one in which children are no longer attending schools segregated by law. The elimination of dual school systems, in this view, results in the end of segregation—hence *de*segregation. Although schools may be segregated in this definition because of zoning lines or residential patterns that feed all-one-color schools, the total system is legally desegregated.

A second definition looks beyond the elimination of dual systems to schools in which children of both races are found in attendance. The statistics drawn from this definition describe total school enrollment; they do not describe the racial composition of specific classrooms. Thus a school that is racially mixed may be racially segregated in its classrooms as a result of tracking or other grouping methods.

A third view of desegregation concerns itself with affective issues that are difficult to describe with numbers—that is, *affective* desegregation. In this view, desegration is found if all children within the system, the school, or the classroom receive the same treatment and hence have an equal opportunity to learn to their individual potentials. But desegregation is not possible when teachers have unconscious expectations that black children will not perform and cannot learn. Desegregation is not possible if black teachers are fired or not hired for a variety of reasons that have subtle racial implications, resulting in all or mostly white faculties. And desegregation is not possible when discipline codes are promulgated that have the effect of inhibiting the expression of legitimate issues by black students. In short, desegregation is not possible in the presence of racism. There are boundless examples of methods by which a system blocks the ability of black children to learn in a classroom.

One might add a fourth definition of desegregation: a situation in which black and white children have exactly equal achievement levels. This definition, however, never had national policy ramifications, although the presence of a skewed distribution of achievement by race is a common signal that problems related to race are in existence.

But *right* could also be defined independently of the *desegregation* question. It could also mean a change in procedures for allocating federal monies in education—change in federal procedures and, as well, change in the allocation of funds within local communities and procedures by which states divide the money among school districts. It is extremely difficult, however, for anyone to know when such a change has occurred or how to measure it. Although changes in the racial composition of students in a system might be an indication that new inputs are involved in the decision-making process, these changes may be merely token indicators. They do not guarantee that steps have been taken toward equal access to the education decision-making system. For example, numbers describing the racial composition of classrooms and schools have been promulgated with a double-edged set of expectations. They are considered meritorious on their own terms (as indicators of some sort of desegregation) and, at the same time, are expected to stand as fuzzy, symbolic indicators of change in procedures in state or local decision-making.

Even if educators, administrators, politicians, parents, and students within a school system could agree on a single strategy to achieve more equity in the distribution of educational services in that system, this strategy could not be reduced to a formula that would fit conditions across the country. Many of the questions that surround local debates about desegregation and the question of rights take on special meaning in a specialized local context. To bus or not to bus, to track or not to track, to impose discipline codes or not—all these are questions that must be hammered out in discussions based on local realities, responsive to local needs and demands. As long as blacks (or other minorities) are kept out of the decision-making process, however, almost any policy adopted by a school system will be tainted by racism and will inhibit affective desegregation.

School Desegregation: How to Measure It?

For these and other reasons, performance criteria have been in dispute since the efforts at school desegregation began. Part of the dispute stems from the inability of educators, administrators, politicians, parents, and students to agree on the causative factors that allow children to learn and, beyond that, on the role of education in the broader society.

For the past decade, the debate in educational circles has been hot and heavy over the extent to which education makes any difference in achieving socioeconomic mobility and, if it makes any difference at all, the implications for the organizational forms of a school system. But although some factors are disputed,[5] the problem does have certain agreed-upon descriptive components: educational performance is correlated with the socioeconomic status of a student and the community in which a student lives. For a variety of reasons that seem to have little to do with the attributes of schools as presently constituted, middle-class students of any race do perform more successfully on standardized tests than do poor students.

Serious reservations have been voiced about the use of performance criteria by both opponents and supporters of school desegregation and civil rights policies. Simple numerical accounts of the racial composition of classrooms and faculties have been used as indicators of success or failure. Although superficially straightforward, these statistics cannot solve the evaluation problem. The variation in definitions of desegregation makes comparative evaluation of success based on numbers difficult.

Much of the dispute is simply a question of whether a half glass of water is viewed as half-empty or half-full.

Since the federal government began desegregation efforts, it has released statistics that describe an end to hundreds of separate-but-equal school systems in the Southern and border states. Although the specific figures are usually contested, there is little disagreement with a general statement that more black children are attending school in Southern desegregated school districts than was true when the Civil Rights Act of 1964 was passed. Up through 1962-1963, less than 1% of black students in the eleven old Confederate states attended school with white students. By the school year 1965-1966, the figure was up to 6.01%.[6] Although the U.S. Commission on Civil Rights, the Southern Education Reporting Service, and the Southern Regional Council could agree that some progress had been made, these groups were more likely to concentrate on the high percentage of students who continued to attend all-black schools.

But the dispute was less often over the number of children attending desegregated schools than over the number of school districts in compliance with formal nondiscrimination federal requirements. The argument over the "numbers game," as it was called, came to a peak in 1969, when the U.S. Commission on Civil Rights frontally attacked the statement of the Attorney General and the Secretary of Health, Education, and Welfare "that there is 'a steadily shrinking core of resistance' to school desegregation, and that 'most Southern and border school districts. . . have come into voluntary compliance'."[7] According to the Commission, these statistics presented "an overly optimistic, misleading and inaccurate picture of the scope of desegregation actually achieved."[8] Yet another attack on the statistical reports by HEW on compliance was waged in 1970 through a case filed by the NAACP Legal Defense Fund, challenging HEW's administrative enforcement of school desegregation in the South and alleging a "calculated default" in the implementation of Title VI.[9]

It is probably no accident that non-governmental interest groups made public and full-blown attacks on school desegregation efforts by HEW after the Nixon administration took office. Although a good case might be made that the transfer of partisan political power did change the thrust of the implementation efforts, it was easier for individuals and organizations with ties of support to Johnson and the Democratic party to wait to criticize until the administration changed hands. To judge by the public criticisms, the problems given partisan interpretations after 1969 were created by the transfer of power from a Democratic administration to a Republican one.

But the question remains: was "default" a new turn in policy implementation in 1969 or was it the logical outcome of policies (and problems) that had been in existence from 1965? Although this study does not argue that the 1969 decisions were "inevitable," it does focus on the points of implementation of Title VI in school desegregation that appear to be precedent setting and decision limiting. These involved attempts to define the relationship between the Title VI policy as an education issue and as a civil rights matter and, flowing from that, the administrative decisions that were appropriate to the dual definition.

The Study as an Implementation Problem

The coincidence of time between efforts to implement desegregation policy and efforts at major education policy change created a situation of uncertainty and chaos in HEW that might best be described as a maze. The story of the implementaton efforts involving Title VI cannot be told separately from that of other efforts at federal education activity. As such, the story is a difficult tale to unravel. As in most political battles, the opposition to school desegregation was waged on a number of fronts. That opposition often seemed to be symbolic opposition, arguing less about the specifics of the case in point and more about the idea of the conversation itself (or the changes that the new relationship would require). Opposition sometimes focused on substantive components of an issue but appeared to be concerned over procedural matters—increasingly so as time went on. That is, the debate focused on the specific details of the policy but the controversy was equally (or essentially) concerned about the process of change involved in carrying out the policy. It was not always clear what opponents perceived to be the underlying problem: school desegregation as a racial issue or the general fear of federal "intrusion."

During the period between 1964 and 1968, relationships in the educational system as well as in the civil rights world were in flux. It was difficult for anyone to make predictions with much confidence when the fabric of political, social, and economic relationships appeared to be shifting rapidly. Some have argued that the story of the Title VI implementation in education may eventually be told simply as a footnote illustrating the decline of power of Lyndon Johnson and the "old politics" in the age of the VietNam war. This argument focuses on the underlying theme of the erosion of presidential authority and the will to take action within the bureaucracy.

The interrelatedness of the civil rights issue and the more general questions of federal education policy meant that a policy decision in one or the other area always affected the other policy sphere. If civil rights requirements were enforced, federal funds would flow much more slowly, if at all, into many school districts and through state education agencies. Conversely, efficient and rapid distribution of federal education monies would make enforcing the nondiscrimination requirements much more difficult. On the one hand, the government would have to sacrifice existing Southern school programs to the goal of desegregation; on the other, the government would sacrifice the improvement goal to desegregation.

Although both desegregation policy enforcement and implementation of federal education programs were opposed or criticized by some who argued for "local control of schools," the slogan was occasionally a smokescreen for the defense of another power base: *state* influence over education. Following the *Brown* decision in 1954, conflict between state education agencies and local districts was not uncommon in some Southern states. In some cases, the state interposition policies were used to stymy local efforts to move toward integration. In New Orleans, for example, the local school board attempted a moderate move toward compliance with the Supreme Court decision. Those efforts were stopped by state action.[10] In that case, although opponents of desegregation were talking about local control of schools, in reality they were worried about federal action destroying state power and, at the same time, setting what they perceived to be an unwanted precedent in the local authorities.

What Was the Reality?

In retrospect, it is difficult to understand how a realistic policy strategy for civil rights implementation was devised as separate from other education matters. But rarely were the two worlds programatically entwined; although linked in the legislative arena, the realities of the multiple administrative actors in the story were very separate. The local school people might have been involved in pitched battles with state officials, but the federal people rarely knew the details of what might be going on. A group of local parents might have been involved in negotiations with a local school system; the feds rarely knew that was happening. A local superintendent might have been on the verge of convincing a board to move toward compliance, but federal officials had no way of knowing whether that was so. Conversely, local school officials had little sense of what was happening in Washington or, if they had a glimmer of some activity, why that action was taken.

This unavoidable inability of any actor in the story to see all the various aspects of the policy world in which he or she operated—or at least to have a sense of the outline of that world—drastically affected the way that implementation activities were conceived and unfolded. All the actors within the federal bureaucracy had world views that in reality defined only a segment of the world. They based a number of assumptions about their jobs on those views, resulting in expectations about the behavior of state officials, local school people, and community and parents groups. These assumptions provided the basis for expectations about each other. Although the responding behavior often was not what was expected, that behavior was usually explained by questioning the commitment and values of the parties involved.

It is more difficult to summarize the assumptions, and hence the expectations, basic to the responses of state and local education officials affected by the implementation of the civil rights compliance program. Although people in the field may have viewed the action of some federal authorities as crazy or prejudicial, that view had to be weighed against the risks of noncompliance. Federal behavior might have been more or less constant over time, but the signals to local districts about the political seriousness of compliance demands sometimes changed independently of the federal official behavior. Elections, votes in Congress, and other administration demands created their own political calculations, which affected local school administrators' determinations about the credibility of the demands of the federal education and civil rights officials. In a situation of miscast expectations, friends did not always turn out to be friends and enemies were not found where they were expected.

The Study

Every administrator approaches his or her job with an underlying conceptualization of the job to be done that flows from a world view that is usually intuitively and experientially based. This perspective helps the administrator select administrative tools, shapes a model of internal organization decision-making, and provides the basis for relationships with individuals and groups outside the agency. This study argues that the individual and collective perspectives of the administrators involved with the implementation efforts stemmed from assumptions that were inappropriate to the job to be done and, as a result, made an extremely difficult task even more difficult.

Consciously or not, the implementors of Title VI chose a series of administrative tools from the bureaucratic bag of tricks that moved the process away from possible success through actions that did not "fit" the policy at hand. When decisions were made about the structure of the organization, federal decision-makers assumed that they could control policy from the top reaches of the organization. Although authority in the education world was dispersed throughout multiple jurisdictions, federal officials developed procedures that depended on Washington-based taut control. Although it was extremely difficult to separate civil rights considerations from other matters, officials tended to treat the issue as a specialized, technical function.

When faced with policy choices, officials tended to make decisions that were narrow, formal, and rigid. The rules that were formulated treated civil rights as a consistent, stable, and predictable issue. Successful desegregation was defined in prepackaged forms with the expectation that the package could be easily adopted and fit into local school districts across the country. When the package met with resistance, federal officials had boxed themselves into an either/or situation. They either accepted the resistance (most often by ignoring it) or took the drastic step of invoking the only sanction available to them: the cutoff or deferral of federal funds to the district. Experience with that sanction proved its ineffectiveness; of the 600 administrative proceedings undertaken against school districts between 1964 and 1970, funds were terminated in 200; in all but four of these 200 districts, federal aid was subsequently restored, often without a change in local procedures.[11]

Public Issues

This study deals with the issues and perceptions that constrained the federal officials within the bueaucracy. Most of the examples that have been used in the following pages do not involve activities that were highly visible to those outside the immediate decision world. Two incidents that have received detailed attention in other sources, however, were visible and public:[12] the substantive policy determination to rely on "freedom-of-choice" compliance plans and the political ramifications of the administrative decision to defer federal funds from the Chicago school system.

Freedom-of-choice was the method of desegregation that placed the burden of change on the family and the student in the school system. Students who were formerly assigned to schools on the basis of race were given the opportunity each school year to choose, on a nonracial basis, the school they wanted to attend subject to limitations imposed by overcrowded facilities.[13] This requirement was attacked by civil rights advocates almost from the first moment it was promulgated by HEW. According to the U.S. Commission on Civil Rights, "such plans did not eliminate

the racial identity of the schools and placed the burden of change upon
Negro parents and pupils who often were reluctant to assert their rights
for fear of harassment and intimidation by hostile white persons."[14] Although the requirement was originally developed as conceived by the
federal court system, it appeared to be much easier to scrutinize the
effects of a freedom-of-choice plan in a specific, unique community (as
courts were able to do, relying on counsel for the black parent or child
to report on compliance) than to know whether thousands of paper compliance forms submitted by the local education authorities realistically
described opportunities for black children in local communities. It is one
thing for white school officials to certify the existence of a freedom-of-
choice plan and quite another (and more risky) matter for black parents
and children to exercise that choice and live with its consequences. Thus,
according to critics of the policy requirement, local freedom-of-choice
plans were not adequately evaluated because HEW officials lacked
adequate staff and procedures for detecting violations. The "proof" of the
ineffectiveness of the requirement, the critics argued, was that "white
families almost invariably choose to have their children attend the predominantly white school, and most Negro families choose to have their
children attend the all-black school."[15]

The Chicago "fiasco" (as it was known) represented a bench mark in
Title VI enforcement efforts and raised serious problems for all actors
involved. The original provocation, according to the Office of Education's
critics, came when the federal agency unfairly decided to defer ESEA
Title I funds because the Illinois city failed to comply with civil rights
requirements. The decision provoked rage on the part of city and state
education and political figures. The responding decision was pushed by
the White House to back away from the deferral decision and release the
funds. That infuriated civil rights activists both in Chicago and inside
HEW. The forced release of the monies in the absence of compliance
indicated that the Title VI enforcers were on tenuous political grounds
and that a number of formerly latent issues in the Title VI efforts could be
activated. Political pressure could be used (by and on the president down)
to stop desegregation efforts. School districts could push resistance to
federal implementation outside the education profession. Enforcement
officials had limited authority to justify their requirements. The message
was clear: elimination of discrimination in education was limited to
Southern and border states. If HEW officials did not want to be burned,
they were wise to handle the Northern and Western states with care
and some distance.[16]

Although the Chicago incident and the controversy about freedom-
of-choice plans were well aired and subject to public discussion, the two

issues also raised a number of administrative problems. These problems are illustrated by several cross-cutting themes—the authority of HEW's regional offices, the development of information sources, and the view of a school system as a system. These are questions that are frequently raised in the following pages and that provide another dimension to the basic argument of the study: namely, that officials in an administrative setting have a repertoire of administrative tools from which to choose, and some of those tools are more appropriate than others for the task at hand.

The Question of Strategy

Although one might argue that the officials involved in the implementation activities had a more or less common view of the world in which they were operating, it is more difficult to argue that these officials had a common strategy for dealing with that world. Some of the officials had conscious and even articulated plans of action; these plans ranged from a *voluntaristic* approach (cajoling the school districts in one fashion or another to lure them to change) to an approach that approximated *warfare* (the feds battling against state and local education authorities). Still other officials—whether consciously or not—appeared to be using *confusion* as their strategy. In these cases, multiple approaches (some may be viewed as simple incompetency, others as purposefully capricious or rigid) were used to keep local and state officials off their guard and, as a result, unable to predict federal official behavior.

Yet other officials were using *bluffing* as their strategic approach. Without an appropriation to finance enforcement efforts, without a large staff, these officials tried to give the appearance of strength in Washington to provoke change in the school districts. As some points, the strategies involved both civil rights and ESEA program officials, operating independently but from the same strategic base; but at other times, the two programs were sending out conflicting messages at the same time to the same state and local officials.

Organization of the Study

The study is presented in three parts. The first section—Structure—looks at the ways in which the administrators perceived their political and organizational environment and, based on these perceptions, how they dealt with the internal relationships within HEW and OE as well as with Congress on issues involving organizational structure. The second section—The Law—looks to the role of the law as an important tool in the implementation attempts, particularly the establishment of administrative rules of procedure and legal questions involving the substance of enforcement requirements. The last section—Constituency—details the methods used by administrators to develop outside support for their activities and the reciprocated assumptions and procedures used by the potential supporters to relate to the officials.

Three general themes run through the study. Each illustrates one aspect of the inappropriate decision repertoire: (1) determinations made by the implementors in handling *conflict* (conflict involving the racial aspects of the implementation attempts and conflict concerning the federal education role); (2) decisions by the officials about the predominant *consumers* of the program (important as a redistributive problem because administrators had to determine whose rights would be honored, how much of them, and how soon); and (3) how the officials dealt with *uncertainty* (was the effort viewed in existential proportions reflecting the uncertainty of the political environment?).

Although this study covers the activities of the HEW Office for Civil Rights as well as OE's enforcement program, the analysis emphasizes the beginnings of enforcement activities within OE. By the time the HEW staff had official authority for Title VI actions, a number of decisions had already been made and a political climate created that limited the autonomy of the administrators and circumscribed their choices.

It is not the purpose of this study to write a script for a melodrama; heroes and villains exchanged roles too often for such a simple story line to be developed. It is much easier to criticize the behavior of federal officials than to give them accolades for the courage to act at all. Criticisms are not offered to place "blame." Rather, they are presented in the hope that an understanding of this decision process will be instructive to those responsible for public policy development in other areas and at other times.

II
Structure

2
.
NEW WINE
IN OLD BOTTLES

Any organization, by definition, has a patterning of relationships commonly known as structure. An organization's structure provides those inside as well as outside its boundaries with a series of messages about the *raison d'être* of the organization: an implicit view of the goals of the activity, the kind of work to be done, and the relationship between those within and those outside its boundaries.

Although the political dimensions of the Congressional and Presidential roles in Title VI implementation activities have been well documented and analyzed,[1] almost no attention has been given to the *form* the activities took within the bureaucracy and the relationship between decisions about form and the substance of the nondiscrimination requirement. This analysis will concentrate on the relationship between form and substance; that is, on the effect on Title VI policy enforcement efforts of administrative structure questions. Although many of the same social forces found in public legislative and judicial battles over the civil rights issue were at play in the less open bureaucratic setting, the peculiarities of administrative issues created a situation that at times exacerbated political wounds and at times opened new sores.

Although Title VI policy represented a new basis of authority for the federal bureacucracy, the nature of the issue did not allow the implementors of the nondiscrimination requirement to take the simplest organizational path in a new policy area. A new agency was not set up, distinct and separate from existing operations. New structures could not be created afresh to carry out the Congressional mandate. Rather, Title VI policy depended on the ongoing procedures, policies, and programs already in the bureaucracy. Even though this dependence seems obvious, it was not always acted upon or perceived. Although local and state officials recognized that they had to juggle civil rights issues in the context of their own existing organizational relationships, they were not aware that a similar juggling act was going on in Washington. Responsibility for civil rights issues was handed to the Office of Education (OE) and the Secretary's Office of HEW at a time of expansion of authority and demands. Existing federal agencies were expected to change their patterns of program design, distribution, and administration in a manner that was consistent with civil rights responsibilities. And these changes were expected to occur without additional appropriations. The administration did not want to request funds for implementation of Title VI from Congress. Thus, although OE did set up a special staff to work on civil rights issues, that staff was dependent on the actions of other federal officials.

Consistency was very difficult to achieve in the consideration of structural questions within OE and HEW. Sometimes decisions about the patterning of relationships within the organization were framed solely in response to the imperatives of the civil rights dimensions of the issue. These decisions represented the implementing official's attempt to ascertain how Title VI could best be implemented. Other structural decisions reflected the demands of the organizational environment of the issue. Given the history of OE and that of HEW, some implementors attempted to determine where and how the issue could be handled most "realistically." Still other structural decisions indicated the tension between the new issue and existing activity in OE and HEW. It was always difficult to sort out whether attitudes and responses were based on internal structural considerations, on problems related to education programs, or on issues related to civil rights. And even if the forces were defined, it was difficult to determine the balance between the competing considerations.

The multiple dimensions emerging from this policy setting did, of course, reflect political values of individual actors and their distinctly different social orientations to the civil rights issue and to the federal education posture. For the purposes of this analysis, however, the locational perspective of the policy-maker is the pivotal point in understanding the processes of implementing Title VI in federal education policy.

The locational perspective of a policy-maker is so crucial that two individuals who are twin images of each other in values, techniques of implementation, and personality will come up with different evaluations and diagnoses of policy needs if they are located in different parts of an organization. Where a policy-maker stands does, indeed, depend upon where he or she sits.

This analysis attempts to offer detailed accounts of the structural struggles that took place as Title VI was tossed first to officials within OE and then to officials located in the Office of the Secretary of HEW. As such, it has two goals. First, the detailed descriptions of implementation efforts and policy decisions surrounding structural questions seek to convey the climate of ambiguity, confusion, and political intrigue that characterized Title VI activities and to communicate the importance of the interplay between the literal and the symbolic within the policy setting.

The second goal of this part of the study relates to the question of organizational decentralization and centralization. Too often, discussion about this dichotomy focuses solely on the geographical dimensions of authority dispersal. Usually this issue is viewed as an either/or matter. The determination of a centralized or decentralized structural form is based on an attempt to ascertain the "correct" balance of power between a central headquarters and its field branches. Rarely is the issue discussed as a tension between central headquarters and the functionally autonomous units within it.[2]

In the case of Title VI policy, the tension between centralized and decentralized authority is illustrated through debates about area as well as function. Function refers to the specific activities with which an agency is charged. Within the Title VI context, function involved both enforcement activities and distribution of funds. The tension between both forms of authority are pervasive in the discussion about implementation activities and are illustrated in a number of specific areas: the conflict between HEW and OE; between Washington and the regional offices; between the Office of the Commissioner of Education and the operating agencies and bureaus within OE; between the Office of the Secretary of HEW and the Office of the Commissioner of Education; between the HEW Regional Directors and the regional officials of the HEW family. In each case, the problem is one of determining the location of the authority base, with the centralized actor or function attempting to exert control over the decentralized actor or function.

The story in the following pages can be viewed as an extended answer to the question, "Where is the authority to act and who can use it?" The civil rights staff members in both OE and HEW assumed that they could locate the authority base and, thus, use it. Others in OE and HEW either felt that the authority base was theirs to use or, in some cases, believed that there was no way for anyone to locate the authority source in a single place.

In order to give some sense of the divergent perspectives on the enforcement activities, this section of the study is divided into three parts. The section begins with an account of the structural status of OE and HEW at the point at which the civil rights issue was "dropped" into their jurisdictions. The centralization-decentralization theme runs through this discussion. In OE, the theme is illustrated by the problems faced by the Commissioner of Education in attempts to get control of the operating programs and, also, by the difficulties involved in determining Washington's relationship to the regions. Similar problems are discussed in the HEW context, where the Secretary of HEW was striving to gain control over the largely autonomous HEW agencies and to attempt to work out a satisfactory arrangement with HEW regional officials. An account of an unusual regional experiment concludes the discussion, serving to illustrate the state of structural considerations within HEW at the time civil rights activities were taking place.

The second part of the section centers around the early period of civil rights activities; that is, the activities located in OE through the Equal Educational Opportunities Program (EEOP). This discussion includes consideration of the initial assumptions about the task to be performed, the structure necessary to carry it out, early signs of political trouble, and the organization's response to this conflict.

The final part of the section deals with the shift of civil rights activities involving school desegregation from OE to the Secretary's Office in HEW. This was done through the establishment of an Office for Civil Rights (OCR) operating directly under the authority of the HEW Secretary. The shift took place in two stages; initially, control over OE was exerted primarily through informal policy direction (negotiations, "suggestive" memoranda, and politically rationalized procedures). After Congressional action, OCR was required to assume the formal operational responsibility for civil rights activities throughout the Department.

As the focus for Title VI activities moved up the formal organization structure, it became more difficult for implementors to relate civil rights questions to educational matters and, more importantly, to operate in a quiet, non-politicized atmosphere. When the President called the Secretary of HEW or when a Senator registered a complaint, federal staff officials were less likely to be able to operate anonymously.

Civil Rights Enforcement Activities:
A Structural Skeleton

The following three diagrams depict the shift of power within HEW relating to civil rights responsibilities in education. The first figure characterizes the power relationships in the early days of civil rights enforcement (1964-1965), when the major responsibility and authority for action were found inside the Office of Education. The second period (1966) characterizes a time of shared authority; the last period (1967-1968) indicates the centralization of authority within the Office of the Secretary.

Although organization charts frequently mask the complexities of organizational change, a series of these charts over time provide a shorthand account of that change. These three charts offer a skeletal account of the tensions that are discussed in detail in the subsequent chapters in this part of the study. The skeleton outlines the shared responsibility within the Washington-based structure for civil rights enforcement throughout the entire period. A comparison of Figures 1 and 3 indicates the growing centralization of authority to the Office of the Secretary during the period between 1965 and 1968. That is, the enforcement activities involving school desegregation were moved from the Office of Education to the Office of the Secretary, away from the education-specific program focus.

Figures 1 and 2 also show the separation between the enforcement activities within the Office of Education and the day-to-day activities of the regional representatives as well as the staff of the operating agencies. The Office of the General Counsel appears within the cast of characters in Figures 1 and 2. Part III of the study—the discussion of the role of the law in the Title VI enforcement program within HEW—provides a more detailed account of the substantive role of legal decisions and of lawyers in the civil rights enforcement activities.

Figure 4, a listing of the actors discussed in the study, is offered in the tradition of the nineteenth century Russian novel. Many individual and organizational names are presented in the subsequent chapters of this work. This array is somewhat confusing to a reader who is unfamiliar with the cast of characters, particularly because the cast list shifts frequently within short periods of time. Figure 4 also provides a reader with a sense of the diversity of characters involved and concerned about structural decisions in the area of school desegregation enforcement. That diversity is particularly important because it is superimposed upon the frequent change in top leadership within the Department and the Office of Education.

FIGURE 1   CIVIL RIGHTS RESPONSIBILITIES IN OE AND HEW,
1964–1965

Λ *Primary civil rights authority in education*
O *Some civil rights authority in education*

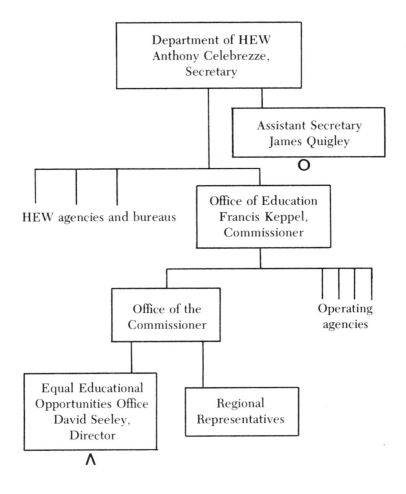

FIGURE 2 CIVIL RIGHTS RESPONSIBILITIES IN OE AND HEW, 1966

∧ *Primary civil rights authority in education*
O *Some civil rights authority in education*

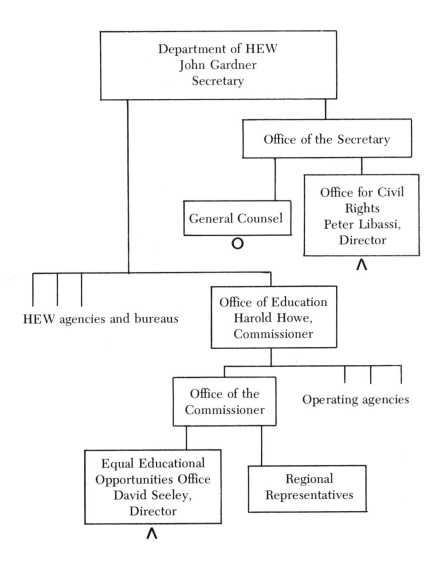

FIGURE 3   CIVIL RIGHTS RESPONSIBILITIES IN OE AND HEW,
1967–1968

∧ *Primary civil rights authority in education*
O *Some civil rights authority in education*

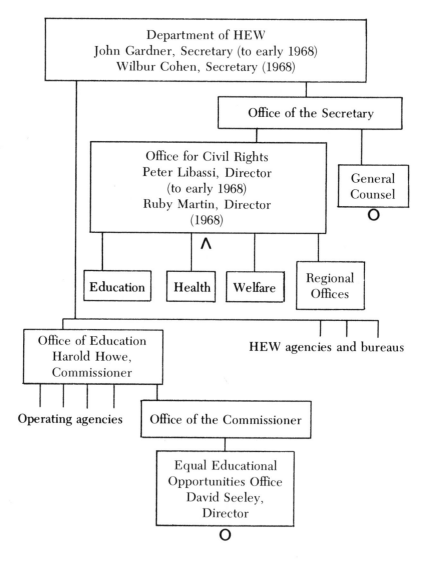

FIGURE 4   ACTORS DISCUSSED

Office of Education

Commissioners of Education
    Lawrence Derthick, 1956-1961
    Sterling M. McMurrin, 1961-1962
    Francis Keppel, 1962-1966
    Harold Howe, 1966-1968
Deputy Commissioner of Education
    Wayne O. Reed (to Keppel and Howe)
    Henry Loomis (to Keppel)
    Graham Sullivan (to Howe)
Assistant to the Deputy Commissioner of Education
    Walter Mylecraine (to Loomis)

OE Field Staff

Directors of Field Services
    Arthur Harris
    Herman Offner
Associate Commissioner for Field Services
    James Turman (to Keppel and Howe)
Regional Representative, OC
    George Hann (Regional Representative, Dallas)

OE Civil Rights Staff

Director of Equal Educational Opportunities Program
    David Seeley
Other staff
    Stanley Kruger
    Allan Lesser
Consultants
    John Niemeyer
    Robert Kriedler

Other—OE

Dwight Ink, Chairman, White House Task Force on OE
    Reorganization
Stephen Trachtenberg, White House Fellow assigned to Howe

Figure 4 (continued)

Department of Health, Education, and Welfare
Secretaries of HEW
Olveta Culp Hobby, 1953-1955
Abraham Ribicoff, 1961-1962
Anthony Celebrezze, 1962-1965
John Gardner, 1965-1968
Wilbur Cohen, 1968-1969
Under Secretary of HEW
Wilbur Cohen, 1965-1968
Assistant Secretary of HEW
James Quigley, 1961-1966

HEW Field Staff
William "Pete" Page, Regional Director, HEW, Atlanta
Alvin Cohen, Regional Attorney, HEW, Chicago

HEW Civil Rights Staff
Director, Office for Civil Rights
F. Peter Libassi, 1966-1968
Ruby Martin, 1968-1969

HEW Administrative Staff
James Kelly, Comptroller and Deputy Assistant Secretary,
1961-1966
John Corson

White House
Douglass Cater, Special Assistant to the President for Education

Congress
Congressman Adam Clayton Powell, Chairman, House Labor and
Education Committee
Congressman John Fogarty, Chairman, House Appropriations
Subcommittee for HEW
Congressman Daniel Flood, successor to Fogarty

Chicago actors
Richard Daley, Mayor
Benjamin Willis, Superintendent of Schools

3

•

THE NUCLEAR FAMILY: THE U.S. OFFICE OF EDUCATION IN WASHINGTON AND IN THE FIELD

To impose any sort of change on the tradition-bound U. S. Office of Education has been viewed as a task of Herculean proportions. But to attempt to use OE as the means of implementing a national policy (Title VI) that so blatantly violated the ideology of local control of schools seemed to be suicidal to many observers of the federal education agency. Created in 1917, OE wheezed along to the 1960's without much indication that the staff and its attentive public recognized there were major changes taking place in American social arrangements. During the New Deal, the autonomy of local school systems was acknowledged by a formal commitment to limit the Office's activities to gathering statistics and supporting some research. Despite the post-Sputnik growth of federal monies for education, OE looked much the same in 1960 as it did in the pre-World War II years. Major shakeups might occur in the White House but OE continued to be what a former OE official called a "daisy chain that resulted in an interchangeability between people using OE services and the people on the OE staff." According to Walter Mylecraine, a former Assistant to the Deputy Commissioner of Education, "OE was intended to be the ensconcement of every variety of educational specialist that existed. OE would reflect the panorama of talent in the education field, and, in a system of mutual back patting, people could call for specialist assistance as resources for state and local educators."

The system tended to work to bestow the rewards of federal jobs on aging educators who wanted a quiet place to spend their last working years. And the process was somehow biased to populate the federal agency with a disproportionate number of Southern, Southwestern, and Midwestern staff members. The agency was so inbred that one could not differentiate between the interests of state and local educators (and their organizational representatives) and those of individuals who were paid by the government. Indeed, in many cases federal staff members picked up supplementary salaries by consulting, as free agents, for individuals and systems that received federal grants. As one management official put it, "no one knew what conflict of interest was about."

Until circa 1958, when the passage of the National Defense Education Act (NDEA) was imminent, the system was managed entirely from Washington. At that time, the U.S. Commissioner of Education, Lawrence Derthick—a former president of the American Association of School Administrators—concocted an organizational change that amazed his education establishment friends. NDEA would give OE vastly increased funds to administer; it was, according to Derthick, "one of the great milestones in the history of American education—a great new program touching individual schools through states." Derthick was concerned about the ability of the existing OE structure to administer this program. For what he described as efficiency and administrative reasons, he created a system of Regional Representatives of the Office of the Commissioner, with sites for these individuals corresponding to the existing regional offices in the HEW structure. "With so many titles, programs and institutions involved in NDEA, we wanted expertise closer at hand. This staff would do what a larger Washington staff might have done, but people were near at hand to help interpret the new programs," Derthick has commented.

But, despite Derthick's credentials as "one of the boys," the education groups—particularly the major education organizations known as the Big Six—raised major resistance to the move. The association of Chief State School Officers (CSSO) felt that regional offices were an intrusion on the principle of state and local control of education. Their primary objection, according to Derthick, was that "the federal government would be closer to local schools and state education people." These groups "wanted to go straight to the top, thus they argued that the regional system would create more red tape to obstruct them."

Others have given different interpretations to the opposition by the Big Six. One OE staff member has argued that the opposition to regionalization stemmed from the location of OE within HEW. "OE regional people sit in regional offices headed by a HEW Regional Director. That Regional Director tends to spend time and be responsible to the governors of the states within his region. The close relationship to the governor is feared by the chief state school officials—21 of whom are elected independently and are not a formal part of the governor's administration. Thus the chief state school officials—even in states governed by state boards of education—are fearful of control by the governor over the education turf."

Although the education groups were not apprehensive about Derthick personally—he was the father of the federal education slogan "leadership without domination, assistance without interference"—they *were* concerned that the Commissioner was setting up administrative machinery involving regions that would haunt them for a long time after he left.

Regional Representatives, Office of the Commissioner

Although Derthick had originally proposed that the new job category he created be called Regional Assistant Commissioner, the job title that was accepted was Regional Representative, Office of the Commissioner (hereafter called Regional Representative OC). The accepted nomenclature indicated the touchy relationship between the Commissioner's office and the existing Assistant Commissioners—the heads of OE operating bureaus—who wanted it clear that the regional staff was not on a par with them, and so the Commissioner's Regional Representatives took their place alongside the regional staff from OE bureaus already assigned to regional offices.

OE staff members had first been assigned to regional offices with the passage of the federal impacted areas aid program. The program authorized federal grants to areas supposedly "impacted" by tax-free federal property and installations, Indian reservations, or government contractors. Within a few years, the single OE person in each region was joined by a representative for vocational education; subsequently several other positions were created. According to one long-time OE staff member, the Regional Representative OC position was established as an administrative device: "There was a need to have someone sit in the regions to keep

Washington informed. Clearly the program direction was from Washington. The Regional Representative was there to fulfill an administrative position." Thus, to the Washington hierarchy, the Regional Representative OC was not the conductor of the small regional OE band.

If the new Regional Representatives OC did not enjoy high rank within the Office of Education hierarchy, they did bring status to the job as a result of their previous experience. None of the nine men named to the position had been in the federal government before their regional appointments. They had, however, been in positions of power within the educational establishment. Derthick consciously appointed individuals "that people—especially the chief state school officers—had confidence in." The men included former chief state school officers, presidents or deans of colleges, and former local school administrators. All had advanced degrees—either M.A.'s, Ed.D.'s, or Ph.D.'s. In one or two cases, the individual appointed had good political connections with the Congressional delegates from the area. The former Commissioner noted that he "tried to select regional office heads that were acceptable to the state people so that the state people would trust them more than they would D.C.-based bureaucrats. I tried to make it profitable for the chief state school officers to go through the regional offices—although nothing prohibited them from going to Washington."

Derthick's method of dispelling the education constituency's doubts about regional OE representatives created an unanticipated difficulty. In his attempt to fill the jobs with top-level individuals, Derthick had, in effect, placed first-level players on a third-rate team. A policy paper circulated among the top OE staff in 1960 attempted to clarify the roles of the Regional Representative OC and the program-related regional OE staff members. The men in the year-old positions were concerned about maintaining their "hard won professional status." The position paper characterized their feeling as being "run over by a truck."[1] For, the position paper noted, "each of these men has achieved wide recognition and professional status in positions of broad and varied responsibility before coming to the Office of Education. They have much to contribute, but much to lose if the opportunity to achieve and to make that contribution should be limited or denied, and their loss would be the loss of the Office, of American education, compounded."[2]

The policy paper was hardly a revolutionary document. One of its major contributors was Dr. Arthur Harris, then Director of the Office of Field Services within the Commissioner's office. (Harris was subsequently appointed Assistant Commissioner for the Bureau of Elementary and Secondary Education when the Elementary and Secondary Education Act of 1965 was enacted—a program operating job that required close relationships with the Big Six.) The text of the policy document was careful not to step openly on the toes of Assistant Commissioners with program responsibility and functioned to deny any rift between Derthick's new men and ongoing program officials. The paper made it clear that the regional representative positions were not to compete with the operating authority of program people in Washington. To emphasize the point, the document reiterated the Commissioner's decision "as sound administrative practice" to delegate to program people "authority essential to the effective discharge of their respective responsibilities."[3] Indeed, the Commissioner's "overt exercise or display of a means for effecting compliance with his policies, plans and objectives is seldom necessary and seldom used, for these are determined cooperatively in almost all instances."[4]

In contrast to the specific broad responsibilities given the program. staff, the job of Regional Representative OC was defined very imprecisely. Regional representatives were given four areas of duty and responsibility for management, coordination, short-term special assignments, and promoting the cause of education. Numerous examples of each "duty" area were included in the paper, but each was worded carefully to avoid crossing the authority of the program officials.

Clearly, the job of the Regional Representative OC was to fill in the cracks. The real motive for circulating the paper may have been to voice a warning found in a sentence toward the end of the memo: "The Commissioner. does not hold the Office of Education Regional Representative responsible in any way for the direction or the performance of the program field staff in the discharge of their assigned program functions."[5] It appears that the grievances of the new staff were to be dispelled with a statement of autonomy, a loose job description, nonresponsibility for regional program officials, and travel budget that was almost entirely discretionary. Although OE's organizational diagram indicated that the Regional Representative OC had line responsibility to the Commissioner through the Director of the Office of Field Services, fear of trespassing the program manager's turf made that linkage relatively inoperative.

When the new OE Commissioner, Sterling M. McMurrin, took office following the change of administration in 1961, he received a status report on problems of current significance from the executive officer of OE. In the section on field offices, the new Commissioner was told that "the establishment and staffing of these [Regional Representative OC] field positions was strongly supported by the Office of the Secretary. However, recently Secretary Ribicoff has expressed doubt about the usefulness of these field representatives of the Office of the Commissioner."[6] Because of Ribicoff's skepticism, the Department requested that the Office of Education delay appointing anyone to fill a vacancy in one of the regional offices.

McMurrin's response to the field service question was to name a committee of representatives from several OE bureaus and offices and from the Bureau of the Budget to take a look at the field apparatus and to make recommendations to him. The appointment of this committee may have been a way to put off making any decision; this Ribicoff-appointed Commissioner was known throughout HEW for his disinterest in administrative issues. The report of the committee called for the establishment of "a direct supervisory line from the Commissioner to the nine Regional Representatives" but acknowledged the dilemma "of the necessity for recommending increases in authority and responsibility for that [Regional Representative] position and yet maintaining unimpaired program direction of the other field representative directly from headquarters."[7]

The committee looked to additional responsibility in "program and legislative planning and review and information activities" for the Regional Representative OC, and suggested that additional staff assistance be provided to "assure the flexibility that is necessary." The Commissioner's relationship with these offices was criticized and he was told to "attend more to the task of developing direct relationships between himself and his Regional Representative."[8] Although "encouraged by the caliber and ability of the present field representatives," the committee concluded that it had been "dismayed by the under utilization of the Regional Representatives, Office of Education, positions in many cases, and particularly by the misconceptions that prevail about these positions at headquarters."[9]

Keppel and the Regional Offices

The report to Commissioner McMurrin was submitted in late August 1962. In December of that year, McMurrin was replaced by Francis Keppel, Dean of the Harvard School of Education, appointed by President Kennedy to concentrate on the legislative education program of the New Frontier, which had been destroyed by Congress earlier in the administration. The White House wanted a successful drive to get education legislation through Congress before the 1964 election campaign.

Unlike McMurrin, Keppel was a personal appointee and friend of the President. His entrance represented a Presidential commitment to an increased federal education role. Also unlike McMurrin, Keppel was personally known by leaders of the education establishment, although according to one educator, Keppel's role was on the "fringes." (The leaders of the education family were drawn mainly from public institutions, not from private schools like Harvard or Stanford.)

Keppel's major concern was in building support for the pending federal education legislation; this goal made it impolitic for him to tackle any of the internal practices within the office that might have upset potential legislative allies. Personally, he was less interested in the mechanics of day-to-day operations within OE than in the planning and development of a new and grand federal role in education. His concerns were not always appreciated by staff members. In one known case, a staff member expressed his displeasure in a memo suggesting changes in Keppel's conduct of program planning discussion meetings. The author of the memo quotes the Commisioner as saying in a staff meeting that he is "not interested in administrative structure." The author, Jack Ciaccio, a member of the Program Planning Branch, notes that Keppel's comment "leads some to feel that he is 'naive' and that program planning won't succeed because he's ignoring the realities they have to deal with in program planning. It seems better to say that program planning has to be grounded in administrative reality as well as fiscal and political reality."[10]

If Keppel failed to focus on administrative issues in general, he was even less interested in matters affecting the OE field system.[11] Herman L. Offner, former Regional Representative OC in the New York region, had replaced Arthur Harris as director of the Office of Field Services. His experience in the field made Offner a more vocal advocate of increased responsibility and accountability on the Regional Representative OC. In a March 1963 memo to Keppel, written a few months after the new Commissioner arrived, Offner transmitted a suggestion from the Dallas Regional Representative, George Hann, that Keppel (or Offner for Keppel) write a note to each chief state school officer expressing appreciation for cooperation with the Regional Representatives and inquiring how the Representative might more effectively be of value.

After quoting from Hann's report, Offner commented parenthetically that Hann's suggestion had been made to McMurrin but no action had been taken on the matter. Furthermore, wrote Offner,

> Mr. McMurrin's lack of close identification and association with the field staff dried up almost completely the confidential and diplomatic types of two-way communication [which Offner says existed under Derthick] and reduced field representation to handling public information, assisting OE programs without field representatives upon request, representing OE upon Office, Department or Congressional request, recruiting, distributing OE publications and films, and securing precise information desired by Chief State School Officers and other leaders in education.[12]

Although Offner's memory of past glory under Derthick might have been somewhat faulty, he did express the concerns of others within the field system about their role under the new Commissioner.

Keppel's reaction to Offner's memo was transmitted to his deputy, Wayne O. Reed: "I am hesitant to take any action on the suggestion made by Mr. Hann until I have a much stronger grasp of the nature of the field services and their present duties and future possibilities. Ordinarily I dislike turning down a suggestion . . . but I should think that even a 'casual, information note' [the specific form of Hann's suggestion] might imply commitments that would not be wise at this time."[13] Because of his concerns and the pressures on his time, it might have been rational for Keppel to put off dealing with the field system. But to the men in the regional offices, the new Commissioner was continuing a pattern; clearly, the Regional Representative OC was a stepchild within the Office of Education.

The pattern was to continue through Keppel's term as Commissioner and into that of Harold Howe. Although the field staff was on the front line, easily accessible by and vulnerable to state and local officials, it was thrust on the battlefield without much in the way of policy ammunition. Given the past relationships between the Regional Representatives OC and state and local officials, the situation was particularly embarassing to them.

Ironically, Derthick had set up a system that kept the individuals in this job from being socialized into the federal family. Although they were sitting in a federal office, representing a federal agency, and clearly identified as individuals on the federal payroll, the Regional Representatives OC were cut off from the day-to-day transactions of the Office of Education. They had no opportunity to contribute to the discussions that were taking place within the agency about proposed legislation. When they arrived in Washington for their semi-annual staff meetings, they sat passively and listened to reports from representatives of OE bureaus. Sometimes bureau chiefs would pay the visiting Regional Representatives a "social" call; but more often the bureau second or third in command was in charge of low priority reports to the Commissioner's field staff. Although Keppel's arrival did signal a new turn for the Office of Education, the regional officials attached to the Commissioner's office continued to be excluded from the mainstream of the federal education bureaucracy.

The primary method of communication between Commissioner Keppel and the Regional Representatives OC was through the monthly activities report submitted to the Washington Director of the Office of Field Services, who excerpted them for the Commissioner. This communication procedure did not begin with Keppel; Derthick also relied on the passive memorandum form to keep in touch with his regional staff members. It was rare for the Commissioner to pick up the telephone to request direct assistance from his Regional Representatives. The chief state school officials tended to be the sole source of information about state or local conditions, and their advice was often sought about OE policy matters. From the formal letters occasionally sent by the Commissioner to "his" men in the field, it would appear that personal contacts between them were extremely limited.

Because their policy relationship to the Commissioner was defined in large part by the monthly field reports, the items in the reports provide some insight into the views held by the Regional Representatives. These reports indicate that the field officials were forced to give out information about the civil rights issue, whether or not they were involved in formulating the dimensions of the policy. These items can be seen as the response from field officials to what they perceived to be in the mind of the Commissioner and as a fishing expedition for increased responsibility.

Although there was minimal discussion in early 1964 within Washington OE offices about responsibilities if the 1964 pending Civil Rights Act were passed, monthly reports from the field began regularly to include items on integration and civil rights from January 1964 through the passage of the Act in July.[14] The appearance of these items and the position on desegregation they implied was curious. Most of the items came from the Dallas and Atlanta regional offices, which covered the majority of the massive resistance, anti-integration states. Both the Dallas and the Atlanta Regional Representatives OC were native to the regions they covered. They had been educated and socialized to the values of the South and Southwest; the chief state school officials with whom they dealt were personal and long-time friends. One does not know, of course, what the Regional Representative OC and the chief state school officials said to each other in private. But the messages transmitted to Washington emphasized the willingness of the Southern school officials to talk about, if not to accept, the probable law of the land.

The regularity of these reports up to the time of the passage of the 1964 Civil Rights Act indicates that the Commissioner's field men—cut off from so much of the significant OE policy-making and program planning—were asking to be included in the implementation of the civil rights policy. They recognized that OE's traditional method of policy implementation—turning the federal policy over to the states to operate—would not work when traditionally, state officials in the South and Southwest were bound to practices that flouted federal policy. Although they were federal officials, the Commissioner's field representatives had close relationships with the state school officials. The descriptive material included in the monthly reports shows that, whether Keppel had planned it or not, the Regional Representatives were being used by state officials to transmit policy questions, information, and requests for interpretations of federal policy.

By the end of 1964, however, the field reports to the Commissioner no longer included civil rights items.[15] For by that time, Commissioner Keppel had set up a civil rights policy enforcement process that excluded the Regional Representatives from an ongoing role and effectively closed them out of policy formulation. The system that was devised reflected Keppel's bias against regional office utilization in general and his distrust of handing civil rights enforcement to locally-based, Southern bureaucrats. From time to time during the period that OE had responsibility for Title VI enforcement, individual Regional Representatives OC emerged, only to sink again. Infrequently they were used for information-gathering purposes. But the EEOP—the Equal Educational Opportunities Program—distrust of the Commissioner's Regional Representatives was strong enough to prompt the OE civil rights operation to bypass regional staff and to enter into a separate contract with the Southern Education Reporting Service for general statistics involving Southern school systems. Occasionally, the Regional Representatives relayed questions about school desegregation guidelines that they had been asked (and were unable to answer) by state or local school officials. But the policy door had been effectively closed in the face of the Commissioner's field staff.

Between the end of 1964 and December 1965—the period of the first, intensive civil rights push in OE—the Office of Field Services was in effect eliminated from the Commissioner's Washington organization. As one regional official put it, "for more than a year, the field people just sat." Without a Washington-based coordinator, the Regional Representatives OC were stripped of their single communication device; there was no one in Washington to read the monthly reports or, indeed, to acknowledge their existence in the field.

Promises, Promises

Unlike those of many other agencies,[16] OE's decentralization pushes have coincided with the addition of new responsibilities for the agency. Derthick had created the Regional Representative OC job when the NDEA surfaced from Congress. In 1965, following the passage of the Elementary and Secondary Education Act, Commissioner Keppel brought in a new management team to work out the administration of the massive federal education program. The "new look" was led by a new Assistant Commissioner, former Voice of America director Henry Loomis.

Loomis' appointment signalled a new view of administration within OE toward the politics of the Washington establishment. In the past, the second level job in the Office had been a permanent civil service function. Wayne Reed, a former chief state school officer, had served as Deputy Commissioner under Derthick, McMurrin, and Keppel. Both White House interest in and Congressional concern about the new legislation created a new political game for OE, and it was decided that a political Assistant Commissioner position would be most effective. Loomis was thought to be a persuasive political figure; he had a reputation in Washington as a strong bureaucratic manager. To his dismay, Keppel later learned that Loomis had lost favor with Lyndon Johnson during his Voice of America term and that the President was livid to find his enemy appointed second in command in OE during the administration of the "education President."

The reorganization plan devised by Loomis and his assistant, Walter Mylecraine (plus the Ink task force), emphasized a new role for the regional offices of the education agency—an emphasis heard some months later in directives for the decentralization of the entire HEW family from Secretary Gardner's office. The desire for decentralization and for increased political clout for the field were responsible for the creation of a new position within OE—an Associate Commissioner for Field Services. (The Loomis-Mylecraine plans had called for a restoration of a Washington field service position, but the desire to court favor with the White House pushed the planned job to both a higher federal grade and a more prestigous title.) A Texan, James Turman—an educator, former speaker of the Texas House of Representatives, a defeated candidate for Lieutenant Governor, and a known personal friend of Lyndon Johnson—was appointed to the new associate commissionership in December 1965.

The entrance of the genial and political Turman into the field office job signalled a new day for the Commissioner's Regional Representatives. Turman's victory in achieving an equal grade position with the OE bureau chiefs indicated that the field office spokesman might be able to be more than a messenger boy from the Commissioner to the field. (According to Turman, the new look in the regions was the second phase of Keppel's reorganizing program, which had begun with headquarters reorganization in Washington.)

Among old-timers in OE, the reorganization scheme that swept the Office was drastic; the year of the Loomis-Mylecraine regime was known as the "year of the locust." The Loomis/Mylecraine team saw their job as pushing a sloppy, sleeping organization to do something with a lot of money. Up to that point, it was argued by the new managers, OE did not have the capacity to handle large amounts of money. With more than 300 job vacancies at the time, they concocted the idea of appointing a White House Task Force to look into education management. (Commissioner Keppel, described by one official as "quite a Byzantine," saw the task force as an effective way of relating to President Johnson. Because Keppel was always known as Kennedy's man, his relationship to Johnson was, at the best, distant. Whereas Kennedy had used Keppel as his link to HEW, Johnson dealt directly with the HEW Secretary, especially after his man—John Gardner—assumed office.) Johnson appointed AEC official Dwight Ink to head up the task force team on reorganization; but Loomis and his staff controlled the substantive recommendations involving the details of the reorganization.

Supported by the larger reorganization, Turman used his political ties to push ahead and create new responsibilities for the Commissioner's Regional Representatives. Among his first acts was a move to change the title of the job from Regional Representative OC to Regional Commissioner—connoting that the regional official was acting as "little commissioner" in the field structure. Turman recalls that former Assistant Commissioner Wayne Reed opposed that idea, arguing that it was a "facade" since it was a title without authority. A compromise was reached at that time, and the Commissioner's regional staff members were called Regional Assistant Commissioners (the name has subsequently been changed to Regional Commissioner).

Although Turman did have line authority from the Commissioner, he had neither program responsibilities nor the dollars that flowed from programs to deal out to field staff. For the most part, he used staff members as men without portfolio who reported directly to him; Turman termed them his "eyes and ears." Recognizing the limits of nonoperating functions, the Associate Commissioner attempted to give the regional staff members sign-off authority on some programs. The chief program target of both the Turman and Loomis schemes for reorganization was the Bureau of Elementary and Secondary Education—the bureau with the major dollar responsibility under ESEA and the bureau with the strongest lifeline links to the major education groups, especially the chief state school officers. Like Derthick, Turman attempted to use the divide-and-conquer technique to dispell criticisms of the decentralization programs and cultivated the chief state school officials and big city school superintendents, who were convinced by his argument that OE would be able to deliver better service from the regional offices than from headquarters.

Despite Turman's efforts, there was no rebirth of the regional office staff. Indeed, the gestation period was hardly completed when Loomis— the advocator and protector of the OE shakeup—left the agency, soon after John Gardner assumed office. According to some of Loomis' friends, the departure order came straight from the White House and was a condition of Gardner's job. Loomis' departure was difficult for the advocates of reorganization in OE. For some time, Loomis as Deputy Commissioner had been effectively running OE and Keppel was fading into the background. Soon after, Keppel was "kicked upstairs" to become Assistant Secretary of HEW for Education, and Harold Howe assumed the office of the Commissioner. Turman stayed in the job until the Nixon Administration came in (and once again the field offices were left without a spokesperson in Washington). Loomis' plans for field office strength did not materialize after he left OE, however.

The Office of Education regional offices have yet to be given responsibility and formal authority in the decision process and thus their potential value has yet to be tapped. By dint of their proximity to the state and local setting, active and alert regional staff could provide Washington with information that is detailed and attuned to localized perceptions. Information collection skill is usually developed as one side of an equation, however; individuals and organizations are effective informants when they believe that they will receive something in return. If regional officials have no authority to effect changes in programs or to distribute funds, there is little reason for them to be connected to an information network in a region. Ten regional offices, spread around a large and diverse nation, do not constitute a full-blown field system. But ten offices do have the potential to help construct a national program that might be effectively administered in the country.

4

OE'S EXTENDED FAMILY:
THE HEW STRUCTURE

In 1953, during the Eisenhower administration, the U.S. Congress approved the first major reorganization of a federal domestic department since World War II, and the U.S. Department of Health, Education, and Welfare (HEW) was created. (The other monster department, the U.S. Department of Defense, was created in 1947.) On paper, the HEW Department's structure implied that the Secretary held formal authority over the agencies and bureaus subsumed within it. Despite the new creation, however, the historical autonomy of the affiliated groups continued. The titular centralization of authority within the Department had to be interpreted within the reality of survival. Thus the Congressional alliances that the operating agencies and bureaus had developed over the years and the strong professional identifications that bound the public servants to predictable behavior, made welfare, health, and education bureaucrats responsive to a different drum from the one beat from the Secretary's office. The Secretary was up front; he sometimes played a significant role in the legislative battles that involved the creation of new responsibilities for the Department. But the affiliated operating agencies, such as the Welfare Administration, the Office of Education, the Public Health Service, and the Social Security Administration, continued their business as usual, changing practices slowly, on cue not from the Secretary but from their Congressional and professional allies.

Robert McNamara's organizational and belt-tightening successes with the Department of Defense in the early 1960's made Lyndon Johnson and his advisors optimistic about a similar domestic try. In terms of Johnson's desire for tighter control, HEW was ripe for the effort. John Gardner, who was considered the domestic counterpart of McNamara, came to head HEW in August 1965. Like McNamara, Gardner was not only a strong individual with a considerable reputation outside the government; the HEW Secretary also brought with him technicians (kin of the Defense Department Whiz Kids) to establish control mechanisms. The Office of Program Planning and Evaluation—the most prominent control device—was considered meritorious on its own technical terms but could also assist the new Secretary in his attempts to exert critical control over the independent operating agencies and bureaus.[1] Gardner's new arsenal included the establishment of an Office for Civil Rights— another office that not only served a function on its own literal terms but also demonstrated the Secretary's desire for control of the HEW affiliates.

Gardner's HEW inheritance included a field organization that had given earlier Secretaries cause for concern. HEW's regional activities were an outgrowth of the original Social Security regional offices, supplemented in 1948 by a Congressionally-mandated regionalization of other departmental offices that was intended to save a half million dollars. By 1954, all HEW activities had regional offices, with the exception of the Food and Drug Administration, some public health functions, and area offices of the Old Age Survivors Insurance program (OASI). When the Department was created in 1953, the control and authority tangle in Washington was miniaturized in the regions. The job position of HEW Regional Director was conceived and directors were appointed in each of the HEW regions.

The field problems faced by the Gardner administration were essentially the same as those described by management consultants Cresap, McCormick, and Paget in a contracted report to HEW Secretary Olveta Culp Hobby late in 1954—just a year after the creation of HEW. In an appendix to the study, the firm noted that "During our interviews and observations at headquarters and in the field, we received more unsolicited comment about Regional Directors and their functions than about any other segment of the HEW management organization."[2] Although the regional apparatus was not a formal part of the management study, the report included a nine-page analysis of regional office problems, especially issues involving Regional Directors. An exhibit detailing the regional structure, viewed from the field level, emphasized the separation of the Regional Director from the substance of the Department's activities. The Regional Director, according to the study, was so far from the technical core of the Department's work that he was not able to play any kind of substantive role. In effect, the management team found the opposite of what the OE field people had argued—that is, the Regional Director operated in a narrow administrative funnel, divorced from any policy-making functions.

The Cresap, McCormick, and Paget report rejected the "headquarters staff" concept as the method of characterizing the role of the Regional Director. Rather, they commented:

> Were HEW a single-purpose agency with a high degree of interdependence among its several program activities, this approach [putting Regional Directors fully in the chain of command as line commanders] would be feasible and productive. However, HEW is a collection of separate, main-purpose program activities, some of which have a mutual interest, but none of which is highly dependent on another. . . . Viewed realistically, we do not believe that HEW can function as a "single command" operation, since its field forces do not merge their efforts to accomplish a single mission, as is true, for example, of the Armed Forces in a combat theatre. Using the military analogy, HEW field activities are more comparable to those of a Naval District which contains a shipbuilding and repair installation, an aircraft overhaul and repair installation, an ordnance activity, etc. . . . It is our conclusion that HEW, like the Navy, must accept the reality of vesting command in headquarters constituents over technical, main-purpose field activities, using over-all field executives in a coordinating relationship.[3]

On paper, at least, Mrs. Hobby accepted these recommendations. When the Democrats came into power in 1961, the rhetoric of Regional Director coordinating multi-function authority continued to be proclaimed. Despite the words, however, there were few substantive areas over which the HEW Regional Directors exerted control, coordinative or not. Thus, after the passage of the Civil Rights Act in July 1964, the field system of HEW seemed an obvious untapped resource for HEW Assistant Secretary James Quigley, the top Department official charged with enforcement of the new legislation. Quigley, a former Pennsylvania Congressman, served as Secretary Celebrezze's right-hand man—someone who could assume responsibility for the Secretary. As one of Quigley's former staff members described it, "Quigley's idea of regional office involvement was based on the practicality of the situation rather than any philosophical basis of involvement of regional people. There was no money appropriated to enforce Title VI since a deal had been made by Congressional liberals that brought votes of moderate Congressmen in exchange for a promise of no appropriation for enforcement of Title VI.

Quigley was trying to bootleg enforcement by making agencies responsible for the civil rights program. And since the regional agency people exerted a lot of power, he looked there."

Coming from the Secretary's office, Quigley could not deal directly with the regional representatives of the numerous HEW operating bureaus and agencies without going through their Washington chiefs. And although the staff in the Secretary's office was loyal to the Secretary, the sense of loyalty was considerably diminished in the operating bureaus and agencies. Recognizing the impossibility of that effort, Quigley utilized the resource attached directly to the Secretary's office: the multi-function Regional Directors in the nine HEW regions. With a sparse staff, Quigley visited the regional offices, flying around the country in an attempt to get Regional Directors involved in the enforcement effort. Within days after the President signed the Civil Rights bill, Quigley was in and out of the regional offices, meeting with every federal, state, and local official he could corral.

The powerlessness of the Secretary's office was soon indicated by the response to Quigley's efforts. Although he gave Regional Directors some authority in the review of compliance efforts, his bombardment of memos to regional officials of HEW affiliates was effectively useless. Quigley, according to one observer, "expected to convince regional people on the basis of memos from Washington. He thought his memos would argue convincingly that if the regional program official didn't comply, he'd be in trouble."

But the HEW Regional Directors were not powerful advocates for Quigley; the regional agency program officials had no reason to assume the credibility of the otherwise low-grade, powerless Regional Directors. Both Washington-based and regional officials within OE had special abilities to resist Quigley's enforcement attempts and to flaunt their independence.

Gardner's Push: "To the Field"

Less than a year after Gardner took office as the third Secretary of HEW in the Democratic tenure, he launched a major effort to "strengthen our field operations, especially in the Regional Offices."[4] The move followed the passage of the Great Society legislation, which gave HEW affiliates vastly expanded programs. Although the memo to agency heads announcing the intent to strengthen field operations was couched in the language of decentralized activities, its underlying motive was less clear.

On one level, Gardner argued:

Strong representation in the field can provide us with closer informal communication with our clientele—officials of State and local government, representatives of non-goverment institutions and the general public. Day to
day responsiveness by Federal officials to State, local and institutional problems can resolve problems at an early stage before they escalate to the
Washington level.[5]

Yet, at the same time, the Secretary called for "coordination of all Federal
programs at the grassroots level." Such coordination would appear to
require increased authority within the Office of the Secretary to pull the
parts together, authority that could then be decentralized to the coordinator within the regions—the Regional Director.

Thus the decentralization argument could not be taken at its face
value. Program operators could (and did) effectively argue that their operations were already decentralized; Gardner's variation on the "power to
the people" cry was, in reality, a means of attaining centralized control.

In this case, geographic decentralization was only one aspect of a
battle between the generalists (the Secretary and his Regional Directors)
and the specialists (the agency program operators and their regional representatives). Gardner was buttressed by recommendations for regional
coordination issued by staff members of the Bureau of the Budget. The
BOB officials shared Gardner's concern to increase the abilities of the
Secretary's office to plan programs, formulate policy, issue regulations
and instructions, supervise field operations, and control overall administration.

Gardner's strategy was also indicated by the civil rights enforcement
program he established. Gardner hired F. Peter Libassi, former deputy
staff director of the U.S. Commission on Civil Rights, to head a new
Office for Civil Rights operating within the Secretary's office. Although
the centralized civil rights office was eventually required by Congress,
Gardner's action can be viewed also as a part of his struggle for authority
for the Secretary's office. The result was a rather convoluted situation for
Libassi: civil rights enforcement would not be achieved until it became an
integral part of all of HEW's programs. If the monitoring of this responsibility were given to the generalists (i.e., the Regional Directors), Libassi
and his staff were not assured that these individuals would have either the
time or the inclination to follow through on enforcement scrutinizing.
They were especially skeptical when it came to giving authority to the
regional directors in the Southern states. Libassi eventually came up with

a structural arrangement in which regional representatives from his Office were assigned to the Regional HEW offices, reporting not to the Regional Director, however, but to Libassi in Washington. Without appearing to be conscious of the effect of this structural decision, Libassi's regional staff turned into a replication of the fragmented, technical approach to policy influence that Gardner was attempting to deter in other parts of the Department.

A Regional Experiment

One of the first regional actions taken by Gardner when he came to the Department was the appointment of William (Pete) Page to the Regional Directorship of the Atlanta region (the states included were Georgia, North Carolina, South Carolina, Mississippi, Florida, and Alabama). Page was not a typical regional official. A Southerner by birth, he had spent considerable time in the Office of the Secretary within the Office of Field Administration. From this vantage point, Page had witnessed the generalized lack of trust toward regional people characteristic of the Secretary's office. Although some people within the Department considered his decision to go back South "wildly insane" and a career sacrifice, Page saw the move as a creative opportunity to show some of his Washington colleagues that a native Southerner could be an effective advocate of the national policy on civil rights. Page felt that the new Great Society federal programs, many of which were located in HEW, would have enormous impact on the socioeconomic condition of the South.

Page not only knew the South, he was also familiar with Department activities and programs to an extent unusual for a regional official. His appointment was made within the career service; he was not a political appointee. For some time Page had advocated a stronger role for regional officials, including the authority to make decisions on a regional level within bounds understood and known by Washington as well as by regional staff. Because Page was willing to make some personal investment in the job and to take the risk of exerting authority that was not formally authorized, he jumped into policy arguments that other regional officials feared to enter. Page's initiative was sanctioned by the Secretary; when he went to Atlanta, Page had an understanding with Gardner that his tenure there would be an experiment in which his region would be given the opportunity for decentralized responsibilities.

Page reviewed and advised on policy matters that had never crossed the Regional Director's desk before. When Gardner advanced his organization scheme for the strengthening of field operations, he requested an upgrading of the Regional Director job. The request to the Civil Service Commission was based on the argument that the Secretary was planning to rely more heavily on the regional men. Despite Gardner's advocacy, the Commission recommended against the upgrading, requiring that the Department itself make an investment in its regional people and institute the change before the Civil Service Commission gave formal approval. The Commission told Gardner that they would evaluate the impact of the various Regional Directors' performances and, on the basis of that evaluation, recommend promotions on an individual basis. Page was the only Regional Director promoted as a result of that process.

"Pete" Page considered himself a strong advocate of the civil rights responsibilities given to HEW through Title VI; he bristled at the assumption by some on the civil rights enforcement staff that a Southerner could not effectively work in the South. Although he challenged Libassi's move to establish regional positions for civil rights attached to the regional office but with line responsibility from Washington, Page went along with the arrangement on Gardner's request. The Atlanta Regional Director had argued that, whether Libassi liked it or not, the enforcement efforts were dependent on program operators and that he was willing to hold program managers within his region accountable for Title VI implementation efforts. Page felt that the civil rights program and assurances were as much a responsibility of the program operators as were fiscal responsibility and other rules and regulations. "Although this would have been traumatic and costly," Page has commented, "I was willing to take the difficult actions to remove the personnel and the other barriers in order to act. It beats ten years of hassling."

Thus, to Page, it was possible to create a situation in which native Southerners, who knew the schools, the hospitals, and other local facilities, would be responsive to the federal policy. Page noted that there were 500 people in the regional offices but only 50 involved in the civil rights efforts; "you won't really accomplish desegregation and other desirable ends until the 500 are extensively involved in what the 50 do as a specialized performance."

In the spring of 1966, just months after Page arrived in Atlanta, he read about a petition circulated within the Senate to pressure HEW and the Office of Education to rescind their enforcement efforts involving school desegregation. In a move unheard of from a Regional Director, Page wired Gardner, asking him to hold strong against the Senate pressures. It seemed to Page that, if the Senate could cause the executive branch to pull back from the Act's enforcement, it would remove the legal authority for action and, as well, would invalidate the Department's previous actions. Although he came down forthrightly in favor of the existing school desegregation guidelines, Page used the opportunity of the telegram to emphasize his regional perspective:

> Compliance cannot be achieved by efforts of personnel in Washington alone, regardless of their good intentions. They do not have and cannot get the local information and sensitivity requisite to full performance. Local people respond more positively to federal personnel stationed in the area than to personnel remotely stationed in Washington. Even if they could perform that function centrally, we cannot operate sensibly in the regional office— this one, particularly—without having immediate information and capacity for response.[6]

The morning after the telegram was sent, the text of the message appeared in an Atlanta newspaper. Since Page knew he did not leak the message, he was concerned about the leak from a management standpoint. "I was just sending a wire to my boss," Page noted, and considered it a breach of confidence that the text was made public. Although the cause of the leak is still undetermined, several theories have been advanced. One theory attributes it to someone in a Congressional office; it was known that copies of the wire were typed, put in HEW envelopes, privately stamped (not franked), and mailed to all members of Congress the same day the wire was received by Gardner. Another theory set forth suggests that, since copies of the wire were distributed within the Office of Education, one of the education officials resistant to the desegregation policy made the text of the wire public. But once the message was made public, Page acknowledged his position, considering that his views were supportive of Gardner and did not represent insubordination of the Secretary's policies.

Page's tenure in Atlanta did represent a new style in the way Regional Directors proceeded. As a symbol of federal policy (operating as a miniature Secretary), Page used his special position to serve the larger Department goals without belittling the unique needs and style of the South. The Regional Director was able to do this and still be considered (as was described by one former member of the civil rights staff) "strong on civil rights." Already socialized to the broader Department policy through his Washington-based tenure, Page used the platform of the regional position to reiterate federal policy on nondiscrimination.[7] With the support of Secretary Gardner (assumed through personal contact if not formal delegation), Page was able to withstand the regional pressures to remove him from office that were generated through the political system.[8] Always willing to talk, Page attempted to show recalcitrant state and local officials that the requirements of federal law were reasonable and simply required "fair play."

HEW: An Overview and a Structural Summary

Approximately a decade old at the passage of the 1964 Civil Rights Act, the Department of Health, Education, and Welfare was in a fluid state during the period between 1964 and 1968. Although described on paper as a Department with centralized control and authority, HEW was actually a confederation of independent affiliates, each with its own cluster of goals, constituencies, and methods of attaining public support. Although the Secretary provided some symbolic leadership—primarily in a public relations fashion—the gut work of the Department was done through its operating bureaus and agencies, each with its own decentralized system. Promises by the Secretary affecting existing operations thus had to be viewed with some skepticism about his ability to deliver.

The Regional Directors of HEW—serving as regional Secretaries— inherited the powerlessness of the Secretary vis-à-vis the regional program affiliates. In addition, they existed in a no-man's land within the Office of the Secretary. Protective of their limited powers, the Secretaries—through several administrations—were dubious about giving the Regional Directors authority to exercise discretion within the regional setting. The Atlanta experiment with "Pete" Page appears to be the single case in which a Regional Director was given some measure of trust by a Secretary and allowed to operate as a federal official on a regional level.

5

•

THE CIVIL RIGHTS
ENFORCEMENT STRUCTURE
IN OE

The two sections of the 1964 Civil Rights Act affecting OE operations involved issues that had actively surrounded discussions of federal education policy for a decade. During the 1950's—following the Supreme Court's *Brown* decision—attempts to legislate federal aid to education were blocked by Harlem Congressman Adam Clayton Powell's insistence that increased federal monies be tied to compliance with the Supreme Court decision. Powell's position caused a number of headaches for Democratic politicians; according to one student of the legislative battles, "Powell's action seemed like needless and damaging obstructionism."[1] Until the Kennedy Administration, there were concerted attempts in Congress to keep the civil rights issue separated from the administrative apparatus and confined to the courts. Not only were Powell's amendments opposed, but there was scant support for authority for the Office of Education to give technical assistance to desegregating schools. Failing the support of both the Republican administration and the Democratic establishment, the 1957 Civil Rights Act passed with the education technical assistance section deleted.

Although the policy situation within HEW and OE had changed during the 1963 and 1964 Congressional civil rights debates to the extent that there was some official administration support for desegregation, there was a general uneasiness about the form and extent of administrative action. Pressure from Powell, who was now no longer a "loud mouth" Harlem Congressman but the powerful chairman of the House Labor and Education Committee, pushed HEW Secretary Ribicoff to insert a non-discrimination clause in college contracts under the National Defense Education Act (NDEA).[2] But the major administrative action within HEW, prior to the 1964 Civil Rights Act, was Ribicoff's decision to withhold funds from local school districts that required children of families living on Southern military bases to attend segregated schools. Ribicoff was acting under the impacted aid program, which compensated local school districts for the loss of property taxes arising from federally-owned land or from the operation by the Department of Defense of schools for children of federal officials. The result of this action was the threatened building of desegregated schools within the confines of military bases.

The decision to withhold these monies was a significant federal breakthrough in the application of national standards to local school districts. It was a special case, however. First, the decision to withhold was made within the Secretary's office. Assistant Secretary Quigley orchestrated the situation; and although the letter informing local school systems of the cutoff was signed by the Acting Commissioner of OE, the political determination of the action centered in the Secretary's office. Second, and more important, this case involved an OE program that, despite the opposition of the large education organization, was built upon a direct relationship between the local school district and the federal government.

This is not to say that the cutoff decision was easy. Rather, the full force of opposition did not come into play in this decision. The impacted aid program affected a relative smattering of schools around the country and involved a relatively small appropriation; it was a limited threat to the education establishment. Additionally, the debate around the decision centered on the authority of HEW to effect the cutoff.

After the decision in the military base situation, there was little attention given at HEW or by a new Secretary to the administrative apparatus that would integrate that policy decision with the rest of OE's and HEW's programs.

When the Civil Rights Act emerged from Congress in July 1964 including Title VI—the section calling for the expenditure of federal funds in a nondiscriminatory fashion—OE's preparation for the implementation of that section was nil. The title had been originally inserted into the bill by the Kennedy Administration for bargaining purposes; the John Kennedy assassination and the subsequent Johnson honeymoon gave the section real life. Assistant Secretary Quigley's action on the impacted aid program provided precedent for the assumption that Title VI enforcement in HEW would be located in the Secretary's office. And many of the OE meetings, memos, and conferences involving the Civil Rights Act were focused on Title IV, the section of the legislation that called upon the Office of Education to provide technical assistance to desegregating school systems.

Although the planning for civil rights policies centered in the Commissioner's office, the strategizing for the Title VI program assumed that it, like other OE operations, would work as a specialist, technical service. From the beginning, civil rights activities within OE were the responsibility of a small, compartmentalized group of dedicated OE officials. When Keppel had assumed the Commissionership, he had pulled David Seeley from the Office of General Counsel in HEW to be his special assistant. Seeley combined a Yale law degree with studies at the Harvard Graduate School of Education and was known by Keppel. As special assistant, Seeley acted as a troubleshooter for the Commissioner and was assigned a number of areas of responsibility, including the civil rights projects. Stanley Kruger, a specialist in local school system administration, also had a succession of civil rights assignments, serving first as executive secretary of OE's Prince Edward County, Virginia, task force,[3] then staffing the Luddington task force (a group appointed by Keppel to investigate OE's responsibilities under the proposed 1963 Civil Rights Act). Kruger recalls that none of the planning discussions prior to the passage of the 1964 act dealt with what became Title VI. Discussions of Title VI were taking place in the Office of the Secretary, however.

Implementation Startup

OE civil rights planning lay dormant for about six months in 1964 until Keppel appointed John Niemeyer, president of New York's Bank Street College, and Robert Kriedler, a vice president of the Sloan Foundation, to come to OE as consultants to develop the substantive implementation plans for Title IV. Although both men were expert in the education field, they came to it with a limited perspective. Their interest was in innovative methodology, centered around the classroom itself. They did not bring any special knowledge of administrative issues surrounding education or of the politics of school systems. Thus the plan that emerged from their consultancies concentrated on the use of Title IV monies for general upgrading in integrated schools to dispel the bugaboo that the quality of education would be diluted if integration took place. They looked to plans for faculty integration and projects in which blacks and whites would work together on curriculum development.

According to political scientist Gary Orfield, OE's disinterest in the Title VI efforts was quite predictable. He quotes Assistant Secretary Quigley as saying "I couldn't believe my eyes" when he read that the Kennedy Administration included withholding provisions in its civil rights legislation.[4] He notes, also, that "it was clear that both the leaders of the major education grant programs and the HEW legal staff were hostile to the fund withholding idea."[5] Not only were some administration spokesmen aware of the political traps ahead in such an effort, but they were also protective of what they considered the implicit authority within the executive branch of the government to determine whether such an administrative decision would be made. If cutoff provisions would be triggered, they argued for a determination by the executive branch rather than Congressional action.

. Thus, up to October 1964, the formal civil rights organization within OE was charged with the administration of Title IV—focused on technical assistance programs through workshops and institutes (run by institutions of higher education) and grant programs to local school districts. The staff working with these efforts continued to be small, reflecting the operating assumption that additional assistance developed in the field through the institute program would act as a large bank of consultants (not regular civil servants) to be deployed as needed. Although this arrangement indicated some acceptance of diffused responsibility away from Washington, Stanley Kruger has recalled that "we didn't feel that OE had existing competency in the regions so we hired new people to be paid by the federal government but acting without the stigma of federal employees."

Although OE did not have a budget allocation to support a separate Title VI staff, the requirement did receive some attention in the late summer and early fall by other OE staff members. In the late fall, Allan Lesser, a former Senate committee staff member, joined the OE civil rights staff to "worry about Title VI enforcement." Although the situation was still fluid, the message had come through the Secretary's office that OE would be required to write its own regulations for the enforcement efforts. Quigley's bootlegging operation was of limited effectiveness; he had neither the funds to develop an adequate monitoring staff nor the structural clout from the Secretary's office to require compliance. The funds that had been appropriated by OE to administer Title IV were the only monies specifically designated by Congress for civil rights activities within HEW. Thus, common sense seemed to dictate that the education enforcement program be located in tandem with the technical assistance functions.

Although Quigley's office pushed all HEW agencies and bureaus to take in-house action on the civil rights enforcement, OE's separate source of funds flowing from Title IV gave the education agency a kind of independence that other bureaus did not have nor did they attempt to develop. And after unsuccessful attempts to bring in someone from outside the federal government to head the Equal Educational Opportunities Program (the major candidate was the State Superintendent of Schools from Michigan, but he refused the job), Keppel asked David Seeley to assume the formal responsibility for the activities that had been expanded beyond the original technical assistance functions in the OE unit called the Equal Educational Opportunities Program (EEOP).

The small staff assembled to mount the civil rights enforcement activities within OE was joined by a few consultants—chosen, for the most part, because of experience or knowledge of school desegregation litigation, which had preceded legislative action. Although a staff of six and consultants were, indeed, "puny resources for the administration of a social revolution," as Orfield has argued,[6] the composition of the staff reflected the prevailing view of the resources available for the job. Although there are probably never enough resources to mount a social revolution, the Title VI enforcement staff walked into battle without much armor. In retrospect, it may have been more important for the OE staff members to make a stronger argument for additional staff and a larger appropriation. But the officials decided to plunge ahead into field battles rather than into Congressional battles.

For, as some members of the original EEOP recall, the proportions of the task ahead were shrouded in gray mystery when the first set of regulations was published in December 1964. One member of that first team remembers that "at the time we started, nobody had any conception of the number of school districts in the country. Nobody had that information—not OE, the unions, the NEA. The only information we had was from a five year old census—and OE bought that information from the Census Bureau."[7] Another staff member described the expectations of the first civil rights efforts: "We assumed that the plans would just flow in. We thought that the government would receive plans and accept them—it wouldn't be a big job. We were thinking of a potential staff of about 10 or 15 people."

If this is accurate, one might, with the advantage of hindsight, characterize the expectations of the OE staff as pure fantasy. It is difficult to believe that they were able to ignore the complicated system of past federal, state, and local relationships, which was bound to be disrupted at any sign of change. And there were few changes as drastic as those implied by a federal requirement for assurances of nondiscrimination to qualify for federal monies. Indeed, there was more planning and strategizing for compliance efforts related to the public accommodations section of the 1964 Act—a relatively simple section of the Act geared toward the private sector of society instead of toward the marble cake political structure of federal programs, especially in education.

Complexity and Good Intentions

Most interpretations of the Seeley years within OE have focused on the good intentions of the civil rights staff in OE. The pressures on this staff have been characterized as alien forces that caused the dissolution of a beautiful moment in federal policy formation.[8] In 1965, a conglomeration of political and bureaucratic forces made OE the focus of the civil rights education enforcement. The officials charged with enforcement made a number of assumptions about their job that were precedent setting. These assumptions had a part in nourishing the problems that subsequently limited the role of the federal government in achieving school desegregation. These assumptions acted to deny the complexity of the problem involved, both by simplifying the substance of the issue and by cutting off the organizational relationships that necessarily surrounded the problem. An understanding of these tensions is necessary to comprehend the structural machinations that followed the 1965 activities.

Three clusters of assumptions worked to simplify the mission of the civil rights efforts and to shut off the organization from support:

1. *The problem was defined on its own terms.* This assumption meant that the civil rights staff within OE proceeded as if the solution to the problem could come from their single efforts. This belief tended to isolate the staff from others within OE—both program individuals in Washington and regional staff—and led to heavy-handed relationships with state education officials and local educators. The issue was implicitly antagonistic to Southern school officials. The inward-looking view of the OE civil rights staff (seen as arrogant by some state and local officials) made the federal government's job more difficult. Federal heavy-handedness did not jibe with the "reality" of past relationships among state, local, and federal school officials.

When the state and local officials complained to their Congressional delegates, the impact on OE became increasingly unsettling. Although some Congressional opposition was to be expected from known anti-civil rights members, criticism was beginning to come from unexpected quarters, and the Congressional majority began to show some signs of crumbling. This, in turn, limited the policy, structural, and financial independence of the enforcement effort. Yet OE continued to deal with Congress on an *ad hoc* basis; no skilled Congressonal liaison operated out of the federal agency.[9]

2. *The requirements for compliance were conceptualized, written, and administered as a simple, standardized operation.* Although Seeley and Keppel both acknowledged the variation in school districts within the country, they were under pressure to establish clear requirements for compliance as soon as possible. They seem to have accepted the argument that the only way to defuse the issue was to reduce it to terms that were as simple and prepackaged as possible. Although ideas on the method of achieving compliance differed in HEW (Seeley's operation assumed from the beginning that formal requirements would be promulgated, but Quigley thought that initial plans would be negotiated), it was believed that OE requirements would be accepted as clear-cut precedent. The belief in standardization led the civil rights staff to locate their operations completely in national headquarters in Washington and to view the process, once the bugs were eliminated, as a rather mechanical operation. In a few atypical situations, the development of school desegregation plans for compliance was achieved through bargaining and face-to-face relationships. The rule of thumb, however, was to rely on formal or informal canned plans and on impersonal telephone calls or memo relationships. In a country with 25,000 school districts built upon the ideology (if not the reality) of local control, these assumptions were supportable on neither efficiency nor policy grounds.

Even if one accepts the *need* for standardization of activity, it is difficult to believe that it made any sense in this policy context. Indeed, the procedures that were developed would work only if change were inevitable; that is, if Presidential and Congressional support meant that public norms and values would be quickly changed. The Title VI policy, however, was hardly conflict free. It was very easy for opponents of the policy to point to arbitrary action by the feds.

3. *The formal authority of EEOP was focused on school districts in the South and border states, whereas informal activities covered the North and West.* In part, this schizoid attitude throughout EEOP operations emanated from the Congressional mandate surrounding Title IV; Congress stipulated that federal monies could not be used to require the elimination of racial imbalance. But OE officials were also convinced that

it made more sense to deal with the problems in the South first. This strategy was justified on two grounds: the problems of segregation were clearer and more blatant and, second, the national political support for action confined to the South was stronger than it would be for the rest of the country.

The legal cloud that surrounded the differentiation between *de facto* and *de jure* segregation also provided ammunition for HEW's Office of General Counsel to argue that OE had no authority to operate in the North. The EEOP operation never really dealt with the legal limitations; the cover of Title IV was used to devise a series of almost clandestine activities in the North, and fast-talking negotiations with the General Counsel's office detached the "purely" educational issues from legal ones. Although the compliance forms were distributed nationwide, the review procedure for Northern districts was limited to a few large city systems.

The Chicago Fiasco

All three of these clusters of assumptions were early signs of problems within OE, signalling that the threshold of support was eroding. Then came Chicago.

The infamous Northern case was the Chicago complaint, brought to OE by the Coordinating Council of Community Organizations (CCCO) in Chicago. That complaint provoked action thought to be responsible for Keppel's OE demise and White House skepticism about the OE civil rights enforcement process. Tangling with Chicago's venerable Mayor Richard Daley is not an easy job for anyone—but HEW found itself in particular difficulty when it was disclosed that the careful procedures for termination of federal funds that had been rigidly devised for the South were, in effect, ignored in Chicago. The differentiation between fund cut-offs and deferral of funds was clear to some HEW officials, particularly to Quigley, but the informal procedures that were used to rattle the sabre in front of Chicago School Superintendent Benjamin Willis gave Daley ample ammunition to charge capriciousness on the part of OE officials.

The story goes that Daley and Lyndon Johnson met in New York during the official welcome for the Pope. In conversations that day, Daley threatened to pull votes from Lady Bird Johnson's beautification program if the termination of education monies from Chicago was not rescinded. When Johnson returned to Washington, he gave the "fix-it" assignment to White House aide Douglass Cater, who worked directly through Wilbur Cohen, then Undersecretary of HEW, to wiggle OE out of the situation.

Although the action in Chicago was tragic in itself, frustrating achievement of equal educational opportunity for the children of that city, its repercussions were far reaching. Keppel's relationship with Lyndon Johnson further deteriorated. Even more important, the White House action on the Chicago matter gave out a clear signal to Southern politicians that the President was no longer playing a hands-off game on the school segregation issue. As one HEW staff member put it, "The Chicago incident showed Southerners the political vulnerability of the program. Thereafter anybody could call the White House and complain." Before Daley's run to Johnson, Southern Congressmen centered their informal authority and relationships around agency officials within the bureaucracy. The rules had now changed. Until Chicago, the grievances that surrounded internal OE civil rights procedures had been held in abeyance. Chicago gave the cluster of inchoate complaints new life.

6
.
THE SHIFT
TOWARD HEW

After Chicago . . . A New Game

Secretary Gardner began his job at HEW in August 1965. He no sooner sat down to confront the octopus-like Department than the Chicago school complaint was thrown upon him. By the end of August, the new Secretary appointed an HEW team to study the Chicago allegations. The press release issued from HEW noted that Gardner was calling for the investigation of complaints of racial discrimination in schools in Boston, Chicago, San Francisco, and Chester, Pennsylvania. Although the White House intervention in the Chicago matter had not yet fully developed, officials in both OE and HEW handled the CCCO complaint from the beginning with some recognition of the political sensitivity and potential vulnerability of the situation.

Although Commissioner Keppel was the recipient of the original Chicago complaint in July, he quickly turned the 12-page document to Assistant Secretary Quigley. For more than a month the complaint was bandied about within the bureaucracy. The attention of a large part of the OE staff was preoccupied with preparations for the administration of

ESEA, anticipating Presidential and Congressional approval of the appropriations bill, which was actually signed on September 23. But the delay on the Chicago matter also reflected the confusion within EEOP about jurisdiction in Northern states. Because the question hinged on legal interpretations, the HEW Office of General Counsel was involved in the matter from the beginning. Thus, when Secretary Gardner appointed a team to study the Chicago situation, he named Alvin Cohen, HEW regional attorney for the Chicago area, as chairman. Alvin Cohen's appointment was significant for a number of reasons. It was the first known circumstance in which a *regional* official was given public and formal responsibilities for the investigation of civil rights matters, cloaked with the aura of authority from the Secretary. While he was a regional individual, Alvin Cohen was attached to an office that operated directly from the Office of the Secretary. This was a rare occurrence when the Secretary's representative in the field was given a role in negotiating a Washington-generated issue. Like the reorganization later mandated by Gardner, which attempted to prop up the powers of the Regional Directors, Alvin Cohen—as HEW regional attorney—represented a regionally-based effort for control by the Secretary over the HEW affiliate, OE. Cohen's appointment also reflected the general pattern of deference to lawyers when HEW or OE were confronted with crisis situations related to school desegregation and, as well, an attempt to cultivate an on-site relationship with Daley.

The scenario involving Chicago progressed through a fact-finding stage in the early fall and a series of judgments involving the determination of limited HEW authority over Northern style problems of school segregation. "Take it easy" advice came from the HEW legal staff and, as well, from David Seeley, who was attempting to juggle the tasks that were thrown at him. Assistant Secretary Quigley, however, continued to argue for enforcement of the principle of Title VI across the country.

When the civil rights issues involved in Title VI combined with Commissioner Keppel's hopes for ESEA, the bottom dropped out. The Chicago School Superintendent, Benjamin Willis, was not about to have the educational program of his district dictated by the federal government. He meant to proceed as usual, whether or not the submission of a civil rights compliance plan for the use of Title I of ESEA was required by the new education law. Commissioner Keppel, who nourished high expectations for the impact of the ESEA legislation on educational policies, viewed the battle with Willis as a real test—test enough, it turned out, for Keppel to agree to defer ESEA funds to the Chicago district until further investigation determined whether the official stamp of non-compliance with the Civil Rights Act would be applied and require both definite refusal of ESEA funds and termination of any other grants. Officials within HEW and OE attached great definitional distance to the difference between *deferral* of funds and actual *termination* of the monies, but the school officials in Chicago considered that either path robbed them of greatly needed dollars—roughly $30 million—and resisted the legalistic twist that allowed the Department to hold up funds from new grants.

The deferral letter from Keppel to Illinois School Superintendent Page was delivered on October 1. Although Keppel "touched base" with White House aide Douglass Cater before the letter was sent, he set up the contact in a *pro forma* manner that minimized the significance of the deferral decision. It took less than a week for the full cycle to develop: press and public reaction in Chicago, Congressonal pressure in Washington, Daley's meeting with Johnson, the White House directive to HEW, a quick trip to Chicago by Undersecretary Cohen, and official release of the funds and HEW withdrawal of its investigators. By October 9, Keppel sent a mop-up memo to Joseph Califano in the White House, enclosing the Chicago agreement and copies of the documents that followed the receipt of the original July 4 CCCO complaint. The White House was following the case closely.

The Chicago incident was a fast baptism for Secretary Gardner in school desegregation matters. Although the Secretary's office had little relationship to the nuts and bolts of the day-to-day enforcement machinery, the experience of Chicago indicated that the HEW chief would be held accountable for the political consequences of the civil rights policies. Although Chicago might have been a special case, a strong and new Secretary was not about to allow another opportunity like that to occur. HEW's life support system—dollars—was controlled by Congress. If Northern Congressmen should join Southern and border state representatives already opposed to school desegregation policy, the consequences for HEW would spread far beyond the civil rights efforts.

Thus the December 1965 appointment of F. Peter Libassi as the head of a small Office for Civil Rights, operating within the Secretary's office, represented the first attempt by Gardner to take administrative control of the civil rights enforcement program in HEW. Although Libassi knew his way around the government, he, too, had little experience with the administrative demands of a Title VI operation. Prior to his appointment, Libassi had served first as director of the Federal Programs Division and then as Deputy Staff Director for the U.S. Commission on

Civil Rights. While at the Commission, Libassi provided the staff work for the Presidential Council on Equal Opportunity—the coordinating organization created by Johnson and chaired by Vice President Humphrey to tie together the administration's civil rights programs. A lawyer by training, Libassi shared Secretary Gardner's belief that effective leadership was the key to administrative success. The new HEW civil rights chief had little patience with the administrative mess he saw before him in OE. Not only were the civil rights activities capable of pushing the entire Department into a Chicago fiasco and its consequences, but by the time Libassi came to the Department in January 1966, the political pressures from Congress and the White House had intensified. The new school desegregation guidelines for fall 1966 could be expected to create new anxiety.

The EEOP . . . Through Libassi's Eyes

Although Libassi's appointment represented a new chapter in the Department-wide concern over the civil rights programs, the problems he inherited in the job were familiar to Assistant Secretary Quigley. In a memorandum prepared for the HEW Secretary's meeting with Vice President Humphrey in December 1964, Quigley outlined the principal difficulties he saw in carrying out HEW responsibilities in the civil rights area. He termed one such difficulty "Making our program people conscious of their new responsibilities in the field of civil rights." For, wrote Quigley, "It is not possible to find or to hire enough 'civil rights experts' to do the job that has to be done. Civil rights is now a part of every program we administer but many of our program people simply are not civil rights oriented. Making them so is a necessary but formidable task."[1]

Although there was no alternative to relying on the operating program agencies, the small civil rights staff floating around Quigley was not sanguine about the way OE went about their organization for compliance activities. The agency level struggle between generalist and specialist, reflected in the structural location of the civil rights staff, was a particular problem. When Francis Keppel requested approval from the Secretary for the administration of OE responsibilities under Titles IV and VI, he specified that the staff would include a three-level balanced team: specialist personnel operating from Washington, "a small directorate," and "field representatives operating from five of the Departmental regional offices and from Washington."[2] The balance, wrote Keppel, would be for 19 people in the field, 38 in the specialist units, 11 in the Office of the Director, and two in the Office of the Departmental General Counsel.

Although Keppel asserted that "The work that is done in the field will be of crucial significance,"[3] the field positions never materialized. By May 1965, David Seeley formally requested permission to reassign field positions to the central office. For, wrote Seeley, "until considerable spade work is done in Washington, we will not be in a position to utilize a field staff."[4]

Seeley's organizational view of the method of managing Title VI enforcement activities did not jibe with the schemes that were forthcoming from the Secretary's office. In November, in anticipation of the creation of the position of special assistant to the Secretary for Civil Rights (Libassi's title), Acting Assistant Secretary Kelly—who was shortly named Comptroller of HEW—circulated a draft plan of organization to meet the Department's responsibilities under Title VI. Although modest in scale, the proposal set the scene for the consolidation of power within the Office of the Secretary that Libassi was soon to demand. Much of Kelly's plan harked back to Quigley's program—the decentralization of compliance responsibilities to the operating agencies with policy formulation and coordination in the Office of the Secretary. But the key difference between the proposed setup and Quigley's gadfly operation was the enlarged central staff established to carry out Gardner's mandates—a staff that could mean the difference between idle threats and policy follow-through. Not only would a special assistant be appointed, but Kelly's plan called for the placement in each regional office of a special staff assistant to coordinate all compliance matters in that region.[5]

Although the language of the proposal called for decentralization, the assumptions implied in the document revealed a confusing situation. To the agencies and bureaus within HEW, decentralization meant that the Secretary was going to allow business to proceed as usual—that is, the agencies and bureaus would operate as independent entities, with only occasional contact and opportunity for conflict with the Secretary's office. To those in the Office of the Secretary, however, decentralization meant that authority within the centralized HEW offices would be dispersed to the operating agencies or to the regional offices. Decentralization to HEW thus included the latent agreement that the diffused authority could be reclaimed by the Secretary's office and that the decentralized groups would be *responsive* if not formally *responsible* to the top HEW officials.

The ambiguity of the meaning of the Kelly memorandum was indicated by the response to it from Henry Loomis, then Deputy Comissioner of Education. Loomis certainly favored the principle of geographic decentralization; indeed, he was in the midst of the OE battle to strengthen the authority of the Assistant Regional Commissioners to coordinate programs within OE at the regional level. Loomis knew that straightforward, clear-cut lines of authority were not really possible. Yet, as he wrote Kelly, although "in general we are in favor of the proposed organization, . . . in choosing this horn of the dilemma . . . every effort must be made to minimize its disadvantages."[6] Loomis zoomed in on the regional office situation:

> The chain of command with regard to the "proposed staff assistant" in the regional office must be clarified. Does he report to the Special Assistant to the Secretary, or to the Regional Director, or to the operating agencies (depending on the area involved)? Making a clear decision on this point is more important than the particular alternative chosen. However, considerable confusion will result unless such a staff assistant is subordinated to the operating agencies in carrying out their line responsibilities. If an operating agency is conducting an investigation in the field, for instance, the field team cannot get instructions both from the home office and from the regional staff assistant. Such subordination on operating matters would not preclude the staff assistant, however, from reporting directly to either the Regional Director or to the Special Assistant to the Secretary as to progress and problems in compliance in his region as he sees them.[7]

Loomis' memo to Kelly was followed by a similar memorandum from Keppel to Gardner, reiterating the problems involved in the regional office section of the Kelly proposal and suggesting new language that gave the regionally-based officials less independence than the earlier draft. In effect, according to Keppel's memorandum, the regional special assistant would operate in a technical assistance capacity; Keppel wrote, "the operating agencies cannot be held responsible for carrying out their compliance activities effectively unless there is a clear-cut delineation of their responsibility for the conduct of investigations and compliance reviews."[8]

About the time that Libassi assumed office, Gardner formally circulated a policy memorandum and a statement detailing the Title VI reorganization plan. The policy enunciated was predicated on an insistence on wholeness and the interrelationships between programs within HEW. Gardner's administrative and structural concerns for consolidation and strengthened central authority were built on a conviction (or rationale) that HEW programs were implicitly tied to one another. Not only were there substantive interdependencies between the various agencies and bureaus involved with health, education, and welfare, but Gardner tended to view the political survival of the Department as a whole piece.

Although this made a great deal of sense programmatically, it was hard to fit it into a federalist system.

The arguments for consistency, leadership, and uniformity that flowed from Gardner's analysis of the Department's composition meshed nicely with Peter Libassi's view of the problems that were faced by Title VI implementors. Advising the President's Council on Equal Opportunity earlier in 1965, Libassi focused on the difficulties that would ensue if independent federal agencies imposed inconsistent requirements on the recipients of federal dollars. From the vantage point of the Presidential Council—attempting to look at the problem with the eyes of the Vice President—Libassi sought a rational, tight procedure to deal with the civil rights issue and to justify a leadership role for the Vice President, who was the chairman of the Council. In effect, Libassi jumped from the skin of the Vice President to the skin of the recipient of the program. From both positions he saw irrationality: disorganization at the top (the hodgepodge of procedures within the federal family) and accumulated and unreasonable paperwork at the bottom (where a single recipient—like a university—might have to deal with 17 or 18 departments and agencies in separate assurance procedures).[9]

But the perspective Libassi brought to HEW had little relationship to the "reality" perceived by the actors already involved in the Title VI endeavors there. The arguments for "wholeness" that came from both Libassi (for civil rights efforts) and Gardner (for the HEW package) could not be absorbed into the day-to-day perceptions of the individuals on the front line who had little opportunity to do more than put out brush fires. The new Office for Civil Rights (OCR) in the Office of the Secretary based its structural directives on a view of the organization that was shared by neither the EEOP nor the Regional Directors.

Have Your Cake . . . And Eat It Too

Libassi began his tenure in early 1966 with a firm hand. His resolve to tighten the HEW operations centered on two fronts: the existing enforcement program within OE and the responsibilities vaguely handed to the Regional Directors. In the case of the OE operation, Libassi argued for decentralization; in the case of the Regional Directors, the Special Assistant instituted a more centralized arrangement.

Within weeks after taking office, Libassi received a report from Ruby Martin, formerly his colleague at the Civil Rights Commission and, more recently, a member of Assistant Secretary Quigley's small civil rights staff.

Ms. Martin summed up the structural situation in the EEOP:

> The Office of Education will undoubtedly be the only Departmental agen-
> cy that runs its entire Title VI efforts from the central office in
> Washington. . . .
>   Most of the Commissioner of Education's representatives in the regions
> are not sensitive to Title VI. . . . This presents the central office with two
> problems: [how to train them to be sensitive to Title VI and how to deal with
> them at present] . . . .
>   One thing is certain, they cannot be bypassed when there is an investiga-
> tion or compliance review anywhere in their region because they could
> hamper if not undercut the efforts of the central staff.[10]

Ruby Martin's criticisms of the EEOP organization were shared by
Libassi; he continually argued in favor of the administrative decentralization of EEOP. This view, pervasive in the Office for Civil Rights, was
supported by reports from HEW Regional Directors, who, despite the
bombardment of memos from Assistant Secretary Quigley, never had an
opportunity to influence OE civil rights policies. The situation was described by one observer: "EEOP's dealing with school officials, including
the State agency people with whom OE field staff and DHEW Regional
Directors regularly did business, seemed to the Directors frequently to
have traumatic effects on Federal-State relationships, whose conduct the
Directors viewed as their particular mission."[11]

David Seeley had already been under some pressure within OE to
decentralize his program as a part of the OE reorganization scheme.
Although he had withstood those pressures, the new directives from the
Office of the Secretary were more intense. The call for decentralization of
civil rights activities came directly from Secretary Gardner in early
March; he argued, in part, the opinions of the Regional Directors. Then,
too, the word was communicated through the new Commissioner, Harold
Howe.

Commissioner Howe's response to Secretary Gardner indicated general agreement to proceed with the request. However, wrote Howe,
David Seeley "does have a couple of qualifications which need to be
considered":

> (1) Civil rights is a sensitive area in which we are continually making new
> policy through our handling of specific issues. Consequently, there is more
> need for immediate communication with and control from the central office
> than is the case with other programs.
>   (2) The handling of civil rights complaints is a highly technical enterprise
> involving specialized knowledge, and therefore teams which work in local

school districts should be headed by specialists working in the civil rights effort rather than by generalists from a regional office.[12]

The civil rights organization that Seeley was defending was hardly a tight, centralized effort. Like the other programs in the Office of Education, EEOP was not known for efficiency or organizational know-how. Through the first round of compliance review in 1965, the offices of the EEOP were described as chaotic, piled with papers, impossible for anyone to work in. The ESEA Title I or Title III or any new program effort might have been similarly disorganized, but the critics of EEOP were not interested in the "normal" pattern of doing business within OE. By March 1966, the EEOP staff was gearing up the second compliance review, anticipating a more stringent review procedure under the 1966 performance guidelines. To deal with anticipated demand, the office was broken into five area operations, all located in Washington, with a fair amount of autonomy for each area director. (The area organization meshed the Title VI staff with the Title IV people to increase the pool of talent.)

The new area-based arrangement might have been described as the worst of all possible worlds. Area directors could proceed independently on some issues. For example, Stanley Kruger, the area director for three of the deep Southern states, received the okay to draft and send his own letter of notification of noncompliance with the guidelines after he became impatient with Seeley's delay in sending the drafted letters. It made little sense for formal letters to school superintendents to vary from area to area—for a letter sent to South Carolina to be different from one sent to Georgia. Although variation might be defended, it could only be defended if officials were basing their judgments on similar principles. As it was, it was difficult to find these principles; instead it appeared that the variation that occurred was based on very idiosyncratic approaches.

On other, less prepackaged, issues, Seeley insisted on making all the decisions—picayune or not. As a result, area directors could not predict what demands would be made on them and on their staff members. In addition, the geographical decentralization implied by the development of areas was administratively superficial. Although the arrangement provided the rationale for dividing the work, it gave none of the on-site advantages of real regionalization. Staff continued to depend on the telephone for impersonal contacts and to be isolated from other OE and HEW programs.

The uncertainty within the staff was communicated outside the agency. School districts could not figure out what was expected of them.

Negotiations that had been undertaken with one OE staff member were terminated without notice. Superintendents did not know whom to call in Washington. When they met one another at meetings, they found that they were given conflicting information about minimum demands. Although some variation in requirements was inevitable, the internal organizational capriciousness made the variation appear to be unreasonable.

The arrangement left EEOP vulnerable, and, when Libassi forwarded an 11-page analysis of the EEOP to Howe late in March, Seeley was not able to develop a cogent rebuttal to it. The analysis characterized the administration of the EEOP as untenable: "Because of the lack of administrative personnel and delegated responsibility, all decision-making seems to reside in the director. This applies to all administrative matters, program functions and policy."[13]

> Operationally, the consequences of this conceptual flaw are easy to see. It can be summed up in the maxim familiar to every administrator: "what is everybody's business is nobody's business." Thus, there is no functional responsibility assigned specifically for compliance paper handling and follow-up, for complaint processing, for periodic compliance reviews, for record keeping, retrieval and reporting, for development of staff guidelines for these functions, and a host of other regularized and systematic duties required for the workability of the Title VI compliance program.
>
> Programmatically, not only does Title VI compliance suffer, but all other program phases are fragmented because staff is assigned to emergenices and exigencies. The pulls and tugs on staff is [sic] demoralizing, and any affirmative programming under such circumstances is administratively and operationally infeasible.[14]

Although classical bureaucratic theory might have led to a diagnosis of EEOP's ills that called for even tighter, top-level direction, the prescription outlined in Libassi's analysis was exactly the opposite. Instead, the document called for total responsibility to area directors for all program and compliance activities in the region, with area directors to be physically located within regional offices. The functions outlined for EEOP staff at the headquarters level were negligible; Washington-based officials really would not have an active role until the formal legal procedures against noncompliant school districts would begin. And these procedures were to be controlled not by OE staff but by the Office of the Secretary.

Many staff members within the EEOP agreed with the descriptive analysis of problems within EEOP, but they diverged sharply with the HEW Office for Civil Rights recommendations. Not only did they resent the intrusion from the Secretary's office for its competitive control implications, but hard-liners on the EEOP staff were convinced that increased authority for Libassi's office meant a go-slow on enforcement efforts. Although Libassi strongly disagreed with this characterization (alleging that his plans would lead to greater effectiveness in the long run), EEOP staff reacted negatively, based on their skepticism about Libassi's style and his known political contacts (i.e., the Vice President) and concerns.

The HEW Office for Civil Rights (OCR) advocated increased power for generalists in the regions when decentralization arguments were advanced to the agency and program people. But when it came to responsibilities within the Office of the Secretary itself, OCR developed a different rationale. In that setting, OCR played out the specialist function (that is, civil rights specialists), and the Regional Directors were the generalists. Although their role was limited, for more than a year the Regional Directors had been operating as the Secretary's Title VI men in the field. Although one could hardly characterize their efforts as aggressive (with the exception of "Pete" Page in Atlanta), the Regional Directors had acquired a proprietary concern about the civil rights implementation program. According to one observer, the Regional Directors "knew that implementation was difficult. They had coped with it as a necessary part of their general ministerial and representational function for all of DHEW. For them, the main question had been the proper and explicit relation of Title VI to general field management of all DHEW interests."[15]

Libassi's office within the Office of the Secretary operated on a peer level with the Office of Field Coordination—the Washington-based staff for the Regional Directors. With the plan for regional officials directly attached to the Office for Civil Rights, Libassi was setting up a competitive situation and taking responsibilities from the hands of the Regional Directors. Although some resistance was raised to Libassi's plan—notably from "Pete" Page—the Regional Directors tended to view the new OCR arrangement as some improvement over the *status quo*, despite their reservations, for the proposal might offer an effective way to control the activity of EEOP. Although responsible to Libassi, at least the regional Title VI staff members would be physically located in the regional offices.

That certainly promised less isolation from the regional administration of HEW than the previous EEOP procedure.

A Tenuous Congressional Deal

Only seven months had passed since the Chicago experience; yet the climate in which the HEW enforcement activity took place had drastically changed. The honeymoon period of the civil rights movement was over. The broad-based coalition that had supported passage of the 1964 Civil Rights Act had crumbled into many pieces. A few of the organizations involved continued to view the world in essentially the same way as they had a year earlier. Other members of the legislative coalition, however, were preoccupied with their own, more immediate, business. And some of the participants found themselves less able to accept the optimism implicit in the federal legislative and administrative programs. Urban riots, a new sense of separate and nationalistic consciousness, and unkept promises pushed the younger, less establishmentarian organizations (such as SNCC and CORE) into new concerns.

As organized citizen support for the civil rights effort changed, so, too, did the Congressional climate. The dissipation of support for the measure was probably inevitable; the political debate over much of the legislation was so lofty and unclear that any action was bound to antagonize wavering members of Congress. But the Chicago experience frightened moderate Republican and conservative Democratic Northern members of Congress; political pressure through the White House created a new game for a new coalition of Northern and Southern Congressmen. Although all of the departments and agencies within the executive branch were under the same mandate as HEW, no other part of the federal establishment had made such a visible and exerted effort to do something about enforcing Title VI. And within HEW, no agency involved as much political sensitivity and multi-level administration as the federal education efforts. Thus the Congressional guns were logically aimed at HEW and especially at OE.

Through the years, Congress has developed extremely sophisticated methods of using the power of the purse to control the substantive output of the executive branch. Presidential reorganization schemes come and go; Capitol Hill continues to rely on long-established relationships with bureau and agency-level career officials. Most of the time, the legislative branch has resisted bureaucratic efforts for consolidation, recognizing that those plans would disrupt their predictable patterns of dealing with the bureaucracy. Legislators ordinarily prefer a functionally organized bureaucracy, at least in part because legislative constituencies are organized that way. These arrangements allow the legislator to play a brokering role between the constituents and the agency. When it sees an advantage for itself, however, Congress can mandate forms of consolidation that make legislative scrutiny easier. Congressional consolidating requirements are more likely in new programs, where no structural change need ensue to disrupt existing Congressional alliances and methods of scrutinizing the bureaucracy.

Such was the case with HEW's civil rights program. The diffused location of civil rights enforcement activities throughout the massive Department meant that Congress could not get a handle on them. With this arrangement, the budget—the usual legislative handle—did not provide an effective entrée. Monies for civil rights activities could be hidden within other requests. Personnel assigned to civil rights programs could be masked with other titles. For these reasons, HEW was under pressure from Congress to centralize its civil rights activities, making it easier for members of Congress to pick up the telephone and be assured that without much effort they could speak to the person effectively involved in a particular enforcement action.

The move for consolidation began in May 1966, when the HEW-Labor appropriations bill came before the House of Representatives. Secretary Gardner was able to deal with Democratic Congressman John Fogarty of Rhode Island, who, as Chairman of the Appropriations Subcommittee that handled HEW, was sympathetic to the administrative problems that would occur if the Secretary's plans were undercut. The agreement Gardner struck with Fogarty provided for a measure of flexibility that would allow Libassi to proceed with the plan that he continued to term one of "decentralization." Although some time was given for the HEW program to develop, the handwriting for consolidation was on the wall. During the debate on the appropriations bill in the House, Fogarty justified deletions in the HEW request and told the body that these cuts were due to the consolidation of civil rights activities within the Department. For, noted Fogarty,

> These activities were budgeted in a great many different places in the Department. The Committee deleted these every place they occurred and has consolidated all funds in the Office of the Secretary. The Committee believes that this will provide for a much more efficient and effective program and will make readily ascertainable the level of funding for these activities. I recognize that a period of transition and experimentation will be necessary. A major part of the Department's civil rights effort must be carried out through the regional offices, so the Secretary should have some discretion and flexibility in allocating civil rights personnel to regional offices.[16]

Pick Your Villain

The formal entrance of Congress into the HEW civil rights battle further confused an already tangled situation. Depending on where you sat, the meaning of the structural ploys was "clear." To Libassi, sitting in the Secretary's office, the Gardner-Fogarty agreement was the best deal that could be made. But there was doubt: Congress was curbing the autonomy of the Office for Civil Rights and minimizing its independence and its ability to achieve its mission of Title VI enforcement. Libassi used the term "decentralization" as a catch-all. It represented the ability of the Secretary's office to use discretion and flexibility in allocating staff to operating agencies as well as regional offices. It was the only way, according to the Gardner-Libassi theory, that HEW would be able to tie the civil rights requirements to the allocation of program monies.

Fogarty's grant of flexibility explicitly covered only the regional offices, not the operating agenices as such. Informally, the Subcommittee Chairman told Gardner that he would close his eyes to the exercise of some flexibility toward the operating agencies, but Libassi was wary of overtly avoiding the House directive. Thus the open and strong flouting of regionalizing by the Office of Education civil rights chief was not only a disregard of Libassi's earlier directives; it became a form of antagonism to Congress. And although the Congressional action appeared to be a stronger push to the decentralization of the EEOP, the intrusion of the legislative branch into the scene only clouded perceptions of responsibilities of the HEW Regional Directors. Congress called for regionalization, yet Libassi's "decentralization" plans did not give increased responsibilities to the HEW regional chiefs. Already uncertain about their role, their unclear expectations were only compounded by Congress.

On the EEOP side, the Congressional directive served to reinforce David Seeley's perception of a threatened position. As the recipient of countless memos, studies, and demands from Libassi in the Office of the Secretary and as a part of the Office of Education himself, Seeley could not help but view the pleas for decentralization coming from OCR as arguments for deference to the operating agencies that resisted change. Seeley was already under internal pressure from some of his staff members to proceed more aggressively in the cutoff of federal funds. To him, the Libassi directives were brakes on the EEOP operation; their effect was to "go slow" and to stop the OE civil rights staff from proceeding with their plans. The Congressional action, therefore, was just another force in the pressure against the EEOP. Although no open accusations were made, there was a lingering view, held by some staff members, that the legislative move simply directed Libassi to do what was already implicit in his *modus operandi.*

Seeley's policy reaction to the demand for civil rights enforcement decentralization needs to be seen within the context of reorganization plans already under way within OE. The EEOP director was arguing for functional, not geographic, decentralization. That view was shared by the traditionalists within OE, who, by that time, were able to slow down the massive reorganization suggested by Loomis and Mylecraine. But although those arguments were made to counter the delegation of authority to the regionally-based Assistant Commissioners, there is little to indicate that Seeley would have been any more receptive to the handing of civil rights responsibilities to regional OE operating program officials. Enforcement required a separate, specialist staff. Regionalization, from the EEOP perspective, meant one of two things: handling compliance responsibilities either to the Assistant Commissioners or to the operating programs. The second choice meant giving compliance review authority to the HEW Regional Director. The first alternative was viewed as suicidal; neither group of OE officials were considered to be advocates of the civil rights policy. And the second alternative was seen as an abdication of both power and responsibility to questionably-committed officials outside the OE family. From Seeley's vantage point, neither view of regionalization was possible if the mission of the EEOP were to survive. Resistance to Libassi, thus, was valorous.

Seeley's valor put Commissioner Howe in an uncomfortable position. Survival within the HEW family was essential; so, too, was Howe's success dependent on his ability to manage the cacophony within OE. In July, the Commissioner asked Wayne Reed, former Deputy Commissioner and at this time Assistant Commissioner for Federal-State Relations, to head up an ad hoc committee that would make an internal review of the organization of the EEOP. Reed's opposition to regionalization in OE went back through several administrations but, to balance his view, the three-person team included the former Director of Field Services, Herman Offner.

The report produced by the Reed team was masterful. In that situation, probably no one but a permanent civil servant could have balanced the interests at play with such precarious sensitivity. Without accusing anyone of bigotry, incompetence, or ineptitude, the report zeroed in on the program problems, the difficulties that flowed from the area-organization operation: differences in operating procedures, imbalance of work load, and determination of program action priorities.[17]

The recommendations that flowed from this analysis of the problems outlined a structure that edged into the regionalization mandated by the OCR. Reed's team called for a reshuffling of the five area operations into a three area office setup.

> The placement of Area Offices II and III in the Atlanta and Dallas regional offices respectively would seem to be desirable for many reasons: to expedite action; to decrease the number of requests coming to headquarters, many of which could be handled more quickly nearer the action front; to keep a constant pressure on the schools to improve their performance; to make staff more available for consultation on cases; to cut down on travel time and expense; to improve the public image of OEEO [EEOP] by making unnecessary the processing of every minute matter in Washington; and to establish closer relationships between OEEO staff and school authorities and officials.[18]

At the same time this proposal seemed to meet the OCR specifications, the report included a caveat for Seeley:

> This recommendation is not for immediate implementation. These two Area Offices should be kept at headquarters until the Director of Area Office Operations has been appointed, working relationships between headquarters and the field have been established, consistency of operating procedures has been developed, necessary lines of authority and communication have been drawn, development of present staff has been considered, new staff has been selected and trained, and a plan has been made for the services and coordination to be provided by headquarters through the Area Office for Operations.[19]

One might assume that, if the Office of Education would proceed with business as usual, it would take quite a long time for Seeley to meet the specifications that conditioned the Reed recommendations.

After a few months respite, the formal announcement of the new organization scheme for the OEEO came in early September—released just as schools were opening around the country, and, according to some observers, timed to further muddle the minds of local school officials, who were having a difficult time figuring out what was expected of them by the federal government. At the same time that the regional staff appointments with nonspecific authority were announced, the press release also noted that a unit of the Office of General Counsel of HEW would "be established to work with the Office of Equal Educational Opportunities to coordinate procedures related to enforcement and litigation and provide legal counsel in connection with complaints and investigations."[20] Through the General Counsel staff, the Office of the Secretary was now given the opportunity for a day-to-day influence on the OE civil rights effort.

Although Seeley "escaped" moderately intact from the reorganization (moderate when viewed in relationship to the intent of the original Libassi directives), the sacrificial lamb in the exchange was Stanley Kruger, the area director for South Carolina, Georgia, and Florida. Kruger was one of the few staff members with formal training and experience in education administration. Rarely intimidated by education officials, Kruger—in his own words—was "a strict constructionist on the guidelines." He was the area director whose independence was of greatest concern to Congressional members and the White House. Kruger was reassigned to be in charge of a new unit for grant and institute programs under Title IV.

To many on the OEEO staff and to some in the school districts within his three-state region, Kruger's new position signalled a change in policy intensity if not in the content of OE civil rights enforcement. For more than a year, and because of the pressure from Capitol Hill, Kruger had taken on symbolic value to the program. His presence represented vigorous enforcement. Although Kruger knew that Seeley would take the action to move him when the time seemed opportune, nonetheless the new assignment created a furor within the staff. Kruger became a *cause célèbre* within the office and another headache for Howe.

To Reinvent the Wheel

Up to the fall of 1966, there was little indication of any special imprint denoting Commissioner Howe's entrance into the chief federal education job and the civil rights problems attached to it. At that time, however, a familiar strain in federal education policy began to reassert itself: deference to state government in the administration of the programs. The "new" idea represented some sense within the bureaucracy of being overwhelmed by the administration of the huge new amount of federal education monies. And, as is often the case when experimental verve begins to diminish, a variation on the familiar reappeared. Howe's intention to give the states increased responsibility for education matters had support in two important quarters: Congress and OE itself. Congress, through spokespersons like Congresswoman Edith Green, began to express doubt about the capacity of OE to—as they put it—"run the whole show"; and strong constituents like local representatives of the major education groups voiced displeasure with OE's administrative patterns. So, too, the permanent civil servants within OE—individuals like Wayne Reed—advocated a return to the familiar relationships cultivated between state education officials and OE.

Dealing with the states had both pluses and minuses for OE officials. Southern state education agencies has been the official props of the segregated policy that OE Title VI operations attempted to reverse. Whether or not state officials wanted to desegregate, it was very difficult for many of them to do so and to survive within the state political climate. But the states were there and there were fewer of them than local school districts. It was more "efficient" to deal with 17 state education agencies than with 5,000 school districts in the Southern and border states.

The reassertion of the state role was first emphasized in the Title IV part of the OE civil rights program. In his memo to Commissioner Howe reviewing the organization of the OEEO, Assistant Commissioner Wayne Reed had suggested that the program locate "supporting staff in State education departments to assist the chief State school officers in equalizing educational opportunity."[21] In that recommendation, Reed referred to the presence of such staff in three states, indicating an incipient move (or, at least, an undercurrent) to rely more extensively on the states. Reed's arguments were persuasive; he noted that "such staff could be a most useful bridge for assistance, cooperation, and coordination between EEO and State education departments, particularly in the States having massive problems."[22]

Reed's review was transmitted to the Commissioner in July. By September, Howe was advocating a dependence on state administration of the desegregation activities—what he called "decentralizing the whole show and making it possible for States to pick up responsibility."[23] And the formal determination of a new policy was indicated by a series of papers from Howe "concerning the possibility of a voluntary program of State responsibility for Title VI enforcement and for planning an equal educational opportunity program."[24] The major piece in that package was a document prepared by Stephen Trachtenberg, Howe's White House Fellow, as the result of a conference with "some of our Title VI staff, some outside consultants, representatives of the Justice Department and the Civil Rights Commission."[25] Although the conference that Trachtenberg cited as the basis for his arguments was concerned with urban schools, he culled its theme of local control to apply to the entire OEEO program:

> But equality of educational opportunity has been the issue which local and State authorities have been most reluctant to tackle. Unless they begin to accept a strong role in this area of education—a role which they now claim in all other areas of education—the Office of Education will increasingly and reluctantly find itself in the enforcement business rather than in the business of educational leadership and innovation. If we are to maintain the national

legal and moral commitment to non-discrimination and retain local control of education we must evolve a strategy whereby local commitment and actions in the area of equal education opportunities can be strengthened while at the same time assuring that the national engagement will not be dissipated.[26]

Carried to its logical end, the Trachtenberg analysis would suggest that the Office of Education completely cease the administrative role it had been attempting to play in desegregation policy. "National legal and moral commitment" would need no more than an articulate Commissioner, available legal staff, an able public relations staff member, and an ever-running mimeograph or Xerox machine.

While the basis for the OEEO operation was being eroded within OE through the discussions about state responsibilities, the attack on Seeley's program continued from Libassi's office. The animosity between the two programs not only involved differences of roles; by mid-October, the personal antagonism between Seeley and Libassi could not even be hidden within the language of official memoranda. In October, Libassi wrote a memorandum to Seeley and Robert Nash, the Director of the Office of Equal Health Opportunity, stating that "Three recent criticisms have been leveled at our compliance program which I believe are serious and which should have your immediate attention."[27] All three points specified by Libassi involved the relationship between field personnel and central or regional offices; all indicated conflicting perceptions between the two groups as to the job to be done and the method by which it should be undertaken. Libassi clearly saw himself as the individual to whom Seeley and Nash were responsible. He "asked" them to "take whatever steps are appropriate for your respective agencies and see that these points are communicated to your field staff" but told them to report to him by a date just six days after the memo was sent.

Seeley answered Libassi 15 days after the memo was sent and forwarded a terse reply. After outlining the instructions given to the staff, Seeley wrote:

> your memo tends to limit by its wording some activities that we have found essential and productive in negotiations. We are well aware of the problems emanating from writing suggestions and agree it should not be done in this program. At this time we have no knowledge of our field staff making determinations of compliance in field conferences or expressing disagreement with instruction from the central office. I would appreciate reviewing any information about specific cases that have come to your attention.[28]

One such specific case involved activity within the Atlanta regional office. Regional Director "Pete" Page wanted to center all compliance activity for the state of Florida within the regional staff; he had close relationships with members of the Florida education agency and considered that Florida was a good place to try out a pattern of compliance review that rested on regional initiatives. The request was passed through Libassi's office to Seeley and to the responsible OEEO headquarters staff member. When the communique finally reached the OEEO staff member in the Atlanta region, the message indicated that Page simply wanted to be involved in the negotiations; the OEEO headquarters staff member was still the individual in charge. As a result of this experience, OCR staff member Ruby Martin commented: "decentralization is not in the mind of OE."[29]

OCR: The New Battleground

Although Libassi had gained more and more control over the Department's civil rights policies, by the end of 1966 he was engaged in a major and time-consuming disagreement with Gardner's administrative advisors, John Corson and James Kelly. To respond to Congressional directives, Corson and Kelly suggested an organization scheme that emphasized some of the aspects already implicit in Libassi's operation. They recommended a program that was *centralized* within the Office of the Secretary but operated in a *decentralized* fashion from the HEW regional offices. The Title VI staff still attached to operating agencies would be transferred to the Office of the Secretary and then to the field. Small advisory units would continue in Washington, both in the agencies and in the Office of the Secretary. Compliance activities would be funneled through agency program staff—not civil rights staff—in regional offices. Enforcement would depend on the concurrence of regional officials as well as headquarters staff.[30]

The debate between Libassi and Corson and Kelly took on an either/or pitched-battle cast. Although Libassi was arguing for decentralization to the agencies, he was firmly opposed to the decentralization aspects of the Corson-Kelly plan. He characterized the proposals as a reorganization that would "seriously and adversely affect the implementation of a civil rights program in the Department."[31] Libassi suggested that the plan would overinvolve the Secretary in a controversial and sensitive field operation; would divorce implementation from the power and influence of agency heads; would fragment the program by creating a complex relationship between civil rights units in the field and at headquarters; and was unnecessary to meet the criticisms of the House Appropriations Committee.

To some extent, the Corson-Kelly plan flagged the concerns of those within HEW who were worried that the problems involved with the civil rights issue were keeping agencies within the Department from proceeding with the administration of the other jobs to be done. And in some cases, they argued, the programs that were being neglected might have greater consequences for black citizens than would the civil rights *qua* civil rights issues. The real challenge, thus, was to create a system of federal programs that were administered with federal standards—and among those standards would be the Title VI requirements. Libassi, on the other hand, argued that, although decentralization as advocated by Corson and Kelly *might* free the agencies to use Title VI within their arsenal of program standards, there was no assurance that program individuals within the agencies would not simply proceed with business as usual.

On January 9, 1967, Secretary Gardner met with the entire professional civil rights staff of the Department to announce that he would retain the organizational scheme established and advocated by Libassi. The session, according to some reports, had the character of a pep rally, praising a badly demoralized team and asking the members to go forward with new, invigorated spirit. Libassi told the group that, although no further reorganization would take place, regional operations had to be expanded. When the session was opened for questions, most queries concerned the organizational arrangements of the civil rights enforcement program; evidently the Gardner determination had now alleviated all uncertainties and concerns about the structural setup.

One of the questions raised in the meeting concerned Congressman Fogarty's attitude toward Gardner's decision. Asked whether Fogarty would buy his decentralization scheme, Libassi expressed confidence that the Rhode Island Congressman would agree. The next day, however, Congressman Fogarty died. The tenuous agreement privately arranged between Gardner and the House Subcommittee Chairman could no longer be assumed to be operative. As the spring Appropriations Subcommittee hearings were to indicate, Libassi's victory was a hollow one.

A Mop-up Operation

Despite Fogarty's death, orders from the HEW Office for Civil Rights continued to press for decentralization to the regions. And, despite his increasing isolation within the Office of Education, David Seeley continued to argue that decentralization in his program meant a loss of control and, hence, nonenforcement.

Following the pep rally in January, Seeley was under a steady stream of criticism for his resistance to the Libassi directives. In early February, he forwarded two separate memos to Deputy Commissioner Graham Sullivan outlining his objections to the decentralization program. The first memo started out rather apologetically; wrote Seeley, "I am afraid I must engage in a mild form of 'sit-in' regarding our program for decentralization." The document continued with a recapitulation of his long-standing objections to the establishment of operational units in the regional offices—objections that he had recently reconsidered with the understanding that these units would be adequately staffed.[32] According to Seeley, an increase in staff would be one of the few actions that could offset the skepticism surrounding the organizational reshuffling. For, wrote Seeley,

> There has been a good deal of skepticism among the staff and civil rights groups because of the rumors that "decentralization" is a code name for political scuttling of Title VI—an effort to take the pressure off school desegregation, either by putting it into the hands of Office of Education regional units more sympathetic to southern attitudes, or by rendering the program ineffective through fragmentation and impossible communications and administrative entanglements.[33]

Although Seeley agreed to go along with the regionalization in the offices in Dallas and Atlanta, he argued that he opposed further decentralization "unless the present staffing decisions are reversed. A decision to decentralize under the present conditions would be a decision to seriously weaken, if not cripple, the program."[34]

At the same time Seeley wrote that memorandum to Sullivan with copies to Howe and Libassi, he spelled out a more personal plea to the Deputy Commissioner in a memo he titled "Justification for Seeley's Outrageous Insubordination."[35] Writing on a Saturday morning, the OE civil rights chief pleaded for special treatment. For, he wrote, "our program is different from all others in the Office in essential respects," and, as a result, "*must* be viewed as a different animal from all other Office of Education programs: It is *not* just a small grant program. It is a form of *warfare.*"[36] Seeley described the program as one "as different from our ordinary operations as say fighting the Vietnam War."[37]

He argued that, although all of the OE depended on the success of the OEEO, yet OE's response to the various forms of criticism had encouraged resistance that, in turn, led to further noncompliance. He characterized the past response of OE and HEW as "defensive support" and called, instead, for "an aggressive, positive program to weaken irresponsible resistance and unite support behind the program."[38]

Although Seeley agreed, in effect, to decentralize all the authority exercised by the area directors located in Washington to OEEO representatives in Atlanta and Dallas, he requested that the authority-flow be in a channel from the representative in the regional office to the headquarters Assistant Commissioner for OEEO and then to the Commissioner. This flow continued the separate organizational civil rights program within OE. For Seeley, whatever success was to be found in the federal policy toward school desegregation was "due largely to the concentration of responsibility for Title VI compliance procedures in one organizational unit."[39] Seeley resisted the idea of giving the Regional Assistant Commissioners line responsibility for school desegregation; he argued that if they were responsible for the program, "they would have no time for anything else."[40] Commissioner Howe gave partial approval to Seeley's request for line responsibility from the civil rights regional staff members to OEEO in Washington. He left the door open, however, for the determination of a role for the Regional Assistant Commissioners in policy matters affecting school desegregation. Although the effect of the Howe agreement was a way of saving face for Seeley, he could not anticipate support for his position in the future.

A Strong Congressional Slap

April was the cruelest month for all parts of the HEW civil rights family in 1967. The budget hearings under the House Appropriations Subcommittee were conducted without the protection of Congressman Fogarty. HEW spokesmen were put in the position of defending a request for funds that included increased civil rights staff for operating agencies. Hostile Subcommittee members could not see where the justification material submitted with HEW's fund request jibed with the Congressional centralization directives handed down the previous year. Despite his usual poised and persuasive style in Hill appearances, Undersecretary Wilbur Cohen was not able to convince Congressional adversaries. Although Cohen and Libassi could argue that the Department had consolidated the separate and scattered civil rights staffs found within the Department, they could not meet the Congressional objections. Indeed, without Fogarty's protections they appeared to have flouted the conditions specified by the House Committee.

At the same time the budget attacks were made, an independent attack was developing within the House to question HEW's authority to enforce Title VI. Proposals crippling Title VI were tied to ESEA amendments that attempted to prohibit the OE from directing its monies in any form but block grants. Both sets of objections— to Title VI and to federal administration of education programs—struck at the heart of federal-state relationships and questioned the authority of OE to apply federal standards to federal funds. Although John Gardner had argued hard for the new federalism in his decentralization arguments, Congress had not been convinced.

When cruel April concluded, Gardner recognized that minimal survival depended on his willingness to take the steps toward centralization required by the new Subcommittee Chairman, Daniel Flood. His decision was taken against Libassi's advice. It came about the same time that David Seeley announced his decision to leave OE. The combination of the two announcements made Gardner vulnerable to charges that his capitulation to Flood was a deal taking Title VI enforcement from OE—where both Howe and Seeley were symbols of serious compliance activity—and putting it in a spot where Congress could dictate policy application and substance. Although Libassi and Gardner perceived the action as a tragic but necessary result of a battle with Congress, staff members within OE found it a logical outcome of the plan devised by Libassi some 18 months earlier.

The change mandated by Congress meant that all the Title VI activities were centered in OCR, but OE continued to run Title IV activities. But although one aspect of the struggle was settled, the familiar conflict between headquarters and regions continued to be played out within the civil rights staff now centralized in the Office of the Secretary. Major reorganization might occur and formal authority be diminished, but the struggle appeared to be inevitable. When Ruby Martin replaced Peter Libassi as OCR chief, she, too, confronted the headquarters/regional question. And the story ends, as it began, with a protest from a regional official to a Washington chief:

> It is my strong feeling that once the regional office is operational it must exert the functions and responsibilities which are planned for the regional office....
>
> I think my major problem with your suggestions relates to the means by which Washington guarantees the integrity of the program and establishes proper direction...the best way to assure this integrity and control is not to hold back from the regional staffs for any particular period of time the functions and responsibilities which will be theirs, but rather to make sure that the regional staffs fulfill these functions and responsibilities properly.[41]

7
•
AN EDUCATION
OR A CIVIL RIGHTS
ISSUE?

This section of the study began with a statement that the structure of an organization provides those inside as well as outside its boundaries with a series of messages about the goals of the activity, the kind of work to be done, and the relationship between those within and those outside its boundaries. Thus if a structural form makes "sense," it communicates these messages with some consistency. When architects of the organization's structure attempt to answer the question "What would be the most effective organizational form?", they do so with basic agreement about the implicit but unspoken part of that question, "What would be the most effective organization form *to do* . . . ?"

Because implementors of Title VI policies in education faced so many cross-cutting issues, it is difficult to know how they might have answered the complete question and, hence, where to begin an analysis of decision-making about organizational structure. If one characterizes the Title VI activities as *education* issues, one series of observations flows. But if one characterizes the Title VI implementation as a *civil rights* matter, yet another set of "givens" constitute the analytic mode. Separate analyses of the two inextricable characterizations give some indication of the underlying confusion.

A Civil Rights Issue

To view the Title VI activities as civil rights issues, the following observations might be made about organizational structure:

1. Civil rights issues involved the establishment of federal standards. As such, Title VI could only be administered by a structure in which national control was firmly established. This meant that civil rights policy would be most effectively implemented by individuals who were conscious of their unique, federal responsibility. Structurally, it demanded that a Title VI staff should be separate from other parts of the agency and should be as close to the formal authority of the agency as possible.

2. The political and social delicacy of the change required by Title VI required that it be administered by an organizational structure that was centralized in Washington. Such a structure could respond to political nuances in a strong, united fashion, protecting the implementation activities by its strength, and making the minimum accommodations that it deemed absolutely necessary.

3. Because the regional offices were staffed by individuals who lived within the communities in which the offices were located (and hence were subject to local pressures), it was unrealistic to expect that regional office staff could be a part of the enforcement effort. The analogy was drawn to the FBI field offices; it was not realistic to expect federal officials in the field to administer programs and undertake activities that were opposed in the communities in which they lived.

4. If civil rights requirements were melded into the package of requirements administered by other OE program staff, the enforcement would be severely diluted. As such, the civil rights activities had to be established as a separate program on an organizational level with the operating programs, rather than as an advisory, staff function.

An Education Issue

To view the Title VI activities as education issues, however, the following observations might be made about organizational structure:

1. The Office of Education had no experience in administering a program that would guarantee local responsiveness to federal purposes systematically and efficiently across the nation. Until the enactment of ESEA, the consultative supportive role of the office required an organizational structure that was relatively casual and loose. With ESEA, however, the Office was asked to move into a regulatory posture; that is, to develop procedures that were regulative of local school systems. That new role demanded an organizational posture that was new for OE and

required it to develop accountability mechanisms. Those mechanisms, applied by OE to state and local education agencies, were needed by the Office to justify its patterns of spending federal funds.

2. The Office of Education never had an effective field organization. Although interest was occasionally voiced in regional offices, decentralized field structures were not seriously developed within the agency. All policy questions, thus, had to be sent to Washington for clearance. The historical rationale for Washington-based decision-making was somewhat schizophrenic. Decentralization was sometimes opposed on the ground that it diluted the federal presence; that is, the assumption was made that, if regional offices were given authority, they would be rapidly coopted by state and local officials. At the same time, however, some individuals and organizations argued that regionalization of OE would have a multiplier effect and increase the impact of federal policy. This argument was advanced based on the assumption that a single authority source in Washington was more visible and, hence, easier to control.

3. Until John Gardner's term as Secretary of HEW, the Office of Education was able to operate quite independently of the rest of the HEW family. HEW did not ask much of anything in return for family membership. The organizational relationships that were important to OE involved Congressional committees (and members of Congress) and the education interest groups. John Gardner, however, had an interest in education policy as well as a commitment to deal with the component parts of HEW as a whole.

4. Commissioners of Education were rarely chosen because of administrative ability. Neither of the individuals who served as Commissioners during the Johnson administration had skill or interest in the day-to-day mechanisms of the Office. They perceived themselves as "educational leaders" who used the solo performance, rather than the ensemble arrangement, as their mode of operation. The disinterest in internal operations had pendulating effects; it sometimes meant that permanent civil servants had the delegated responsibility to make the agency run. But it sometimes meant the opposite: permanent civil servants were completely ignored and cut out of influence on policy and administrative development.

Compliance Versus Independence?

It seems quite clear that if Title VI enforcement and the imperatives of administering ESEA had been given to OE at two separate periods, the organizational problems of implementation would not have been as difficult as they were. If Title VI enforcement had been able to establish an independent procedure before ESEA, it might have set up a compliance program that operated out of the Commissioner's office, autonomous from program staff as well as from the Secretary's office. In such a setting, the Title VI program would have been less disruptive of the pattern of OE operations.

But such a victory would have been hollow. The funds available to local school districts under ESEA provided the carrot as well as the stick for a Title VI compliance program. Until ESEA, it would have been much easier for a school district to simply ignore the nondiscrimination requirements and give up the minimal federal support that might have been available to it. Indeed, OE spent many more hours, resources, and effort in the Title VI requirements and policies after the enactment of ESEA— almost a year after the 1964 Civil Rights Act was passed.

After the enactment of ESEA, changes in the historical "givens" in the Office of Education appeared inevitable. Some federal control was necessary if accountability mechanisms were to be developed. Someone in the top reaches of the agency had to be concerned about developing an organizational structure that would move the Office from a passive to an active role. Dollars had to be distributed quickly and targeted as effectively as was possible. School districts were asked to spend the new monies in stipulated ways; the federal government had no procedure to find out if this was happening. It was difficult for a small group of officials in Washington to deal with all these imperatives at once. And on top of that, with no funds to speak of, they were asked to enforce the nondiscrimination requirements.

OE officials took action that they felt promised the most successful path to mesh the civil rights and education realities. The job was extraordinarily difficult. And whether or not they were able to achieve the meshing in Washington, they knew that the local school district had to live with the consequences of both policy demands by the feds.

Diffused Responsibility

Title VI of the 1964 Civil Rights Act emerged from Congress without a definitive legislative history to serve as an explicit directive for administration. It proceeded to the White House, where, despite the creation of a Presidential Council on Equal Opportunity, a vague aura continued to surround the requirements implicit in the Title. Once Title VI was lodged in the Department of Health, Education, and Welfare, Assistant Secretary Quigley began to think about the details of the administration of the nondiscrimination requirements. Because of the relationships between the Secretary's office and the affiliated HEW agencies, Quigley's efforts were dependent on the will of the agencies and bureaus, and the Office of Education became the focal point for the school desegregation efforts. Once in OE, a specialist civil rights staff was created to carry out the Act's mandate for enforcement.

It seemed sensible to have a civil rights staff worry about school desegregation issues. But problems with the specialist civil rights activities meant that the Commissioner of Education—or all of OE—was more directly involved. Difficulties as aggravated as the Chicago incident necessitated the political concern of the Secretary and his office with the OE civil rights administrative enforcement. When an activity had the possibility of jeopardizing a larger administration goal (or if political tempers were short), the White House became active. And, finally, when Congress decided that the executive branch was not carrying out its will in the matter—no matter how unspecified the legislation had been—it took both fiscal and legal action to curb the activity.

Although a shifting locus of authority might be found within other administrative areas, federal activity in education does confront special problems. Ordinarily a new federal program is established with a centralizing tendency; questions of authority, details of administration, and general familiarity with the inevitable administrative "bugs" are confronted in a confined setting. Once the administrators of the new effort are able to anticipate the span of problems they will encounter (including the issues that would potentially incur Congressional wrath), decentralization, in some form, might be undertaken. But the Title VI implementor did not have the latitude to use the traditional administrative timing. The traditional centralization/decentralization dichotomy was an entrapment. Centralized decision-making meant federal control of education; the opposition was predictable. Decentralization meant weak civil rights enforcement; here too the opposition could be expected.

One might, however, use an alternative formulation to ask organizational questions and attempt to devise a structure that meets some specific functional needs. In the context of ESEA, enforcement of Title VI seemed to require:

1. Good information about practices and conditions in local school districts;

2. Methods of relating the civil rights issue to the education issue. This was needed both when the allocation of funds was made (relating civil rights staff to program staff) and when compliance plans were evaluated (since it is difficult to know much about school desegregation unless one also is informed about other aspects of education); and

3. An organizational mechanism that is responsive to people in the field (able to answer questions, provide forms o᾽ technical assistance).

It is difficult to imagine that these needs could be fulfilled by a Washington-based operation. Yet, like so many who identify their politics within the social democratic school, the architects of change in civil rights policies within OE and the Department of HEW seem to have had an ideological predisposition to rely on centralized decision-making from Washington.

Change thus appeared to be a monolithic substance to be directed and controlled from Washington. Control was not distributable; understandably, those who were identified with the change policies preserved and protected their own powers. For the most part, arguments for efficiency were framed within the confines of the Washington offices. Few made and fewer heard arguments for regionalization based on efficient use of the full capacities of the Department. Distribution of control functions was viewed as a deterrent to the implementation of the desired policy.

The control mechanisms that were devised to implement the nondiscrimination policy never seemed quite to "fit." Operations in both OE and the OCR confronted a disparity between the formal authority expected from officials at the top of organizations, and the actual authority implicit in the day-to-day functioning of the federal offices. Closing in on the "essence" of the authority was difficult.

Staffing Patterns

As might be expected, staffing patterns within OE and HEW were related to the centralized view of control and organizational structure. Many of the first civil rights staff members in OE had the view that their activities were a twentieth century crusade. Evil—racism and segregation—was pervasive. A small, committed group of individuals would by their action bring the truth to the heathens. The forces of good would rule; and conversion would be possible. With this moral fervor, a small staff could believe that a few tough enforcement actions would be precedent setting and the walls would come tumbling down. The President gave his blessing to the crusade and the religious fervor around the issue tended to support a simplistic view of the mission and the structure necessary to carry it out. This moral view did not help the civil rights officials view their job as a "normal" administrative endeavor. Although attempts were made to systematize compliance demands, for many staff members systematization meant business as usual—and business as usual meant deference to segregation. This view also supported the tendency in both OE and HEW to distrust permanent civil servants; officials in Washington and in the regional offices were viewed as "a part of the problem."

Zealots cannot deal with day-to-day uncertainty. By necessity, the moralist must close off arguments that logically intrude into a closed and certain view of the world. The civil rights operations in both OE and HEW tended to attract individuals whose strengths were found in conviction rather than in administration—in the civil rights situation, administrative skills included the ability to analyze the uncertain conditions with which the enforcement policies had to live. Uncertainty, in this case, was everywhere.

To survive, the civil rights staffs could not close off their dependencies on outside groups. Although they attempted organizationally to devise control mechanisms that assumed independence, they were continually stymied, by-passed, or overtly flouted. The organizational structures imposed by both OE and HEW were predicated on the assumption that the commodity of discretion was theirs to give and take; but, in reality, discretion was found everywhere in the system.

The Politics of Administrative Structure

All the major actors in the tale of Title VI enforcement in OE and HEW confronted administrative situations in which the administrative issues could not be separated from the substance and the politics of the policy involved. When tensions are high and conflict is inevitable, decisions taken on purely technical organizational grounds (that is, from the point of view of the decision-maker) burst into a larger setting. Individual job changes and structural shufflings have a symbolic character in such a conflict-ridden situation.

As the structural games cannot be viewed out of context from the policies to be administered, so too does the decision-maker confront a "given" when making any structural decision: implicit structural competition whatever the policy involved. Anyone sitting in the Office of the

Secretary of HEW must deal with the tension between the Department and the affiliated agencies and bureaus. Anyone attempting to change the Office of Education must deal with the implicit struggle between the Commissioner and the program people. And wherever a Washington-based individual sits on whatever policy, that person must deal with a competitive situation between D.C. and the regional staff. But although competition may exist, it may be a low enough price to pay for the improvement in information and linkages that comes with a regional set-up.

The civil rights enforcement staffs in OE and HEW searched for consistency and predictability in an organizational structure. Given the world in which they operated, that search was an impossible one.

III
THE LAW

8

•

THE TITLE VI
GUIDELINES

Until the passage of the 1964 Civil Rights Act, those who wished to use legal procedures to desegregate schools were limited to a litigating role in the federal court system. After the Supreme Court's monumental 1954 *Brown* decision calling for the end of separate but equal schools, individuals and groups who wanted to speed up desegregation went through the federal courts. Although some political pressures resulted in limited action within the executive branch, Congress' failure to enact civil rights legislation meant that the other major law-producing source—the legislative branch—was silent.

With the passage of the 1964 Civil Rights Act, however, a new chapter in civil rights law was opened. In that legislation, Congress declared a series of substantive rights, federal remedies, and methods of appeal. But the Congress cannot administer; it can only attempt to require. Therefore it called on the agencies within the federal family to develop regulations to implement that general federal standard.

The legal activity within the Office of Education and the Department of Health, Education, and Welfare aimed at enforcement of Title VI in education is discussed here in the context of the administrative process, the problem of applying federal standards, and the conflict between the authority of the administrative apparatus and that of the courts. The problems dealing with legal issues are highlighted in this study because they are always one of the major questions within the administrative process and because of the relationship between the issue of school desegregation and legal questions. A number of issues involving the law were confronted in the process of implementing Title VI that are important to this study and that emanated from the kinds of choices that were made from among legal tools: the appropriateness of the guidelines, the procedures, the sanctions, and other rules that were chosen to facilitate the goal of implementing Title VI to achieve school desegregation.

Title VI: The Game Changes

The movement of the school desegregation effort from the courts to an administrative agency gave officials an opportunity to play a new game. That new game called for a new playing field, new rules, and a new lineup of players. School desegregation, as it had been carried on in the federal courts, had a number of assumed attributes: the activity occured on a case-by-case basis (involving individual school districts); the players involved were representatives of school districts and parents of black children in the districts (and attorneys for both sides). For ten years after the *Brown* decision, a slow and tedious process was carried out. Frederick Wirt described the situation of relying on the federal courts for enforcement:

> these courts had in some cases not been helpful, southern school districts delayed and evaded, and decisions were hard to apply beyond the district in which they arose. As Burke Marshall wrote in 1964: "It is as if no taxpayer sent in a return until he personally was sued by the Federal government."[1]

The court approach demanded that black parents take the initiative—an initiative that was not only expensive and slow, but that also carried risks of intimidation to the parents and children living in a community when a suit was brought against officials of that community. There were, however, certain advantages to the judicial process. The court system provided an opportunity for both parties involved to present a case, describing the local conditions as they perceived them. The information presented about the case (and the remedy that was eventually structured to change conditions) was tailored for the specific district. And if a black parent or officials from a school district felt that satisfactory treatment was not accorded during the initial hearing, the appeal process provided an opportunity for higher-level federal courts to review the case.

Shifting to the administrative setting did establish a new game. The location obviously changed from the courts to the administrative agency. The approach shifted from a case-by-case basis to an attempt to establish policy that could be applied to a large number of cases—that is, making for numbers. The players in the game involved some replacements; the federal government, instead of a group of black parents, was the primary opponent involved in an adversary relationship with a local school district. (It was not clear at the outset, however, what role state education agencies and spokespersons for black parents might play.)

When an administrative agency is given authority by Congress to implement a new policy, a number of considerations are usually confronted. The administrative decision-makers must evaluate the legislative history leading up to the policy, attempting to ascertain what constraints are established or indicated by the Congressional action. Although this search always takes place in the context of the decision-maker's own preferences, certain basic questions must be asked. The decision-maker must determine if formal rules are to be promulgated, outlining the basis for administrative policy. Although an administrator does have some discretion to determine whether formal rules must be issued, agencies are generally on more solid ground to justify their action if contested in the courts when action is based on established rules. If the agency determines that rules are to be established, it is expected to issue those rules pursuant to certain established procedures (usually based on stipulations in the Administrative Procedures Act). The procedure considered minimally acceptable has been the requirement that the rules, once written, are published and open for comment by the affected parties involved in the policy determination. After the affected parties have the opportunity to comment, the rules may be revised. If not, they stand as the basis for the agency to administer the policy.

Title VI: The Problem of Developing Rules

Although school desegregation policy turned out to be a specialized and quite discrete aspect of Title VI enforcement within HEW, the rules that were first developed inside HEW gave minimal attention to its special nature. The rule-making process involving Title VI in education did not initially take place within the Office of Education. In the months following the passage of the 1964 Civil Rights Act, the focus of attention on Title VI was organizationally centered inside the Office of the Secretary, specifically in Assistant Secretary James Quigley's hands. Thus the attention to Title VI was Department-wide. This Department-wide orientation was reflected in the December 1964 regulations, published in the Federal Register, setting the ground rules for Title VI enforcement in all the programs within HEW's jurisdiction.[2]

The regulations defined the coverage of the discrimination prohibition. (In this case, the regulations covered 69 grant areas outside the state-administered continuing programs and 25 areas that involved grants to states.) They stipulated the assurances required under the prohibition, and the procedure by which compliance would be affected (reviews, investigations, hearings, decisions and notice, and judicial review). After they emerged from the Justice Department-led task force, the regulations traveled the official prescribed path: approved by the Secretary of HEW, signed by the President, and published in the Federal Register.

The legal biases of those drafting the first set of regulations to govern the agencies administering Title VI meant that the set of imperatives that concerned them had little to do with normal problems involved with administrative law. A task force of representatives from the White House, the Civil Rights Commission, the Justice Department, and the Bureau of the Budget hammered out a model set of procedures, which were then individually tailored with minimal variations to meet the demands of 22 agencies and departments. The Justice Department, as well as the White House, was concerned with consistency within the federal nondiscrimination requirements.

According to one observer, there were three important ideas in Title VI:

(1) Public funds spent for the common good should be distributed equitably among the members of the public for whose benefit they are intended;

(2) Some racial discrimination is unconstitutional;

(3) The granting of Federal funds to a racially-discriminatory institution may constitute Federal participation in some of the discriminations practiced by that institution, some or all of which may be unconstitutional.[3]

The sanction available to administrators to implement the Title VI requirement was the possibility of terminating or refusing to grant or continue assistance to a recipient if noncompliance were found.

Although the regulations issued by HEW were general in form, one stipulation in the document did indicate the special character of the education programs. Part 80.4c in the regulations contained a stipulation that exempted elementary and secondary schools under court order from filing plans for desegregation under Title VI. The exemption was written into the regulations, according to participants, because the legislative intent was clear.[4]

School desegregation, as demanded by Title VI, did provide an unusual case. For more than ten years, the court system had been acting as a quasi-administrative agency in the school desegregation area. It was not only handing down decrees setting standards for local school districts to conform to the requirements of the Fourteenth Amendment, but at several levels within the federal judiciary, judges were supervising the day-to-day response of the schools under court order. Lacking an administrative agency to carry out the mandate of the court and with justification for action under Constitutional rather than statutory grounds, courts had no alternative to performing these quasi-administrative functions.

Because of the experience of the courts in the school desegregation field, it was understandable that neither the supporters of Title VI in Congress nor its administrative allies gave much thought to differentiating between the judicial approach to the problem and an approach that fit the administrative setting. Prior to the enactment of the legislation, the bulk of the work on the statute was carried out by Justice Department lawyers, who were more sensitive to the issues involved in litigation than to the problems encountered in administrative law. In addition, the lawyers within OE and HEW who had any civil rights knowledge (as well as those playing lobbying functions outside the government) tended to be experienced in school desegregation litigation and, whether knowingly or not, appeared to view the Title VI efforts as an extension of their litigating role.

When the HEW-wide regulations were issued, Assistant Secretary Quigley argued that they provided sufficient basis for OE to proceed. He did not feel that it was necessary for OE to issue its own formal rules for implementation; the HEW regulations, according to Quigley, met the basic requirements of administrative procedure.

Staff in OE, however, did not agree with Quigley. Although the HEW regulations provided the general outlines for departmental responsibility, they did not answer questions that arose as officials attempted to devise procedures for specific programs within the Department. How were legal standards to be devised to carry out the goal? How could these standards be defined and applied? Lawyers could draw up a neat and abstract set of standards that might be used to condition the allocation of grants and other funds, modeled on a simple contract between two business partners. But that two-party model did not speak to the complex relationships among the federal government, the states, and localities in education. Most of the contractual relationships between the feds and the schools were funneled through the state education agencies; in the few programs where Uncle Sam gave funds directly to local school districts, those monies were given without many strings.

Development of OE Guidelines

By early 1965, OE staff were beginning to feel pressure from state and local school officials, who wanted to know what was expected of them under Title VI. And as the passage of the Elementary and Secondary Education Act became imminent, the pressure increased.

According to Gary Orfield, "No one was able to give authoritative guidance to school officials asking questions left unanswered by the regulation and the instructions."[5] Because the Office of Education staff was hardly geared up to provide those answers (David Seeley had been appointed the chief of the OE civil rights program just days after the regulations were issued), a group of legal consultants was pulled together to set the standards for the administrative effort. The consultants were headed by Professor G. W. Foster, Jr., a native Southerner who was teaching at the University of Wisconsin Law School. Foster saw the new administrative authority as a chance to take the school desegregation effort out from its "goldfish bowl" position within the courts. Foster wrote Seeley:

> For more than a decade the implementation of *Brown v. Board of Education* was conducted in a goldfish bowl, where in adversary proceedings before the courts the civil rights position could be publicly asserted and brought to bear on the decisional process. From this came a series of standards upon which our present administrative procedures will be forced importantly to rest. It is evident that we can stall the administrative process to a halt if either the fixing of standards or the day-to-day administrative decision process is hampered by the kind of knock-down, drag-out proceeding which we have so long watched in the courts.[6]

Working feverishly, Foster's group hammered out the first set of standards that OE would use as its rule of thumb to measure compliance. For the first few months, the emerging requirements were communicated by word of mouth, reflecting an on-going struggle within HEW about the approach to be used by the agency to demand school district compliance. Opposition to the development of formal standards was led by Assistant Secretary Quigley; Quigley did not believe that the agency should issue public, written standards—or guidelines—that would be distributed or available to local school districts outlining OE's expectations for compliance. He was not only concerned about political reaction from opponents of desegregation but was also opposed to setting minimum standards that would act as the lowest common denominator and invite opposition from civil rights supporters. After a series of negotiating go-rounds with school districts, Quigley expected that a clear pattern of

OE requirements would emerge and districts would have a fairly good idea of what the agency would accept.

The other position, argued by Foster (with Seeley and OE Commissioner Keppel in agreement), spoke to a different problem. They thought that there was no way to turn the school desegregation issue into an administrative operation unless it was regularized, formalized, and made predictable. They were uncomfortable with the fluidity that the Quigley approach demanded; they wanted to be able to tell state and local school officials that they were applying known standards in the process of reviewing an assurance form or a desegregation plan.

Because the Department would not support the position argued by Foster, the first set of policy requirements issued by OE came out in a strange form. Consultant Foster—speaking for "himself"—published an article detailing the OE requirements for compliance in a March issue of the *Saturday Review of Literature*.[7] Although publication of the article hardly met normal due process requirements of notice nor did it call for official approval of the Secretary or the President, it did provide a written statement of OE expectations. The article was circulated in reprint form to school districts throughout the country, financed by the Potomac Institute, a private, foundation-supported Washington group concerned about federal civil rights activities. The *Saturday Review* article was initially viewed as a quasi-official way for the agency to circulate its standards without getting the Department's formal agreement. By April, however, the substance of the article was formulated into a "General Statement of Policies Under Title VI of the Civil Rights Act of 1964 Respecting Desegregation of Elementary and Secondary Schools." Those policies—including requirements for faculty and staff desegregation; nondiscrimination in other school affiliated services, facilities, activities, and programs; preparation of pupils, teachers, staff, and community for desegregation; and notice of desegregation plans—were to be the OE standard for approval of plans that would affect school opening in fall 1965.

The question that was debated inside HEW throughout the period of the Quigley-Foster *et al.* conflict was one that posed an either/or situation: should there be rules (or guidelines) formally issued by OE for Title VI enforcement or should no rules be issued? Very little attention was given to the second level question that had to be asked if it was decided that rules (issued in some manner) would be developed: what would be the substantive content of the rules?

In the earliest discussions, Foster did appear to be concerned about the substantive requirements that would be issued by OE as they attempted to work out a pattern of administrative feasibility. A number of questions seemed obvious: Would the agency accept a grade-a-year plan to desegregate schools? Under what conditions was "freedom of choice" acceptable? What responsibilities did the district have to make it easier and less embarrassing for a black student to transfer to a white school? These were the kinds of questions that had been confronted by the appellate court system, particularly by the U. S. Fifth Circuit Court of Appeals (covering Georgia, Florida, Alabama, Mississippi, Louisiana, and Texas), known as the most liberal of the appellate courts in matters related to race. To Foster and his band of consultants, the court experience provided the authority for the education agency to act and gave the basis for the codification of the most current Fifth Circuit rulings into administrative requirements.

Although there is no evidence that anyone involved in the substantive development of the first guidelines considered any other approach to school desegregation than that hammered out by the federal courts, one might question whether any alternatives were available to the decision-makers. Those involved in the choice of the court-based requirements justify their action on several grounds. They argue that, since Congress required HEW to accept a court order in lieu of any other requirement for desegregation, it made sense to devise administrative standards that were as close to the court rulings as possible to minimize the possibility that a school district might play OE against a court. The officials have also argued that school desegregation had been defined in a judicial setting, and, as such, it was "sensible" for an administrative agency charged with carrying on that task to use the court definitions as a beginning point. Use of the court definitions also provided the officials with an argument to use to finesse the question of Northern school desegregation. To the point of the passage of the 1964 Civil Rights Act, case law had not been developed for *de facto* segregation—that variety of segregation in the North and West that was not supported by law but that, nonetheless, did result in denial of opportunity for millions of black Americans. The Civil Rights Act prohibited policies that required racial balance; although this was also a slippery question, OE staff could avoid it if requirements for compliance were constructed around the Fifth Circuit's definitions of Southern style segregation.

Although one might argue that legislation that has traveled the political path of Congress should be given equal weight with law produced through the judicial system (and, hence, be able to satisfy an administrator's worries about authority to act), it did not appear that the authors of the first OE guidelines for school desegregation were satisfied with the weight of their enabling legislation. Title VI was ratified by Congress with minimal debate; as a result, volumes of legislative history could not be invoked when authority to act might be questioned. In such a case, an administrator might feel comfortable with independent authority of case law to justify particular requirements for administrative compliance.

Although an argument might be made for the use of case precedents by administrators on the grounds of tenuous authority, it is probably not the reason that compelled administrators in 1965 to formulate the requirements as they did. The substantive requirements generated through the court hand-me-down procedure probably closely approximated the authors' view of what needed to be done. Not only were they more sensitive to the judicial experience than to other possible approaches, but they also wanted to move the federal government toward a uniform, tightly constructed posture. Although the authors knew that some flexibility was necessary as the standards were to be applied, they viewed the court decrees as reasonably sensitive to that need.

The intuition that guided the OE officials in a straight path toward the Fifth Circuit decisions also led them away from consideration of procedural questions. Although they wanted the predictability that went along with the issuance of rules, there does not seem to be any evidence that the authors of the first policies were sensitive to the due process questions raised by their failure to allow the opportunity for comment on the agency standards. Although spasmodic conversations were held with representatives of both school districts and civil rights organizations, OE civil rights staff attempted to avoid relationships with either group that legitimized them as parties with an interest in commenting on rules.

Applying the Guidelines

By the end of April 1965, when Foster's *Saturday Review* article took a more formal shape in the General Statement of Policies Under Title VI of the Civil Rights Act of 1964 Respecting Desegregation of Elementary and Secondary Schools, it was clear that a school district might follow three possible paths to satisfy Title VI requirements:

1. If the school district were fully desegregated it could simply file a Form 441 with HEW;
2. If a school district were subject to a final order of a U. S. Court to desegregate, it could submit the order to HEW together with an agreement to abide by it and any modification thereof; or

3. It could submit a desegregation plan for the school system subject to acceptance by the Commissioner of Education.

But despite the General Statement's detailing of requirements, Southern school officials continued to have some difficulty reading the mind of OE staff members.[8] In part, mind reading was not possible because the administrators had not really thought out their procedure for dealing with review of the compliance forms. Toward the end of March 1965, HEW Secretary Celebrezze wrote a memorandum to White House aide Douglass Cater, asking the presidential assistant's advice on subsequent action in the school area. Referring to Georgia, Alabama, Virginia, Tennessee, and Texas, the HEW Secretary noted that "the problem is that hundreds of school districts signed HEW Form 441 [the statement of compliance with nondiscrimination policy] . . . despite the fact that it is well known that the districts operate a dual school system. The motives for signing probably ranged from good intent coupled with misunderstanding to deliberate intention to evade the Act."[9] Celebrezze singled out the Georgia situation and acknowledged that the federal government had little alternative to accepting the good intentions of school board members who signed the forms and proceeding from there; he suggested that the White House deal directly with the governor to ask his advice and to suggest steps toward compliance.

By the summer of 1965, the small OE compliance staff was inundated with piles of paper forms, but the legal remedies for enforcing the guidelines stated in the General Statement of Policies were still unclear. While administrative chaos continued, the legal advisors within OE and HEW found that they were faced with the necessity of changing their standards because of new court decisions within the Fifth Circuit. Almost from the moment they were written, the OE guidelines were out of date. The courts—proceeding on a case-by-case basis—were continuing to hand down decrees that fit the special needs of the school systems involved in litigation. Accordingly, even by the time schools opened in the fall of 1965, officials within OE were looking to changes in the agency requirements to effect desegregation the following fall. One requirement that was particularly troublesome was the policy of accepting freedom-of-choice plans. There was no way for the federal officials in Washington to know why black children were not using the option open to them. The paper forms submitted gave few clues to understanding the local situation.

Some progress had been made in conditioning local school officials to accept the idea of federal standards as a requirement for funds. Funds through the Elementary and Secondary Education Act, made available that summer, gave local school districts a real incentive to follow the carrot of federal funds to some desegregation.

There was widespread dissatisfaction within OE and HEW civil rights staff, however, over the actual progress toward desegregation to be found in local school district performance. Although the staff could not realistically devise requirements that provoked school districts to desegregate in one fell swoop, they were uncomfortable with the step-by-step procedure apparently acceptable under the April 1965 policies. According to one interpretation, the 1965 agency requirements simply reinforced the tendency of the courts to allow school boards "to play the game of the frog, who jumps half-way between here and his rock, and half-way again, and again, and never reaches it."[10]

The truth was that the federal government—whether through OE, HEW, or the legal apparatus of the Justice Department—had real problems determining whether schools were really desegregating. The paper assurances and plans gave little guide to such an evaluation. And the guidelines issued by OE did not help a staff member—even one who visited the site to evaluate performance—decide whether the system was making substantial progress toward desegregation and not simply leapfrogging around the requirements.

Although the goal of the effort was school desegregation (a slippery concept in itself), there were also major political and organizational obstacles present that inhibited legal advisors from determining whether districts were in noncompliance and, as such, whether termination proceedings could be instituted. Congress had never really disassociated itself from an on-going watchdog role in the area. In an unusual requirement, the legislative body had included a provision in Title VI that required agencies to give Congress a 30-day notification of intent to cut off funds before such a termination took place. Thus a decision to proceed with termination required a substantial political investment of agency resources with Congress. The White House had eliminated the coordinating authorities of the President's Council on Equal Opportunity (dissolving it in September 1965) and, instead, provided the Justice Department with authority to oversee Title VI implementation within the executive family. In addition, the Office of General Counsel within the Secretary's office was taking control of the formal hearing procedure before termination of funds—a procedure provided under Title VI. This meant that those who were involved in negotiating plans were not a party to the formal procedures—that is, conducting hearings—used to determine compliance. Although the civil rights compliance staff had to take responsibility for the decisions of the legal staff, they had little opportunity to participate in the formal deliberations.

New Guidelines

The guidelines written for the 1966 school year showed the effects of the numerous problems faced during the first go-round. During November 1965, David Seeley indicated to Commissioner Keppel the procedures he would use for determining changes in Title VI guidelines and policies. He listed seven steps:

1. Circulation of policy issues to appropriate staff members of HEW and Justice;
2. Development of position papers;
3. Solicitation of views from civil rights groups (using the White House Conference on Civil Rights as the gathering point);
4. Solicitation of views from Southern educators;
5. Clearance of recommendations developed to that point with the White House, Attorney General, and the Secretary;
6. Publication of the requirements for a 30-day period of reaction; and
7. Final issuance.[11]

The intention of Seeley's memo was to evoke a clearance to begin a process of guideline development early enough so school officials would have knowledge of HEW's expectations early in the new year. But this timetable collided with unanticipated difficulties. Seeley was under pressure from his staff to take a tough position with the school districts; that view, however, did not mesh with the agenda of the newly established civil rights program within the Office of the Secretary. Reorganization within the civil rights staff of the Office of Education further delayed the process. As a result, the new guidelines were not issued for comment until early March, and they did not have official status until April.

Unlike the first set of requirements developed by OE, the guidelines for the 1966-1967 school year were treated in a formal manner, signifying a less sanguine attitude in OE about authority to proceed. Instead of publication in the *Saturday Review*, these policies were published in the *Federal Register*, reflecting both Department and White House formal concurrence. The first set of policies were about one-fifth as long as the 1966 guidelines.[12] The new policy statement signified the decision within OE to attempt to control school districts more "effectively" by making specific statements of requirements. The 1966 policy stipulated that percentages would be used as the measure of compliance—i.e., whether a school district had achieved 15% integration by the time the school year opened.

Attempting to keep up with the contemporary decisions within the Fifth Circuit, the guidelines included more rigorous specification of use of free choice plans, more attention to the problems of black teachers, and included 1967 as the target date for desegregation. The guidelines also included ten attachments—fill-in-the-blank forms for compliance, "sample" texts for public notices of the desegregation plan, a series of letters to parents, and forms for school transfer.

Opposition to the New Requirements

The formal publication of the new guidelines in the Federal Register opened the opportunity for comment; resistance to the new guidelines was apparent during the 30-day period when the requirements were circulated for comment. As a result, Secretary Gardner sent a letter to members of Congress, governors, chief state school officers, and local superintendents the same day that the guidelines were published in the Federal Register. The Secretary attempted to use the communication to clarify the intent of the policies and remove (or diminish) the confusion and resistance they engendered. According to one commentator, the Secretary's intentions were honorable but ineffective:

> Notwithstanding Gardner's assurance that the percentages were administrative guides tending to field review and thence to the due process of enforcement; notwithstanding the fact that neither Gardner nor any other competent DHEW or Justice official gave any support for views of the percentages as punitively-intended absolute adjudicators of compliance; notwithstanding what Gardner left unsaid about free choice plans and field reviews; nevertheless school officials generally continued to view the percentages in the grimmest light possible—assisted inadvertently in this exercise by occasional misapplication of guideline policies by EEOP staff.[13]

There were few supporters of the guidelines, even among the traditional civil rights advocates. The opponents of desegregation—especially those closely tied to school systems—found the new requirements extremely capricious. The all-out resistors sang their familiar tune. But some local school officials had spent months attempting to move local community leaders toward a compliant posture based on the 1965 guidelines. Just as school was coming to an end in the spring, a new set of requirements was thrust forward. These requirements appeared to generate new resistance from on-the-border officials who had just recovered from their encounters with hostile school board members, local politicians, and others who counselled all-out resistance. In addition, some members of Congress were worried about the coming fall elections and the effect of the new federal requirements on their 1966 campaigns.

The new requirements within the 1966 guidelines attempted to gloss over the disparities within the court system. The substantive changes were drawn from appellate court orders—but derived mainly from the Fifth Circuit. School officials from systems within the possible jurisdiction of the Fourth District Court of Appeals saw that their neighbors under court order were not required to include provisions for black teachers in their desegregation plans; neither were they told by the court to step gingerly on the free choice requirements. As a result, some school officials and Congressmen who had formerly voiced only perfunctory public opposition to the desegregation standards now were convinced of the irrationality and unreasonableness of the federal officials.

Although the OE civil rights officials had convinced themselves that they were acting in the interest of the civil rights organizations and their constituencies, one year of operation had diminished reciprocated support from these groups. Granted that the civil rights movement had dissipated during that year—but even the traditionalists who continued to identify themselves as members of a movement found the federal education civil rights efforts footdragging and disorganized. The agency continually accepted pieces of paper that were known to be fabrications, and there appeared to be few alternatives to the agency decisions. Even when "bad" federal district courts ruled against black parents, there was still some hope that these decisions could be reversed by the U. S. Supreme Court. The administrative process—as carried out in OE and HEW—had extremely limited room for appeal by a black parent (or a parent's advocate), and thus offered little hope for change once a compliance form was accepted.

The depth of the resistance to the 1966 guidelines was indicated by an exchange of communications between Arkansas Senator J. William Fulbright and then Education Commissioner Harold Howe. Fulbright had sent two letters to Howe during April. In the first, he passed on a letter written to him by the President of the Board of Education in Stuttgart, Arkansas, and requested that the Commissioner discuss the differences between the 1965 and 1966 guidelines, the reasons and authority for the changes, and specifically comment on the Stuttgart situation. The second letter (apparently the first was not answered) represented a statement of exasperation about the way the Office of Education was operating and a request that regard be paid to the differences among the school districts of Arkansas.

Although Fulbright was never known as a supporter of integration, up to that point he had not projected an active antagonistic posture vis-à-vis the administrative operations. The seriousness of the situation was acknowledged by Howe; a May 24, 1966, letter to the Senator was nine pages long, answering in detail each of the twelve charges advanced by the Arkansas school board president. Three of the assertions give some sense of the problems perceived by this individual; he stipulated that the 1966 policy did the following:

> (1) It changes our plan of desegregation which we accepted last year and which we have kept in good faith after approval from the Department of Health, Education and Welfare.
>
> (7) It destroys all confidence on the part of those who have thus far worked to meet the law with courage and sincerity because we find that we cannot trust the authorities who approved our original plan.
>
> (12) We feel that we should be able to continue with the three year plan which was approved by the Commissioner of Education and which the schools and its patrons have accepted. Continual and more stringent regulations will but lead to resentment and possible rebellion.[14]

Howe attempted to answer these charges by minimizing the effective differences to the local school district between the 1965 policies and the new requirements—a theme that echoed through the pages of the letter.

In addition to the nine-page reply to the questions about the specific Arkansas situation, Fulbright was also given an 18-page memorandum titled "Authority for the 1966 School Desegregation Guidelines."[15] The extensive memo represented the best legal defense that the Department could devise to counter the attacks on its misuse of authority. It recapitulated the Congressional stipulation within the legislation and quoted from the 1964 Congressional floor debate to justify OE's exertion of authority to require school desegregation. Despite Fulbright's seeming request for a response that clarified procedures, the memo read like a legal brief for a school desegregation court case. The attack on authority was viewed as a questioning of the substantive requirements included in the 1966 guidelines, rather than a questioning of the procedure of changing requirements suddenly. Thus the arguments presented were a detailing of court decisions relevant to the specific substantive issues included in the 1966 guidelines, especially those that were not found in the 1965 requirements.

The attacks on the 1966 guidelines increased during the summer; by the end of September, Commissioner Howe had been formally called to appear before the House Rules Committee. The effect of the Congressional attention to the authority issue, according to one observer, "had so far succeeded in the public opinion area as to support a strong, and widely-accepted case, that DHEW's Title VI operations and agents and policies were improper if not illegal."[16] Although the attacks were focused on the entire HEW enforcement effort, the charges leveled against the Department were primarily drawn from education activities.

In October, a month before the November election, White House aide Douglass Cater sent Secretary Gardner a list of 21 grievances about HEW civil rights activity brought to the White House by Congressmen and generally believed by the public. Of the accusations leveled by the presidential assistant, *four* involved substantive policy questions.[17] Another *four* points dealt with formal procedures and formal methodology of operation. The rest of the 21 points—that is, *13* items—dealt with the operating style of the aggregate program or of its individual practitioners.

Cater's reading of the authority challenge thus hardly gibed with the authority questions answered by OE and HEW lawyers in their May memorandum. Rather than questioning the legal substantive authority of the agency to act, the Cater case rested on the procedural and operating questions that flowed from a tenuous political authority base. Even the so-called substantive questions included in Cater's compilation related to the continually changed requirements of the education enforcement efforts. Cater argued that the agency failed to specify requirements; changed the definition of adequacy; gave like recipients of federal funds different sets of requirements; and specified percentages or quotas, only to deny compliance because the percentage was too low.

It seemed that, although OE and HEW officials perceived the challenge to be directed toward their substantive authority to act at all, both the Cater and Fulbright queries were pointed in a different direction. Whether as a tactic or not, neither query challenged the right of the agency to demand change in the racial patterns of local school districts. Rather, the queries argued about the methods that the federal officials used to achieve that change. Both Cater and Fulbright seemed to imply that the methods used by the OE and HEW staff were grounds enough for local school districts to mobilize opposition to the compliance demands.

9

•

LEGAL ACTIVITY
AND THE
ADMINISTRATIVE PROCESS

Although it seems never to have been discussed in the OE and HEW agency environment, one problem basic to the legal activity involving education and Title VI was that of transferring the issue from the judicial to the administrative process.

According to administrative law authority James Landis, there are several major points of difference between the administrative and judicial processes. Landis points to the ability of the administrative apparatus to "make for number"; "to maintain a long-time uninterrupted interest in a relatively narrow and carefully defined area of economic and society activity"; to develop a body of expertise in an area "where the making of law springs less from generalizations and principles drawn from the majestic authority of textbooks and cases, than from a 'practical' judgment which is based upon all the available considerations and which has in mind the most desirable and pragmatic method of solving that particular problem"; and to have the authority to initiate action rather than simply to respond to claims.[1]

Although these abilities of the administrative process are not to be found within the judiciary, the courts have special facilities—through the rule of the case—to deal with a different set of problems. "The court must decide the dispute that is before it; . . . The court can decide only the particular dispute which is before it; . . . The court can decide the particular dispute only according to a general rule which covers a whole class of like disputes. . . . Everything, big or small, a judge may say in an opinion, is to be read with primary reference to the particular dispute, the particular question before him."[2]

Judicial versus Administrative Processes

The two legal forms operate in very different manners. The judicial process begins with the specific and, through an inductive sequence, proceeds to the general. The administrative process, on the other hand, begins with the general (the rule) and proceeds to the specific (the application and adjudication of the rule) through a sequence of deduction. When a court decides a school desegregation case, for example, it has the latitude to deal with the specific attributes of the educational system that is the subject of the court proceeding and, at the same time, to make statements about a class of problems that apply to other subsequent cases involving school systems with the same characteristics. An administrative rule, by contrast, must be adequately specific to set a floor for compliance that straddles the struggle between too low requirements (for those cases that are close to the goal of compliance) and too high requirements (for those cases that are extremely recalcitrant and must be brought in gradual steps to compliance). Although specific enough to deal with a class of problems, the language of administrative rule-making must provide the flexibility to allow for varying interpretations, depending on the need. In the case of school desegregation administrative rules, the agency was confronted with approximately 25,000 school districts, North and South. And, even if the intent of the rule was focused solely on *de jure* segregation in the Southern and border states, the administrators were still confronted with 5,000 school districts, ranging from quite easily desegregable districts in northern Virginia to totally segregated societies surrounding districts in Mississippi's delta. (*De jure* segregation is the term used to describe segregation supported officially by law; that is, the segregation usually found in the Southern and border states. Northern-style segregation, usually known as *de facto* segregation, is segregation in fact but not sanctioned by state action.)

The decision engraved in the HEW regulations to accept either court orders, agency assurances, or plans for desegregation as proof of deseg-regating intent, meant that agency requirements could not vary signifi-cantly from the prevailing opinions within the federal district court system.

From the beginning the drafters of OE and HEW guidelines looked to the Fifth Circuit—the most liberal of the appellate courts—for guidance. The hand-in-glove relationship between the substantive requirements of the guidelines and the most current Fifth Circuit standards resulted in an interchange of evidence and justifications and continual interaction between the administrative and judicial ends. In several cases, the Fifth Circuit relied on the agency regulations and guidelines to support findings. The most significant case of this series was *United States v. Jefferson County*,[3] in which Judge Wisdom attempted to bypass the tendency of a "number of schools to seek refuge in the federal courts" and evade the HEW requirements. The Jefferson County case resulted in a decree, binding on all cases heard within the Fifth Circuit, that resembled the HEW standards. In that decree, the court declared that "We shall not permit the courts to be used to destroy or dilute the effectiveness of the congressional policy expressed in Title VI. There is no bonus in foot-dragging."[4]

The Jefferson County case represented a conscious attempt by the courts to sort out the separate roles implied in the judicial and administrative processes. As one commentator has noted, the decision had the effect of adopting the guidelines "as minimal procedural standards and emphasized that the executive branch is better equipped than the judiciary to deal with the day to day problems of school desegregation."[5] In its deference to the expertise and legitimacy of the agency-created standards, the court was playing out a fairly usual tendency for the judiciary to rely on the administrative to determine questions of fact.[6] Situations of judicial reaction to administrative action, however, do not typically involve such a developed interest by the courts in the area of regulation nor do they confront an administrative posture in which the agency voluntarily agrees to hand over a part of its regulatory powers to the courts.

Thus, although the reasoning within the Jefferson County decision might have been "normal" for most instances in which courts review administrative action, it was quite unusual for the school desegregation field. Although some courts were anxious to turn over authority, in other cases the administrators and the courts found themselves struggling over the same turf. The tension between the two legal processes was not limited to the question of review; rather, both the courts and the agency were protecting the same authority base, and each wanted to maintain the ability to move independently from the other.

On the administrative side, although the standards required for compliance were drawn from the recent decisions of the Fifth Circuit, the agency often found itself accepting court orders from other significantly less "advanced" federal district courts. The decisions of the Fourth Circuit, especially, presented substantive problems for the administrators. The OE civil rights chief, David Seeley, found the situation untenable enough to query John Doar, Assistant Attorney General, Civil Rights Division, about the matter. Wrote Seeley to Doar, "we continue to find ourselves accepting court orders which we would rather not accept."[7] Seeley asked Doar to "find some way to get these court orders remedied on a routine and almost automatic basis"—a request that was quite impossible given the formal deference to the courts. The problem was not a one-shot affair; as the guidelines were changed to require districts to deal with the problems of black teacher firing and to limit the use of free choice, the HEW and OE officials were continually confronted with a disparity between the agency requirements and the substance of some of the court orders. (Free choice is the term used to describe the desegregating plan in which black students are given free choice to decide what school they will attend within the district. Although the courts allowed the plan to be used in some cases, the evidence became clear that intimidation and reprisals against black students and their families made this procedure of limited use in desegregating schools.)

Some observers have justified the either/or approach included in the HEW regulations on political grounds. According to one agency attorney, "we couldn't have gotten by with ignoring the court order jurisdiction." This political problem was not only felt in relationships with Congress, but administrators also had to deal with the judiciary as a political adversary, protecting its own powers and jurisdiction. The case of *Lee v. Macon*[8] involved a situation in which a three-judge Alabama court made it clear that, although a federal agency could complain to the court about the failure of a district to comply with the court order, it could not hold its own hearing on the failure (a hearing that could result in termination of the federal agency's own funds).[9] Federal District Judge Frank Johnson enjoined HEW from terminating grants to school districts in Alabama (terminations that were already pending) because he issued an order that covered the total Alabama school system and he thus claimed jurisdiction over the entire state. Despite *Jefferson County*, the courts tended to echo the statement of the Eighth Circuit:

> We have great respect for the expertise of the Department of Health, Education and Welfare, and the Guidelines are most useful to courts and school districts in framing acceptable plans. However, our respect for the Department does not demand that we abdicate to it the responsibility for determining proper standards of constitutional protection.[10]

Although the courts obliquely admitted that the either/or approach to enforcement was being used by school districts to circumvent compliance, their sense of "responsibility for determining proper standards of constitutional protection" made them extremely protective of their authority to act. Indeed, as a remedy to minimize the diminution of enforcement (which was at least partially attributable to the court-agency battle), the Fifth Circuit held that a private right to sue is implicit in Title VI when no adequate administrative remedy is available. Thus, in *Lemon v. Bossier Parish School Board*,[11] the court gave a group of black parents in the Air Force standing to sue to require the enforcement of the contract made between HEW and the school district their children attended. In this case, the court recognized the non-enforcement of the administrative requirement but fashioned an order that pulled the responsibility from the administrative setting to the courts and had little effect on subsequent administrative actions.

The Norms of Administration: Control, Rule-making, and Adjudication

The original transfer of authority from Congress to the administrative level represented an unspoken commitment by the legislative branch to support the handling of the inflammatory civil rights issue in a less public, less politically vulnerable fashion. The issues finally included within the 1964 civil rights package had been considered by Congress in various forms for more than 20 years. By the time each house of Congress reached floor debate, a sense of the inevitable surrounded the legislative discussion. Although the Congressional debate on administrative control was minimal, the final version of Title VI did include a reference to the Administrative Procedure Act (APA) and a clause that noted that action under Title VI "shall not be deemed committed to unreviewable agency discretion" within the meaning of the applicable section of the APA.[12] The Congress was concerned primarily with the possibility of judicial review of agency decisions, reflecting the traditional locus of control procedure for independent regulatory agencies. Minimal Congressional debate and skeleton provisions within the act itself, however, did not obscure the thrust of the legislative branch's intention to limit the discretion of Title VI's implementors. Although Congress wanted the volatile issue handed to the administrative level, the legislators took this action with some confidence that agency officials charged with implementation would work out an acceptable level of "fairness" for implementing procedures.

The flexibility to select methods of policy formulation advantageous to the task at hand is considered one of the most distinctive aspects of the administrative process.[13] This flexibility depends on the existence of discretionary authority in the agency and/or in the officials making policy within it. The controls that are applied to the administrative process flow from the assumption of a legitimacy of choice of methods of policy formulation. Once the agency has determined the path it will take in carrying out its mandate, however, the APA specifies that certain procedures follow.

The controls placed on the *policy-making* functions of an agency generally relate to the public nature of rule specification. Administrators are required to publish their formal standards, to give notice and opportunity for comment on these rules, and to develop paths that are conducive to advance planning and uniformity of application. Theoretically, because the rules are thrust into an open, political environment, it is assumed that additional procedural safeguards are not necessary. *Adjudication* controls, however, are assumed to open a private decision chamber to judicial standards of procedure. Court-like provisions of the right to be heard, hearings, and the rights of cross examination and notice provide the control mechanisms for affected parties to question the decision of the agency in the application of policy.

Agency officials are allowed the discretion to determine the form that the administrative functions will take. Having once made that determination, the agency is regulated by a set of procedures that apply to formal and public activities, classified as either policy-making or adjudication. Yet it is recognized that the bulk of federal agency business is neither policy-making nor adjudication but informal activities that are beyond the scope of outside control. The same value sets that are operative in determining the form of administrative functions are the principles that guide the informal, discretionary activities. Neither is subject to outside controls beyond those imposed by the political system.

Although these issues are commonplace legal questions to officials normally involved in administration, they did not inform the architects of Title VI enforcement procedures. The traditional distinctions between rule-making and adjudication provided little insight to the policies evolved within Title VI school desegregation enforcement practices. The original debate over the promulgation of *any* guidelines between Assistant Secretary Quigley and consultant Foster did deal with the rule-making/adjudication conflict: Quigley's advice to rely on the pattern of requirements evolved in specific cases implied a reliance on adjudicative methods. Foster, on the other hand, wanted the Office of Education to issue rules as policies that would bind the relationship between the federal agency and local school districts.

Once Foster's general path was taken, a convoluted situation developed. The first two sets of guidelines in 1965 and 1966 were based on court decisions—decisions that could have some comparability within the administrative level in the adjudication stage. The specifics of the court cases were transformed into *rules*, however. Overly specific rules might make sense in certain, stable situations, but in this case, chaos emerged from the attempt to mechanize the enforcement decision process and to eliminate the area of flexibility.

The inappropriateness of the codification of adjudicative issues into rules made the existing set of administrative controls prescribed by the APA totally disfunctional. Questions of fairness and capriciousness were raised, the discretion of the administrators was questioned, at the rule-making—not the adjudicative—stage. One of the major formal control forms imposed by the APA at the rule-making stage is the opportunity to comment on published rules. When the first set of guidelines was issued outside the formal path—published in the *Saturday Review* instead of the Federal Register—the agency civil rights officials eliminated that control opportunity.

Ironically, although the actual controlling restrictions on the *rule-making* authorities of the Title VI enforcement procedures tended to be less effective than those anticipated by the APA, the controls on *adjudication* under Title VI were more stringent than normal agency practice. The decision to terminate funds—the adjudicative act under Title VI— "seems to offer more safeguards to a recipient than does APA procedure—in terms of notice, review of the decision within an agency, a congressional inspection period and judicial review."[14] The effects of this imbalance of controls were politically difficult. The major flack surrounding Title VI school desegregation activities involved the guidelines (the rules). The agency had few methods of dealing with the conflict that developed around the changing guidelines, few methods of socializing the conflict through participation procedures. At the other end, the controlling procedures around the adjudication were so stringent that actual enforcement of the policies was very difficult. The act of termination required an extreme burden of proof and commitment by the agency to balance the advantages of political clout that could be called on by a local school system.

Basic to the imposition of controls at both the rule-making and adjudication stages of the administrative process is the question of due process—the general way in which a legal system circumscribes the discretion of the decision-maker. But few questions about due process were asked when the procedures were devised to implement Title VI in the school field. Formal due process rights were given only to the recipients of the federal monies: either the local school system or the state education agency. Because of the failure to publish the first set of guidelines in the Federal Register, even those who were considered affected parties in the matter were not provided opportunities to have a formal input in the rule-making stage.

On the informal level, agency officials had perfunctory dealings with both civil rights groups and state and local school officials. But the dependency of the administrators on judicial precedent kept the informal conversations quite undeveloped. The guidelines for the 1966 school year were promulgated with the opportunity for comment, but opponents of the policies (either supporters or opponents of desegregation) were put in the position of arguing against the court system rather than questioning specific agency policy; that is, of disagreeing with the specific requirements handed down by courts.

The formal adjudicative practices specified in the Title VI HEW regulations called for the standard operating procedure of a hearing under the APA. Although the hearing procedure was run-of-the-mill, the enforcement of the funds cutoff required additional steps following the hearing, thus making the enforcement procedure more stringent than the "normal" APA practice. The hearing procedure within HEW was established by a former Federal Trade Commission examiner, who used as his model the standard two-party situation for a regulatory agency. This meant that no third parties were given a seat at the hearing table; the dialogue was between the federal government and the recipient of federal funds. According to one agency member, some discussions were held about opening the hearings to third parties or to the possibility of active *amicus* positions. Officials decided against this procedure, however, arguing that it would open the door to White Citizens Council groups or similar organizations and lead the enforcement proceedings into total chaos.

When viewed in light of the magnitude of the problem, the number of hearings for termination of federal funds was very limited. Many of them held for the purpose of terminating funds to school districts that had openly flouted the federal policies, refusing to file any compliance forms or doing so in a clearly unacceptable fashion. The limited hearing record reflected the strong political constraints on the agency against coming to a decision to cut off monies.

In any case, the effective decision within the agency was not the decision to terminate but the decision to *approve* school desegregation plans. Yet the procedures within the enforcement effort gave no opportunity for a black parent or an organization acting as a surrogate for a parent to question decisions to approve. Plans were approved with no procedure for review of internal agency decisions to accept. Thus, at neither the rule-making stage (construction of guidelines) nor the adjudicating stage (approving or rejecting a school district plan) did the consumer of the program (the black child or parent) have an opportunity to confront the agency.

The lopsided policy that was devised by transforming court decisions to rules played havoc with even the limited due process rights formally specified by the HEW regulations. Denied formal opportunity to question the guidelines (which resembled adjudicative order more than general rules), the school districts appearing at termination hearings almost unilaterally challenged the *guidelines* as the basis for their case.[15] That is, instead of questioning the application of the rule in a specific case, *the school districts were questioning the rule itself.*

Although the supporters of desegregation plans were never given the opportunity to appear at the adjudication stage, similar problems existed. For the most part, due process was flouted in the rule-making stage. Neither supporters nor opponents of the goals of the program had adequate opportunity to be heard in the rule-making stage to determine the enforcement policies, but the adjudication stage provided an opportunity for the opponents of desegregation to question the broad mandate of the civil rights enforcement and the authority of the agency officials to take action. The abuse of fairness principles by the agency lined the thorny path of political criticism, which, in turn, made it more difficult for the agency to enforce *any* Title VI requirements.

At least a part of the agency's reluctance to open its deliberations to due process considerations was the fear that openness would be a way to subvert the goal of nondiscrimination. Clearly, black parents—whether on a local level or through representation by national groups—had fewer resources to do battle within an administrative agency than did Southern school officials and their supporters. But the agency decision, however well-meaning, can be faulted on two counts. First, refusal to accept some measure of participation by affected parties is politically unwise; the political system is dependent on the maintenance of some level of participation by the regulated in regulatory agency activities. Absent even minimal participation, the agency's intent to act as advocate is effectively subverted at the political level. But equally important, the agency failure to open the decision process had the effect of inhibiting the development of on-going capacities of black parents within school systems to deal with the segregation issue. The specific forms of segregation that were prohibited by the guidelines had been devised by local officials to keep the black and white communities separated. As long as these officials maintained their power base within the community, they could act to thwart the opportunities for black children and the black community in multitudinous ways. Free choice plans might be prohibited, but such new devices as firing black teachers and racist disciplinary codes and tracking systems could be (and have been) used to keep the schools racially segregated.

Sanctions

Once the rule-making and adjudication stages were completed, the final resort available to the agency for a school district in noncompliance was the termination of funds to that district. Although this was the only administrative sanction prescribed within the legislation, there were some alternative paths to bring about school desegregation available to the federal government through Justice Department action within the courts (under Titles III, IV, and IX of the 1964 Act). A good number of the cases involving possible termination of funds resulted from clearcut defiances of HEW authority; that is, school districts questioning the rules of the agency and not the application of the rule. By November 1966, 126 cases were pending for cutoff.[16]

The single-shot, politically sensitive sanction available to the administrators has been both praised and damned.[17] Supporters of the sanction defend it on the grounds that a serious and powerful weapon must be available to the federal government to indicate that the agency "means business." Others, however, have viewed the available sanction as less than useful. Some opposition is framed not around the sanction itself, but around the procedures that limit the use of the cutoff.

Early in the enforcement process, OE officials differentiated between the procedures required to *terminate* funds and those required to *defer* payment. According to this interpretation, deferral—the decision to hold up allocation of funds—did not require the hearing process specified within the adjudication stage. Deferral was viewed as permissible when new grants, rather than renewal of grants, were at issue. The decision to withhold funds from the Chicago school system was made as a deferral decision. A substantial part of Mayor Daley's arguments against the determination involved the agency's failure to base its decision on "fair" procedures. Congress soon reacted to the deferral classification; most of the funds available to local school districts were new monies under the Elementary and Secondary Education Act and, as such, could be slotted into the deferral category. The deferral procedure was defended on the grounds that the small legal staff working on enforcement within HEW could not proceed rapidly through the complicated hearing requirements and, thus, could not deal with the number of school districts "known" to be in noncompliance. After a series of intricate maneuverings,[18] Congress finally passed a watered-down version of what was known as the Fountain Amendment, sponsored by North Carolina Congressman H. L. Fountain. The legislation limited the authority of the Commissioner to defer funds without a hearing to a period of 90 days, but specified that if the hearing procedure had begun during that period, deferral of new grants could continue until the final decision of the hearing examiner.

The deferral procedure gave the agency additional time but did not eliminate some of the problems with the cutoff sanction itself:

1. The sanction—termination of funds—was not really related to the goal of desegregation. Recalcitrant school districts that are willing to continue the loss of human resources through segregation and the expenditures required by a dual school system are not necessarily converted by the loss of federal funds. Thus, from the point of view of the recalcitrant districts, no cause and effect relationship to desegregation is implicit in the termination of federal funds.

2. The total cutoff of all funds from a school district may be too drastic a sanction to be credible. The national political consequences of the act are costly because of the publicity given the issue and the notification process to Congress. The termination of total federal monies in a school district may have the effect of disproportionately penalizing the black children within that system (especially if funds are allocated through Title I of ESEA). The blanket sanction does not allow for the determination of partial cutoffs, related to the particular situation within the district—i.e., to cut statewide funds for particular programs, to differentiate within a city between city-wide, school-wide, or special programs. Because of its drastic character, federal officials were bound to be ambivalent about applying this sanction.

3. The decision to apply the sanction is located at a place in the organization structure removed from the substance of the work of

the agency. Although students of administrative law have been wary that "no man shall be judge in his own cause,"[19] the distance of civil rights enforcement procedure from the sanction application was a difficult arrangement. One of the tactics of the compliance staff was based on the carrot theory: the luring presence of federal monies was meant to lead school districts to compliance. Although this approach was not always convincing, its strength was found in the bargaining and negotiating capacities of the federal officials. Without a sanction within their own authority, the officials' threats were less than authentic. After initial compliance reviews and determinations by civil rights staff, formal enforcement was placed in the hands of the lawyers within the Office of General Counsel. At that point, staff members familiar with the specifics of the case were excluded from participation. Although informal conversations could be held between Washington-based compliance officials and the OGC lawyers, the regional compliance officials—often the people most familiar with the situation—were given no opportunity to contribute to the deliberations.

The Problem of the North and West: *De Facto* Segregation

Although the Office of Education rested its authority on the current case law involving *de jure* segregation, the agency was not able to devise an equally consistent rationale for segregation Northern and Western style—*de facto* segregation. The federal courts during the mid-1960's were reluctant to rule on school cases in which the existence of school segregation could not be proven to result from official intent by local school authorities. The legal differentiation between the two forms of desegregation thus gave OE and HEW civil rights staff the authority base on which to focus their attention on the South.

Formally, the Title VI civil rights operation within the Office of Education was a national effort. In OE—as well as other parts of HEW—the civil rights assurance forms were required from *all* recipients of federal dollars, North and South. But from the beginning, agency officials recognized that they were stepping gingerly on their congressionally-mandated authority as they ventured into enforcement in the North and West. Although Congress had not made exclusions for non-Southern enforcement in Title VI, the legislative body had included a specific limitation within Title IV (the section of the 1964 Act that gave the

Office of Education authority to provide technical assistance to desegregating schools) that prohibited the agency from requiring racial balance through its efforts.

Even before the Civil Rights Act was passed, some OE officials were not pleased with the implied limitations on their concerns in the North and West. The educators on the staff had viewed the new legislation as a mandate to proceed with innovative and experimental education integration schemes primarily based within the classroom. The human relations approach to improved understanding between the races (in the classroom between students and between teachers and students) did not accept limitations based on the geographical differences between parts of the country. Indeed, some of the most educationally interesting programs were being developed in Northern school systems. As early as February 1964—a time when OE had hardly focused on the implications of Title VI to their activities—OE Commissioner Keppel queried HEW General Counsel Alanson Willcox for a definition of desegregation for purposes of Title IV that would give the agency latitude to deal with Northern-style issues.[20] An extended series of exchanges between educators and lawyers within the federal family followed; some educators argued for policies dealing with Northern issues within Congressional limits, and some lawyers within HEW and the Justice Department (and others) argued that neither the case law nor Congressional intent gave the agency authority to proceed as if the Southern and Northern situations were interchangeable.

During the early period of the enforcement, Assistant Secretary Quigley wanted the Department to push ahead in the North. He thought that the authority to defer funds would allow the Department to move in that area. When the Department received the Chicago complaint in the summer of 1965, the issue was brought to a head. During the period of discussion about alternative strategies within the Department, Quigley advised Secretary Celebrezze that "we are rapidly approaching the point where our inaction . . . could become bigger news than the complaints themselves."[21] When the issue was resolved to take action against the Chicago school system, however, the rationale for the move was an *educational* one—not a legal or political decision. According to some observers, Commissioner Keppel was forced to view the situation as a test of federal authority to impose educational standards on recipients of federal monies; when Chicago Superintendent Ben Willis (supported by Mayor Daley) refused to accept this authority, Keppel used the civil rights provisions as the enforcing lever.

The substance of the 1965 guidelines had little relationship to the needs and experiences of Northern school systems. The policy drafters, focused on the kinds of cases that had been heard within the Fifth Circuit, did not have an eye out to the set of problems that flowed from housing segregation and other social and economic forms of discrimination that were receiving increased attention through civil rights activity in the North. The lack of an official policy related to the North fueled the charge of the Chicago officials that the federal education office was proceeding in an arbitrary and discriminatory fashion against the Illinois city. The absence of relevant case law to support the OE charges also contributed to the agency's vulnerability. Daley's ability to provoke White House support for his case and reversal of the OE policy clearly indicated that the agency would have to confront major political costs if Northern issues were emphasized.[22]

The gradual move to consolidate HEW's civil rights enforcement in the Office of the Secretary had the effect of diminishing the strength of the arguments for Northern intervention based on educational claims. As the office developed increased operational responsibility for the entire span of Department civil rights activities, policy on *de facto* school segregation was increasingly determined by the Secretary's civil rights officials. When the 1966 guidelines were being devised, consideration was given to the inclusion of minimum standards for Northern and Western school systems. Guideline discussions reflected the concerns of a wide range of administration officials. David Filvaroff, the Justice Department's chief attorney for Title VI issues, argued that Northern problems should be included in the guidelines. Libassi, however, advised separation of the two kinds of situations, noting that pronouncements about Northern situations "should come in a separate document, at a later date, after we have more information and expertise."[23]

The guidelines issued for the 1966 school year were even less relevant to Northern situations than the policies had been the year before. The specificity of the 1966 guidelines gave little latitude to deal with differences between school systems within the South—let alone the flexibility to deal with Northern cases. By the fall of 1967, the HEW education policy could not withstand the increasingly intensive political pressure mounted against it on Capitol Hill. The consolidated Department-wide civil rights office headed by Libassi was spurred to action in the North, according to one interpretation, "because of opposition to Southern school desegregation."[24] The specific impetus was provided by a House amendment to the 1965 Elementary and Secondary Education Act that required uniform enforcement of school desegregation guidelines throughout the nation. The message was clear, and HEW began to give increased attention to school segregation, Northern and Western style.

The 1968 guidelines—the last school desegregation policies of the Johnson Administration—reflected the effects of the Congressional pressures and the difficulties involved in attempting to implement the earlier policies for compliance. The policies, published in the Federal Register in late March 1968, were no longer detailed prescriptions or how-to-do-its distributed to school systems around the nation.[25] The new version was a tersely written statement of general policies, worded to inform school systems of their areas of responsibility but framed to allow the individual system to determine its own method of achieving the broad policy goals. Although the specificity of the earlier guidelines had excluded attention to the North, the new standards were worded more broadly. They were focused on equal educational opportunity in its Southern form (elimination of segregation in education programs, student assignments, and catchment zones) as well as on the Northern variety (remedying concentration of students of one race within schools or classrooms and disparities of educational quality among schools and classes). The standards acknowledged that "these policies do not require the correction of racial imbalance resulting from private patterns," but gave the Department an opportunity to break away from the case law approach to support their Northern activity.

The Role of Lawyers

Because Title VI policy, like many other federal policy issues, relied heavily on determinations framed in legal terms, staff members trained as lawyers were located at many spots within the decision world. A legal perspective was thus articulated in many forms: through the lawyers who were part of the OE and HEW enforcement teams; through the relationship between the civil rights program and the HEW Office of General Counsel; and through the relationship between HEW and the Justice Department. The legal overlay involving the civil rights issue tended to spotlight the role of the lawyers even beyond that normally anticipated within the federal bureaucracy.[26]

The original civil rights staff within the Office of Education was directed by a lawyer-educator, David Seeley. Although one could only speculate as to the relative influence of his legal training compared with his educational concerns, Seeley had spent some time as a staff member of the HEW Office of General Counsel. Apart from Seeley, of the 17 senior compliance staff members in OE, seven were attorneys. During the summer, the regular staff members were joined by several hundred law students, who were sent into the field to do compliance reviews. Although several of the seven regular senior staff members had experience or extensive knowledge of school desegregation litigation, only one of them had a background in administrative law.

Lawyer-administrators were predominant among other staff also in the Department. Although he had never practiced law, the first chief of HEW's Office for Civil Rights, Peter Libassi, was a Yale Law School graduate. In the original OCR staff, three of the five top officials were attorneys. When the OCR became the official centralized enforcement office, five of seven top officials were trained as lawyers. Thus, most of the top HEW and OE civil rights staff members were lawyers acting as administrators. Although the staff represented experience in civil rights litigation, individuals versed in administration or administrative law were a scarce commodity.

Title VI enforcement efforts were dependent on the concurrence of the HEW Office of General Counsel (OGC) on both formal and informal levels. As the Secretary's "lawyer," the OGC staff was used as house counsel to the entire compliance program. Although there were expressions of annoyance about the substance of the legal advice given during the period Seeley was in control of the OE program, problems began to be expressed in a different manner after Libassi took the helm of the Department-wide civil rights effort. In large part, these problems were related to the use of formal procedures for termination of federal monies.

The stipulated procedures for termination of funds required that the OGC handle the case for the government. OGC's presentation would be made in the hearing before the hearing examiner. In the case of a determination of noncompliance, the examiner would make a recommendation for fund cutoff to the Commissioner of Education, who, in turn, reviewed it. The Commissioner could solicit whatever advice he desired and, if he wanted, could appoint a committee to review the determination. In some cases, the Committee and the Commissioner asked for further negotiation. If they agreed with the decision, however, the recommendation for cutoff was passed to the Secretary, who made the final determination. The tendency of the process was to soften the possibility of a strong federal bite—that is, to work against cutoffs rather than to advocate enforcement. Dissatisfaction with this arrangement was voiced during the Seeley period; OGC's activity tended to be viewed as a part of the HEW Secretary's attempt to control the autonomy of the HEW agencies and resisted on those grounds. Later, however, both OE and OCR officials were upset about the procedure through which the civil rights staff lost control over their own negotiations. Cases developed by attorneys within OE and the OCR were handed to lawyers in the General

Counsel's office. In a number of cases, the civil rights staff was discontented with the manner in which the General Counsel defended the government position, particularly when aspects of the defense slipped by because of OGC's unfamiliarity with civil rights matters.[27] Conversely, OGC staff were not always pleased with the prior preparation for the hearing. Although some attempts were made to physically locate staff of the OGC in the civil rights programs to facilitate an interchange of views on the informal level, the formal hearings continued to be the prerogative of the OGC.

The Justice Department's role in Title VI initially involved the drafting of the Title VI regulations as party to intra-agency decision-making; the Department took on new authorities when the President's Council on Equal Opportunity was dissolved, however. Title VI coordination (the euphemism for the Presidential role) was transferred from the coordinating group to the Civil Rights Division of the Justice Department. Although a tight system of coordination was almost impossible within the federal bureaucracy because of the autonomy of the departments, bureaus, and agencies, the Justice Department's role was significant in its use of an effective veto power. The advice of the Justice Department was not merely advisory; rather, Justice had to be considered whenever White House support was needed, and Justice Department concurrence was essential to bargaining with 1600 Pennsylvania Avenue.

Concerned mainly with development of litigation opportunities, Justice's orientation was not attuned to administrative matters. Rather, as a *George Washington Law Review* comment noted, its view of litigation "often runs counter to the idea of administrative means as the primary method of implementation, and fails to appreciate the problems faced by administrators or the potential of administrative enforcement."[28] Justice also posed difficulties for HEW as a competing force within the decision-making process—one that was difficult on its own terms.

> The problems posed for program people by a measure that forces them to act at cross-purposes with their essential obligation to distribute funds are difficult enough to solve when the instructions are issued by superiors within their own agencies; there would be even less reason for these people to listen to the Justice Coordinator, who is at best on an equal level with them, and who has no experience that would seem to qualify him for offering advice.[29]

10

•

TITLE VI AND LEGAL DECISION-MAKING

Legal systems serve society in two ways: in *content*, as a codification of the expectations of human behavior, and as a *process* that members of the society agree to use to channel their grievances. The two attributes are linked; the rules of the game are promulgated with the expectation that the game will be played fairly. When changes are made in the rules, there is an underlying expectation that these changes will not destroy the game itself; that is, that the new game will continue to be played fairly.

Although rarely made explicit, the balanced intertwining of the content and process of rule-making and application is assumed when legislative bodies––frequently the makers of new rules for the game—act to revise the game. Revisions can be superficial or drastic. The procedures by which the game is played can be changed. Even more importantly, perhaps the *players* in the game can be modified; new players can be added, or power distributions of the players changed. But as new or strengthened players enter the playing field, they do so with the assumption that the game will continue to be played under rules approximating some definition of fairness.

Congressional enactment of Title VI of the Civil Rights Act of 1964 was an attempt to change drastically the rules of the game and the role played by the federal government as it distributed its funds to state, local, and private institutions around the country. Before Congress enacted the Civil Rights Act of 1964, federal dollars were not distributed to include black citizens at the receiving end. The revised rules were meant to provide the opportunity for black citizens to get their due from institutions receiving federal monies or, in some instances, for black citizens to develop alternative methods of joining the game.

Like the sports analogy, the model for the legal role (the rules) is one of *managing* a conflict situation. Congressional debate acknowledged that the conflict between black and white citizens was real; its action was not to deny that conflict existed. Rather, the new law was to provide the opportunity for that conflict to be played out within the accepted game. Federal officials would continue to give funds to a wide array of social institutions; regulations limiting the discretion of those officials would continue. But according to the intent of Title VI, institutions receiving federal dollars would no longer be allowed to operate in ways that subordinated an entire class of citizens and excluded them from public benefits.

The experience of officials in OE and HEW involved in translating the general goal enunciated in Title VI to federal education programs indicated that the job was more difficult than anyone had really imagined. Congress had given the officials little more than a vague, general slogan about which there was no consensus. The development of rules and procedures to define the federal role and operationalize that slogan was a monstrous undertaking. As such, it is not surprising that the decisions that were made seem to have exacerbated the political vulnerability of the program.

A number of specific decision points and assumptions made by the decision-makers appear to have contributed to the problem. The legal aspects of the enforcement program were attributes of judicial rather than administrative processes. The form of legal reasoning that was used in the operation was the inductive form of the case method rather than the deductive processes used in rule-making. The lawyers who were involved in enforcement within the civil rights staffs of OE and HEW, the Office of General Counsel in HEW, and the Justice Department took their cues from litigation procedures. The mechanisms for defining the standards to guide federal policy-making were drawn in substance from the courts. Instead of applying case-based decisions to a case-by-case administrative process, during the early precedent-setting years, the court decrees were codified into explicit guidelines.

The first guidelines were open for criticism on a number of counts. To many, these policies did not make sense on their own terms. The specificity of their content made them appear unmanageable and unuseable to a diverse client population within 25,000 school districts. Limited in application to the South, the guidelines created resentment from advocates of change in the North and from Southerners who considered the regional focus discriminatory. Modification of the content of the guidelines to meet the changing court decrees within the Fifth Circuit left the administrators open to charges of capriciousness in requirements.

Whatever the policies devised, the administration of the OE and HEW Title VI effort gave the impression of flouting obligations to proceed in a way that appeared to be fair and in a way that implied that federal government power was imposed with accepted checks on its operations. The controls that were devised to circumscribe the operation were neither democratic (opening the process to input from affected parties) nor effective as a brake on official discretion. The controls were not operative on either the rule-making or the adjudication stages of administrative decision-making. Neither supporters nor opponents of the goal of the efforts—desegregation of schools—felt they had their just day in the administrative chamber. As a result, both forces returned to the open political arena to play out the battle.

The net effect of the effort—both the content of the policies and the process by which the policies were devised and implemented—was a sharp and serious questioning of its *legality*. This questioning included the following issues:

1. the rules that were promulgated were not always publicized in an effective way;
2. changes within the rules gave school systems the sense that the policies could be retroactive;
3. failure to maintain a distinction between rules and adjudication meant that the rules themselves were not always understandable;
4. the seemingly artificial distinction between rules for the South and those for the North provided fuel for the charges that the rules were contradictory;
5. the political relationships that surrounded the public education system meant that the changes required by the federal rules went beyond the powers of the affected party, as it was narrowly defined;

6. the guideline shifts introduced such frequent changes in the rules that it was difficult to orient action by them; and

7. there was a lack of congruence between the rules as announced and the actual administrative ability to apply the not-always-credible sanction.[1]

There are, of course several ways of dealing with these issues. One might argue that the differentiation between the substantive and the procedural aspects of the Title VI efforts represents an obfuscation of the real issue: that is, that both are manifestations of an underlying opposition to the desegregation effort. But even acknowledging that procedural opposition is never completely separable from substantive questions, one might nonetheless argue that the type of legal decision-making in Title VI enforcement courted problems.

Given the specific task to be performed and the political volatility of the issue, it appears in retrospect that Foster, Seeley, and Keppel were correct in their argument that the school desegregation effort needed formal rules on which to operate. But the rules they chose had severe substantive and procedural limitations. Were there any alternatives to the decisions that were made, however? What kinds of rules should have been developed that would have allowed the federal agency to achieve the goals of Title VI?

In some situations, it may make sense to take court decisions and turn them into administrative rules. These conditions might be met if the decisions themselves were general enough to apply to the administrative world and if the range of possible applications was understandable and manageable. Court decisions might be sensibly applied in an area in which the law was not changing rapidly so the administrator would have some confidence that the courts had reached a point of stability and predictability in decisions. And, of course, court decisions would make sense if the administrator had some assurance that the court remedies had proven to be relatively successful in meeting the goals of the administrative policy.

The decision-makers involved in devising rules for Title VI enforcement may have believed that the world they were facing in the implementation efforts was consistent with the world described by the court decisions. But, in retrospect, that appears to have been a miscalculation. The court rulings used by Title VI enforcers as the basis for rules were specific in form, were changing rapidly, and their effectiveness was in question. Thus, again with the advantage of hindsight, the administrative rule *née* court ruling was intrinsically troublesome.

But were there any options?

That question may be answered only by reexamining the goal of the Title VI effort. What was an official in Washington attempting to do? Title VI was viewed as a policy that compelled school districts to put black and white children together in a classroom. It was not viewed as a policy that attempted to develop opportunities for black and white children: specifically, to give black children a chance to do what they wanted (or what their parents wanted for them). As implemented, Title VI became a policy in which the federal government determined what black parents and children wanted or asked the local school district to decide what black children should want. When a school desegregation case would be heard in a court setting, both parties could present their own views of a needed remedy. The administrative posture assumed by Title VI enforcers, however, did not provide any such opportunity.

The federal officials charged with developing Title VI policy in education appear to have believed that the posture they assumed was the only one available to an agency; that is, it was both the strength and the limitation of an administrative role. But they did not explore alternative models that might have been available to them. They did not focus on those issues that might have led them to alternatives. First, they did not acknowledge that no one really knows what desegregation is; it may be black and white children sitting down in a classroom together, or it may be a political relationship in a community that allows black parents to participate in decision-making. Both definitions may be true and both may be false. The reality to test either is the local community. Second, they did not acknowledge that no one really knows why children learn or why they do not learn in school. Washington-defined policy will not be able to resolve that dilemma—even if Washington officials pretend to do so. And third, they did not see the possibility of focusing on the local community as the ultimate and only arena for change. They did not see that a possible way of attacking the complicated questions involved in Title VI and education was to attempt to begin a process of change within the locality. Thus the federal role would be a facilitating posture, providing incentives for various groups within a community to sit down together to work out a program for change.

Although the facilitating role is not the federal government's usual function, there are precedents for this posture. The National Labor Relations Board (NLRB) has prescribed a government role as an enabler—an active third party working to establish conditions for two groups within the society to come to an agreement. Using this concept as a basis, a federal role in civil rights might be devised that would provide the conditions for parties in a community to come to an agreement. The NLRB approach—stressing negotiations and encouraging the parties involved to work out details of a plan—would emphasize the *process* of developing a desegregation plan rather than evaluating the specific details of that plan.

It is interesting that the single member of the original OE civil rights staff with administrative experience had received that experience as a staff member of the NLRB and with the Labor Department. As a result, that individual established operating procedures for his staff entirely different from those of his colleagues. He considered that "most of the other guys were shooting for court cases" rather than negotiating for compliance. He instructed his staff to learn about the idiosyncracies of individual communities and emphasized face-to-face negotiations.[2]

This experience gives some indication that the *style* of dealing with local officials may have some impact on the outcome of the activities. There are, in addition, other interesting precedents to be drawn from the NLRB experience. The Labor Board has developed a procedure by which labor unions are recognized and certified as legitimate parties to be involved in bargaining. Using this model, a federal role might be devised for the Title VI activities in which a policy is established that allows local groups (groups of black parents or groups that could be viewed as legitimate representatives of black parents) to be certified as parties who have a legitimate role in desegregation plan negotiations. Once certification was given a group or groups, a desegregation plan would not be accepted by the federal government without the concurrence of the certified group or groups and the local school district.

Although a procedure developed in this direction is not foolproof (and certainly does not avoid the possible problem of local intimidation), it does provide a framework that allows something called a desegregation plan to be developed that is relevant to the locality. The negotiation process would work out a plan that made some sense to the school officials and to local black parents.

A procedure constructed along these lines would also speak to the due process problem confronted by the Title VI enforcement staff. A desegregation plan negotiated by local parties would be relevant to the substantive needs of the community and, at the same time, would provide adequate opportunities for expression and participation for affected parties in that community. The principle of participation could be applied nationally, making certain that consultation with all concerned parties was encouraged and not avoided during the stage in which the administrative rules for the effort would be devised.

These remarks drawing on the NLRB experience are meant to be suggestive of alternatives; clearly, they do not exhaust the possible options that might have been devised. Rather, they are offered to illustrate the limitations of the world view on which the Title VI legal decision-makers based their policies and the possibilities they left unexplored.

IV
CONSTITUENCY

11
•
OE AND INTEREST GROUPS

To judge by the legislative coalition mobilized to shepherd the 1964 Civil Rights Act through the Congress, the new anti-discrimination legislation had a broad-based constituency to carry it through the legislative stage to its administrative life. Nearly 80 organizations, crossing racial, economic, and religious lines, put together one of the most disciplined and effective lobbying efforts Congressional observers have recalled.[1] Working through the umbrella organization, the Leadership Conference on Civil Rights, the lobbying group concentrated on the moral imperatives of guaranteeing equal opportunity to the millions of black Americans who had less than full privileges of citizenship.

The legislative activity was an acknowledgment of an intensive period of social change, symbolized in its beginnings by the *Brown* decision in the Supreme Court in 1954 and expressed by Southern lunch counter sit-ins and Freedom Rides involving the facilities of inter-state travel in the early 1960's. The ferment took legislative shape in 1963, when, in the wake of a 200,000-strong March on Washington and the growing incidence of Mississippi violence, John Kennedy proposed the first omnibus civil rights legislation of post-Reconstruction days. The tragedy in Dallas and increased Southern resistance evoked the moral guilt of America. With Lyndon Johnson joining in the religious rhetoric of the movement, the 1964 Civil Rights Act traveled along the Congressional paths. Although debated and decried at many steps along the way, nonetheless it overcame conservative resistance to passage of broad civil rights legislation.

United in their expression of moral indignation, the coalition within the Leadership Conference on Civil Rights managed to pull together—at least for that moment—otherwise disparate and dissenting groups within the American society. Despite strains and pulls based on differences in strategy and style, the umbrella organization covered such activist, young civil rights groups as the Student Non-Violent Coordinating Committee (SNCC) and the Congress of Racial Equality (CORE), as well as the older, more "establishment" organizations—the National Association for the Advancement of Colored People (NAACP) and the National Urban League. Grass roots memberships of women's organizations were mobilized—from Women's International League for Peace and Freedom, to the League of Women Voters, to church and synagogue organizations, to black social sororities. And despite some earlier equivocating on the issue, the entire labor movement, from George Meany down, had been organized in support of the legislation.

During the 1964 legislative debates, all these organizations were joined—the less traditionally political organizations morally concerned about the costs of segregation (church groups, social organizations) joined with the regular Washington organizations that had been lobbying for nondiscrimination measures for a number of years. Although the diversity of the coalition meant that a rich array of political contacts could be used to influence the legislative process, it also meant that many of the participants in the lobbying were not directly affected by the outcome of these battles. Although the argument was made that whites as well as blacks benefit from an integrated society, the value of the benefit to whites was an abstract and theoretical one. The day-to-day legislative and administrative business of most of the organizations involved in the civil rights coalition could proceed as usual whether or not the measure was enacted or enforced.

As the 1964 Civil Rights Act moved from a legislative declaration to operation within an administrative setting, the level of concern and sophistication about its implementation by the members of the legislative coalition varied from title to title. Most of the strategy discussions focused on Title II of the Act—the section that prohibited discrimination in places of public accommodation. The violent level of Southern reaction in the past led both supporters and opponents of the anti-discrimination measure to emphasize the repercussions that would follow federal attempts to require equal access to swimming pools, lunch counters and restaurants, public libraries, and other facilities that opened their doors to the general public. But as one individual closely involved with the strategy on the public accommodations issue has recalled, "While we were arguing over public accommodations, we really were talking about a firecracker when—waiting in the wings—Title VI had the effect of dropping a bomb."

There appears to be little evidence that anyone—either opponents of the section or its supporters—was aware of the potential impact of the requirement included in Title VI. As became apparent about midway through the enforcement efforts of the Johnson Administration, procedures that would lead to systematic application of the requirement that federal funds be spent in a nondiscriminatory fashion would require far-reaching changes in all levels of American politics. The apparatus for state and local decision-making would have to be significantly modified to enfranchise new voices and, conversely, to diminish the influence of the existing guard.

A Tenuous Coalition?

To some degree, at least, the delay in the realization of the implications of Title VI was rational for the survival of the legislative coalition. If Title VI had been systematically analyzed and its administrative imperatives understood during the legislative stage, some of the members of the legislative coalition might have found their moral fervor somewhat diminished. That is, they would have been required to face the possibility that existing power relationships—both within local communities as well as vis-à-vis the federal government—might be modified.

For the most part, the individuals who might be expected to be the most direct beneficiaries of the legislation were not organized within the coalition. The black organizations participating in the coalition tended to represent middle-class blacks—individuals who had worked around the system of segregation and discrimination to attain some degree of economic and social security. Although no black American could escape the tentacles of institutionalized racism, the black organizations within the coalition had few participants who could either represent or speak for the two largest groups of American blacks: poor, Southern farmers and urban ghetto dwellers. Both groups—farmers and ghetto dwellers—had strong existential reasons to be concerned with the relationship between federal dollars and nondiscrimination requirements. The urban poor were trapped in a cycle of poverty indirectly supported by federal welfare programs. And black farmers were systematically excluded from the benefits within federal agriculture programs that supported white farmers. Neither group, of course, was an operative Congressional constituency; Southern black farmers were often not allowed to vote and urban ghetto dwellers either did not vote or lived in cities with one-party, no-contest situations. Thus neither category of black Americans was in a position to influence Congressional votes and was of only fringe concern to lobbyists as they went about their business of mobilizing constituent support. At various times, both SNCC and CORE brought the concerns of the small farmer and the ghetto dweller to the attention of the Leadership Conference. But both organizations were tenuous members of the coalition, often criticized by some other coalition participants, who argued that direct action tactics were counterproductive to the legislative process.

The politics of the coalition and the nature of the issue created a situation in which none of the powerful elements within the legislative coalition—the labor unions, church groups, and the NAACP—had a clear picture of a path that would be required for federal officials to proceed from the status quo to the goal enunciated in Title VI. The minimal debate on the measure within Congress also reflected the failures of the contending interest groups involved in the lobbying to focus on the administrative imperatives of the title. The few conditions that were attached to Title VI as gleaned from the Congressional colloquy (such as Hubert Humphrey's discussion on court-ordered school districts) suggested that such conditioning was coming from "expert" advice (such as the Justice Department) rather than from bargaining and trade-offs between contending interest groups.

Administrative Latitude

The combination of all these factors—the nature of the Leadership Conference, the unorganized character of the "real" constituent or consumer of the measure, and Congressional focus away from Title VI— meant that the measure reached the administrative level with the potential for officials to exercise a wide range of discretion in administering the law. On a formal level, at least, administrators had the latitude to carry out the legislative mandate with minimal direction from Congress or the interest groups involved in the Congressional battles. The absence of extended legislative controversy created a vacuum; without specific constraints, officials could proceed with actions of their own choice. The government employees charged with the implementation of Title VI were given undefined discretionary authority. Although all those involved with the measure acknowledged that it was a conflict-ridden, politically sensitive issue, the dimensions of that conflict were not defined in the legislative stage. The bureaucrats charged with administration were thus handed a two-faced situation. The mood on one face was hopeful; the policy directions were vague and loose, and the officials could view their responsibility as one of speaking for an unorganized, undeveloped interest group.[2] The uncertainty of this situation was in the direction of optimism, with emphasis on the possibilities for change in the hands of fairly autonomous administrators. The other face, however, spoke of worry and apprehension, viewing the uncertainty of the situation as a politically difficult problem. To this view, any political reaction was to be feared. Without rules and limits stipulated by Congress, adminstrators had no way to measure the potential legislative reaction and to evaluate its lasting impact on implementation attempts. In addition, administrators had no way to measure the reaction of the traditional education constituency. Would the development of an active set of interest groups for Title VI antagonize the education lobby? And, if so, how might that affect Congressional criticism or support?

Because of the all-encompassing nature of Title VI coverage, any agency official had to weigh the potentially broad impact of Congressional action—that is, a reaction that might affect budgets and procedures of the substantive operational programs as well as the civil rights efforts. Such action would not only be chaotic as it involved Congress and the agency but, to the officials' point of view, would disrupt normal relationships with the constituency of the substantive programs.

The two-faceted potential created by Title VI was clear in the procedures and enforcement attempts involving federal education programs. The civil rights operations in OE as well as the activities attached to the HEW Secretary's office indicated the constant pull between tendencies to plunge ahead, utilizing the authority mandated by the Congressional silence, and tendencies to hold back because of an almost obsessive consciousness of a tenuous political balance on federal education programs. Although the two elements pulling the administrators were separate forces, with independent cycles and attributes, they were potentially interwoven at the point that officials began to recognize that they could, with some skill, use their authority in ways that would effectively modify the existing and somewhat tenuous political balance.

Thus the officials within HEW who sought to enforce Title VI in the education programs were faced with the challenge of devising ways to *politicize* their discretion—that is, to define their discretion in political terms and to use it in ways that had survival payoffs. This involved attempts to develop an active constituency—organized groups that would be attentive to the policies developed, often serving as advocates for the new policies in relationships with Congress and providing the administrators with information. That information might be drawn from grass roots organizations and could provide the administrators with an opportunity to see if federal activities were consistent with the interests of local black communities. This role would be protective to the Title VI administrators as it served to legitimize enforcement attempts. As a result of the existence of such a constituency, a second strategy could be undertaken: the groups in the new constituency might develop political linkages between the Title VI policy and other federal education policies. These linkages could lead to a broadened federal education constituency, including the traditional education groups as well as the civil rights advocates. No matter how limited, movement to that end might minimize the conflict between the civil rights issues and other education policies.

This final part of our study attempts to look at the efforts by officials responsible for Title VI in federal education programs that were conducive to the development of a constituency.

OE: Existing Relationships

The requirement for nondiscrimination in the expenditure of federal education monies came at a time when OE was already pushed to change its relationship with public and private education organizations throughout the country. Although the massive Elementary and Secondary Education Act was not approved by Congress until 1965, at the time of the passage of the 1964 Civil Rights Act the handwriting was fairly clear that at some point—and quite soon—the U. S. Office of Education would assume greater fiscal and programmatic responsibilities for American education.

The increased federal financial role for education had not been reached without pain; the bugaboo that federal dollars meant federal control of the classroom was a strong and persistent belief in the American culture. Powerful and demanding organizations were present to guard vociferously the pattern of federal deference to the states in education.

Until the mid-1960's, the federal Office of Education had presented a minimal threat to the powers of state education. The few federal funds that were offered were mainly funds that could be distributed to "friends" around the country with little expectation that these grants would be used as a leverage for change in education patterns. Although the feds might help fill up the education coffers, the shape and style of that container was completely determined by state and local education policy-makers. Although the National Defense Education Act of 1958 represented an increased federal contribution to education, these funds were carefully allocated in patterns that would not disrupt the existing non-federal controls. Then OE Commissioner Lawrence Derthick—a former chief state school officer himself—involved the Council of Chief State School Officers in the formulation of the guidelines determining the rules for the allocation of funds, allowing the chief schoolmen input in drafting the guidelines as well as an informal veto over the final product. Derthick called all the chief state school officials to Washington at the time the guidelines were discussed to make sure that "the people actually administering" education programs wrote the guidelines rather than "bureaucrats in Washington." Derthick's experience with the NDEA guidelines seemed to indicate that federal officials could minimize the opposition to increased federal responsibilities in education if they systematically deferred to the state powers in education.

As a result, Commissioner Derthick put together a council of the five major education organizations within the country to work with the federal officials on education policy. The five original members of the council were the Council of Chief State School Officers, the National Education Association, the American Association of School Administrators, the National Congress of Parents and Teachers, and the National Association of State Boards of Education—all groups committed to defer to someone other than the federal government in education matters. Although the stated purpose of the council was an advisory, communicating function, the yearly meetings of the group allowed federal officials to show their old friends that indeed they continued to be "old friends." The sessions served to dispel the doubts of the education establishment about the federal administrators. Derthick was convinced that the feds had little to hide; although the organizational roles of his staff might have been different from those of council members, the values and orientation of the federal people continued in the path laid down by the involved interest groups. The solidarity of the two forces was easily established and the organizations involved did not resist Derthick's offer to allow Assistant Commissioner Wayne Reed—also a former chief state school officer—to staff the sessions.

By the 1960's, however, things had changed. Now the six education organizations—the National School Boards Association had been added to the membership—began to be conscious of their potential strength as an independent coordinating lobbying force in both Congressional and administrative policy areas. New participants in the sessions were less than patient with the existing procedure for December sessions in Chicago. As one of these participants described it, "The meetings were gripe sessions with mostly PTA types getting together for a good gab fest." The result of the prods of the new members was a major modification in the way the council proceeded. The formal relationship with OE was severed; although federal education officials continued to attend the meetings in an *ex officio* capacity, they no longer served as staff for the council. Instead, the six members of the organization rotated the staff capacity, minimizing the ability of any one of the groups involved to dominate the program.

The group's solidarity was indicated by its new informal name—The Big Six. It continued to hold an annual fall workshop, organized in the same general fashion as earlier sessions; this meeting was supplemented by a December legislative meeting. During that legislative session, the participants agreed to an agenda for action to be demanded from both the Congress and the executive branch. If any of the participating organizations did not agree on an item, that issue was not included as a part of the action agenda. The recommendations of the session—officially called the Legislative Conference of National Organizations—were then forwarded to the President and Congress and circulated among the state and local affiliates of each of the organizations for their action.

Although Assistant Commissioner Wayne Reed continued to be the major liaison with Big Six members during the years of the Kennedy administration, OE's posture toward the education coalition shifted when Francis Keppel assumed the Commissionership in late 1962. Up to that point, Commissioners of Education had been good friends (like Derthick) or, if not, were otherwise inconsequential to on-going Big Six relationships with the federal education agency. Certainly the interdependencies between the two were strongest at the level of Assistant Commissioners and heads of operating programs. Keppel, according to one informed observer, "had little credibility and not too good a relationship with most of the school people. We felt that Keppel didn't know much about his job." Although Keppel was a well known educator, having assumed the Commissionership from a position as Dean of the Harvard Graduate School of Education, he represented the forces in the education field that wanted to change drastically the relationship of the federal government to the nation's education system. When the education establishment felt that Keppel "didn't know much about his job," they meant that he did not know that it was his place to continue to defer to state control of education. Instead, Keppel saw possibilities in the development of a direct relationship between the feds and local school districts—a relationship that would not only by-pass the traditional state agencies but would also imply an active, conditioning role on the part of a federal education agency.

Thus, rather than the membership of the Big Six, Keppel's potential constituency involved local school officials, especially superintendents in large urban districts. To the traditionalists, at least, the Kennedy-appointed Commissioner was seen as an advocate of change and programs undertaken by "the large foundations" who wanted "to undermine the role of the states, who were constitutionally responsible for education in America." Keppel was associated with the Ford Foundation's Great Schools program—an attempt by the Foundation to do something about the educational quality of inner-city schools. (Ironically, Chicago Superintendent Benjamin Willis was the chairman of the Ford Foundation committee to strategize for change—Willis was the target of the complaint brought by Chicago civil rights groups, considered the supporter of Northern-style segregation. The Chicago complaint was one of the factors that pushed Keppel against the wall.) And style as well as substance defined the differences between the Big Six and the forces Keppel represented. The Big Six organizations tended to be dominated by individuals from Midwestern, Western, and Southern states, who continued regional antipathies to "those Easterners." The suspicions were especially strong in the education area; non-Easterners considered that their counterparts on the East Coast had less stake in public education than did the rest of the country, pointing to a more developed system of non-public schools available as alternative options to East Coast residents. Thus, aligned with Harvard and "the large foundations," Keppel was seen in the tradition of noblesse oblige and was viewed as an elite outsider meddling and experimenting with one of the most important public services in the nation.

Although there was no love lost between Keppel and the Big Six, the common goal of increased federal funds for education provided a meeting ground for the two forces through the period up to the passage of the Elementary and Secondary Education Act in 1965. Keppel recognized that the support of federal aid by the constituent members of the Big Six was necessary to obtain the votes of members of Congress from swing states—especially non-urban areas. Reciprocally, the Big Six recognized Keppel's important political connections, particularly during the Kennedy years and the period he was in favor in Johnson's administration. The bill that did emerge in 1965 reflected both groups' agendas: some funds were allocated by OE directly to local school districts (Title I—the program for school districts with large poverty-level populations—grew out of Keppel's concerns) and others continued the fiscal relationship between the federal government and the states. The staying power of the Big Six was subsequently indicated by the ultimate fate of both Title I and Title III (funds for experimental programs that were allocated from Washington). Although both titles originally included expansive roles for the federal government, continued pressure in Congress led to an eroding of that independent authority and increased powers in these programs for the state education agencies.

As the possibility increased in late 1964 and early 1965 that federal aid to education would be enacted by Congress, Commissioner Keppel, his staff, and interest group supporters were preoccupied with a full-scale mobilization on the education measure. Although the Civil Rights Act had been signed by President Johnson in July 1964, eager administrators were counselled against taking precipitous action before the November election. After the election, however, and the issuance of the HEW Title VI regulations in December, OE staff continued to focus on the historic education legislation that finally emerged in April 1965.

Strategists for the legislation were wary that the civil rights issue would surface to destroy the education bill; memories were still fresh enough to recall the fate of past education measures, killed, at least in part, because of the Powell amendments, which called for desegregation as a condition to federal education monies. Yet the civil rights requirements were necessary to get support. To those groups who made support of education contingent on the nondiscrimination requirements, advocates pointed to such a requirement already enacted in Title VI of the Civil Rights Act. For the most part, however, Congressional supporters of civil rights legislation also tended to be supporters of federal aid to education and thus required minimal assurances about civil rights programs.

Although there had been sparse attention to the Title VI civil rights program before ESEA was enacted, the little thought that had been given to the issue had assumed a direct relationship between the federal government and local school systems. The limited HEW action on civil rights in the impacted school aid program in the period before the passage of the Civil Rights Act developed from the assumption that Washington would hold local school systems (the recipients of the federal dollars) accountable for civil rights issues. In large measure, the emphasis on the direct dealings between the feds and local districts was an attempt by civil rights advocates to dilute the possibility of the organization of state-wide, united political opposition—a development that was feared if state-wide education agencies were involved in the enforcement efforts. Involvement of the Southern chief state school officials in more than perfunctory dealings with the civil rights issue was considered an invitation to another round of massive resistance attempts to stop school desegregation. Thus the civil rights imperatives to deal directly with local school systems meshed nicely with the strong urge of Keppel's OE administration to find ways of minimizing the roles of states in determining patterns of expenditure of federal dollars and, instead, of maximizing the federal government's abilities to condition its funds as a lever for change in local school districts.

The coincidence in time between the school desegregation enforcement attempts and the attempts to administer the ESEA programs involving direct federal relationships to school districts meant that a double level of meaning and, hence, double-barreled politics, were involved in both programs. As a result, it was never possible to sort out two clearly distinct streams for one issue or the other. Supporters of civil rights enforcement were not always ready to take on opposition to the enforcement attempts based on disagreement with an approach that circumvented the role of the state agency. Yet the enforcement attempts were often criticized and blocked not on civil rights grounds but because of the federal agency's by-passing of what were viewed as constitutionally mandated state responsibilities. Too, the advocates of continued state control often found themselves in bed with those who opposed civil rights programs—a cozy relationship nourished by the shared rhetoric defending states' rights. Even in 1972, representatives of Big Six organizations continued to shake their heads and comment that "Segregation is the only issue that could have thrown federal-state relations into such a mess"; "If it hadn't been for the civil rights issue we would have kept the state responsibilities clearly defined"; and "The civil rights issue undermined the federal relationship to the states."

The intermingling of the civil rights issue with questioning of the federal-state relationship created a touchy political situation for the administrators attempting to enforce the civil rights regulations. These officials could anticipate active opposition from those openly opposed to the nondiscrimination requirements—the same forces that had lobbied against the civil rights legislation in Congress. But although the organizations within the Big Six were not opposed to civil rights in some "pure" form, they were wary of the strategy being devised to implement the new equal opportunity legislation. (Indeed, the National Education Association joined the Leadership Conference on Civil Rights in 1968.) This strategy, based on the federal government's compliance requirement directly with local school districts, jeopardized the interests of the education organizations. Thus the officials charged with the civil rights programs had reason to suspect that pressures would be placed within the internal bureaucratic functioning of the federal education agency to inhibit the enforcement of the civil rights program if it clearly by-passed the state role.

The opportunities for subversion of the state-circumventing procedures were manifold in OE. The staffing patterns of the organization, the day-to-day working alliances within the agency, as well as the outreach procedures that involved Congress and its education allies, all supported the existing pattern of relationships between the federal government and the state education agencies.

One strategy would have been aimed at building a strong, vociferous constituency to balance the existing interests; another would be the strategy of avoidance. If Keppel and his colleagues believed that the only way to survive was to stay aloof of both the traditional school organizations and the civil rights groups, the question of building support could be avoided. It is difficult to imagine a federal agency that is completely without a constituency, however. Whether federal officials seek support or opposition, some organization or group is bound to surface to attempt to influence the federal policy.

Toward a New Constituency?

The ability to develop a constituency of support within the bureaucracy was closely related to the ability of the agency leaders to find allies of support in the open political battles with Congress and within the executive branch family. Although the degree of activity within the agency to stabilize an attentive constituency depended on the abilities of that potential constituency itself, there were a series of possible activities within the repertoire of the agency that could be undertaken to produce intervening organizations.[3] These included staffing patterns, formal procedures of dealing with advocates of the civil rights policy, and informal methods of outreach beyond the federal agency.

Staffing

One of the most effective ways of assuring that civil servants comply with a policy is to find procedures by which advocates of that policy are involved in the day-to-day internal decision-making procedures within the agency involved. Although the nondiscrimination requirement applied to all program workings within the Office of Education, it was not possible for top administrators to stipulate that (even if they wanted to) a civil rights loyalty test be given to staff protected by civil service tenure rules. Thus the staffing potential for controlled advocacy was effectively limited to the formal staff charged with implementation of the nondiscrimination policies—the Office of Equal Education Opportunities in OE (most significant during the early part of the administration of the policy) and the HEW Office for Civil Rights (in ascendancy during the latter part of the period studied). As new offices (with the flexibility and freedom that go along with initial staffing), both of these staffs had the opportunity to be shaped by employment decisions that provided for the hiring of competent people and, at the same time, reinforced on an informal level abilities to bring in new spheres of support for the policy.

Of the initial OEEO staff within OE, a large chunk of the senior staff members had some civil rights related experience before joining the Seeley crew. Eleven of the 17 senior compliance staff members and six of the nine senior noncompliance staff (performing technical assistance roles generally involved in Title IV) had been hired with some civil rights activity in their backgrounds. Although these staff members were partially involved in the administration of the Title VI operation as policy advocates, the linkages of the staff were split between two forces with distinctly different definitions of the kind of problem that was handed to the OE officials.

Because the civil rights issue was in a period of transitional definition, the composition of the staff reflected the confusion in its view of the nature of the program goal. One definition of the task at hand was rooted in the inter-group relations experience of religious organizations and state and local human relations agencies. The approach was a no-conflict orientation and fit into a voluntaristic strategy of intervention; crudely characterized, it was based on brotherhood of man considerations, in which advocates strived for an essentially race-less world where all races lived together peacefully. This style of approach had taken some root in Washington federal agencies when no sanctions—only good will—could be used to convince people to stop discriminating. Organizationally, advocates of this group were tied together in NAIRO—the National Association of Intergroup Relations Officials—a predominantly white organization. Individuals who joined the OE staff with links to the inter-group field were often hired because of their skills as intergroup *technicians*— that is, coming to the civil rights field as professionals. As a result, this group tended to define the challenge ahead as a question of providing more technical support—conferences, group sessions, printed materials—to local school districts to convince them to change their practices. Although this group of staff members did have contacts with their counterparts in other agencies and organizations around the country, these tended to be apolitical contacts. Many of the inter-group organizations were non-profit groups, and staff members were prohibited from taking overt political action.

The second definition of the task before the OE civil rights staff grew from the more recent activist demands of the civil rights movement. To this group, the activities of the enforcement staff in OE would only be successful if they were linked to the community organization activities associated with SNCC and CORE. Although the demands of this group were sometimes more rhetorical than rooted in systematic community work, they accepted conflict as an inevitable aspect of the civil rights demands—the conflict that occurs when a new group challenges the powers of the *status quo*. These local organizations were intrinsically political; their very existence threatened the political power alignments in local communities. Because the original staff in OE was predominantly white, the activist orientation was the major push to dealing directly with community-based black organizations. (Four of the 17 senior compliance staff members and two of the nine senior non-compliance staff were black.) The scarcity of black staff members—a problem more pronounced in the OE operations than in OCR—inhibited the development of informal links to other than the activist, young black groups.

The difference between the two approaches to the civil rights problem was largely a generational problem. The older (and often top) officials had been schooled in the human relations approach, and frequently found it difficult to deal with the style as well as the substance of the activist demands. Often these demands came from the younger, lower-level civil servants, who were frustrated not only because they were at too low a level within the organization to personally effectuate change but also because the agency failed to consider the interests of the organizations to which they felt personal obligations.

When the OE civil rights operations were geared up in 1965, the climate of the federal organization in OE was fairly expansive. The staff with civil rights experience—of either variety—was quite free to maintain the contacts developed before coming into the federal agency. The information flow between the agency and concerned groups was loose and frequent; the telephone rang often as OE staff attempted to get as much information as they could about local conditions and, conversely, as organizations geared to some monitoring of the federal operations attempted to find out what was happening in the offices in Washington. During this period, the civil rights staff members were able to utilize the informal level of contacts that were the usual method of procedure (i.e., with contacts in the Big Six) in the federal education agency. Other staff in the Office of Education would get on the telephone to friends to solicit advice on specific policy areas or to try out new ideas on the group representatives whom they considered their attentive public. But unlike other communications from OE, the relationships with local officials were regulative in nature—that is, asking the local officials to change their practices.

Although some staff members with contacts with the activist civil rights organizations had been hired precisely because of these contacts, the first round of attacks on OE civil rights enforcement provoked a punitive atmosphere in the federal agency. Extremely fearful and threatened by the criticisms that followed the initial enforcement activities, OE officials undertook a series of actions to inhibit the informal contacts between staff and the groups now considered civil rights "zealots." Shared information between Washington and community-based organizations became a question of "stealing" information. When the Student Non-Violent Coordinating Committee issued a report criticizing the amount of Title VI enforcement in OE,[4] some of the staff were wary of its internal effect. According to some staff members, Anna Holden—a former CORE activist—was fired as a sacrificial lamb in an attempt to close off sources of information to SNCC. This touched off a series of immediate resignations as well as a demoralized climate that eventually pushed most of the activists off the staff. According to one former staff member, "After the SNCC report came out, Dave Seeley surrounded himself with weak people. There were plenty of vacancies, too; about 14 people resigned in relation to the protest activity."

The series of resignations that occurred within both the OE and the HEW Office of Civil Rights staffs was described by one observer as a "peeling off process." He noted that the first set of resignations involved staff members whose loyalty was never to the federal government but to the activist civil rights organizations. The subsequent resignations were made by individuals with greater loyalties to the civil rights policies than to the agency but who, nonetheless, recognized the difference between the role of the federal government and the posture taken by groups organized to take action that would bring pressure on the officials. This series of resignations usually involved some specific policy in which the staff members attempted to make change and then—for a multitude of different reasons—were stymied in their attempts. This observer has noted that the resignations continued until a final core of the staff was left whose loyalty was simply to the agency and who were willing to undertake the policy directions they were given, regardless of what they might be. Some former staff members perceived the vulnerability of the staff with activist connections to be especially strong when all the decisions involving Title VI enforcement were made in Washington. The accessibility of Congress and the White House to the operations of the OE civil rights staff on Maryland Avenue meant that otherwise innocuous conversations were easily blown up to large political proportions. It was noted that the regionalization of the civil rights operations in the HEW Office of Civil Rights provided a new opportunity for the few organized representatives of groups concerned about Title VI enforcement to restore contacts with middle-level and lower-level staff members. The OCR Atlanta regional operation, in particular, provided access for information and contacts because the Regional Director and the Assistant Regional Director knew individuals involved in local school desegregation efforts. With the exception of this Atlanta Renaissance, however, the first level of resignations in OE effectively left the HEW civil rights operations with few middle- and lower-level staff links to organizations that had specific information, programatic concerns, and concrete knowledge of local school situations.

Outreach Activities

Although the Office of Education had more than 24 public committees advising it on various aspects of the federal education program,[5] no formal group of involved and concerned citizens was constituted to provide advice and counsel on Title VI matters.[6] As a result, both the agency and the concerned citizenry had to depend on the federal officials to call meetings involving the desegregation issue. Although a formal advisory group does not assure representation of all viewpoints, it does provide a communication vehicle. It allows officials to inform a constituency about the particulars of specific issues at hand and, at the same time, gives them access to outside views of the activities of the agency. Regular meetings of an advisory group also encourage agency officials to consider the interests and concerns of group members in the day-to-day activities of the agency.

Throughout the course of Title VI enforcement in the Johnson Administration, officials in both the Office of Education and the HEW Office for Civil Rights held meetings with various representatives of civil rights groups concerned about the enforcement procedures. At one time or another, the sessions included representatives of the NAACP, the NAACP Legal Defense and Educational Fund, Inc., B'nai B'rith, NAIRO, the American Friends Service Committee, CORE, SNCC, SCLC, the Southern Regional Council, the National Urban League, the AFL-CIO, and other groups that participated in the Leadership Conference on Civil Rights. The meetings were held infrequently but were often set up as small group sessions with top administration officials (such as Keppel, Howe, or Gardner). From time to time, the sessions would be planned in response to requests from concerned groups with specific grievances to bring to Washington. Most of the meetings involved national representatives of national groups who had little knowledge of the effects of the school desegregation policies at the point of impact in local school systems. As one participant put it, "the meetings turned out to be a mutual trading of ignorance. Top HEW people didn't know what was happening in the field and the Washington lobbyists also suffered from a similar lack of information." Early in the enforcement attempts, the sessions not only involved civil rights advocates but also included local and state school officials and representatives of educational organizations. As time went on, however, the civil rights issue was separated from other aspects of the federal education program and civil rights advocates met federal officials separately. Although the practice of treating the civil rights issue as a separate problem did provide opportunities for discussion of the intricacies of the desegregation issue (greater detail than would have been possible in a session drawn on broader representation), it also reinforced the tendency within the federal agency to set the issue apart from its day-to-day proceedings. Clearly, the civil rights constituency was not considered a part of the education constituency when no civil rights or civil rights related people appeared on Keppel's listing of names submitted to HEW Under Secretary Wilbur Cohen as individuals to be invited to the White House signing ceremony for the Elementary and Secondary Education Act.[7] Indeed, when Keppel transmitted a list of individuals and organizations whom the Secretary "should see" in his early days in HEW, no civil rights group appeared in his "very important" category, whereas the American Sociological Association, the National Grange, and the National Farmers Union were viewed as "very important" for Gardner to see.[8]

Without an invitation or access to an invitation, an individual or group with questions about the enforcement procedure was limited to a letter of complaint or a query to the federal agency. In the period before the Civil Rights Act was approved by Congress and before he was given clear responsibilities for the civil rights issue within OE, David Seeley had the task of answering questions about school desegregation in letters written to Commissioner Keppel. Seeley took the task to heart and responded with warm, committed prose that indicated concern about the issues at hand while noting that OE—before Title VI—had no authority to act in the fashion requested in the communique. A June 1964 letter from Seeley to John Lewis, Chairman of SNCC, began: "Eternal vigilance is the price of liberty. Good going."[9]

When OE's authority was more certain, however, a new tone was established. By the spring of 1965—just months after OE was geared up to deal with the Title VI issue—letters to the Office of Education inquiring about some aspect of its policies and application in a particular community were answered with a cold, rather terse, form letter. The form thanked the writer for his letter and/or information about conditions in a particular community. It pushed the urgency of the inquiry aside by stating that "Please be assured that OE will give careful attention to the views of _____ in proceeding with its review of the plan for compliance with Title VI of the Civil Rights Act." When a civil rights organization received several of these letters—almost identical to one another—it was hardly motivated to continue written communication with the federal agency.

The method of impersonal treatment indicated by the letters tended to isolate the complaints, treating each as a single, separate issue. In addition, there was a tendency for the complaining letters to be lost in the administrative shuffle within OE; answers were often several months in coming. Although the Office for Civil Rights in HEW was less disorganized than OE had been in answering complaints, it inherited an already demoralized constituency that was less likely to initiate contacts with the federal government in 1966 than it had been in 1965.

The most consistent criticism of all the HEW civil rights activities— in OE as well as the Office of Civil Rights—involved the Department's failure to develop an information program that would help individuals in local communities understand the federal policies. As one individual put it, "HEW never developed a single piece of paper that told people what their rights were." The criticism was heard within the government agency from staff members who were appalled at the lack of information in the field. But the message came to Washington at full strength from both supporters and opponents of desegregation, who were simply asking the officials for a piece of paper that clearly indicated what was expected from local school systems. Misinformation was rampant around the South— especially in the first months of compliance, when official guidelines were not released in a widely distributed public form (not published in the Federal Register). The information that was eventually circulated resulted from the program of the U. S. Commission on Civil Rights or from the activity of private groups. (The Potomac Institute in Washington reprinted the first set of policies, and the AFSC and the NAACP Legal Defense and Educational Fund, Inc. [known as the Inc. Fund] developed a package of materials to be distributed to local communities to assist black citizens in developing the competency to bargain for their rights with local school officials.)

Although the U. S. Commission on Civil Rights had no enforcement authority related to Title VI (nor authority to enforce any other aspect of civil rights law), the independent agency had been given responsibilities under the 1964 Act to serve a clearinghouse function for general civil rights activities. The Commission's first major undertaking resulting from the clearinghouse authority was a national conference on Title VI, held in January 1965 in Washington with several thousand representatives of federal agencies, state and local public and private organizations, civil rights groups, and other interested parties in attendance. Civil rights activists recall the national meeting as the first public acknowledgment by the administration that "something would be done about Title VI." The sessions, keynoted by Vice President Humphrey, provided a definition of the wide coverage of the nondiscrimination requirements, giving many of the civil rights advocates their initial contact with the inner workings of the federal bureaucracy. Although the Washington meeting attempted to paint a general picture of the scope of Title VI, subsequent regional meetings were also sponsored by the Commission. These sessions, held during the spring of 1965, represented a push to dig deeper into the regions for more localized attendance and, hence, greater depth of information from individual communities about the status of federal programs.

A good deal of attention was focused on school desegregation issues during the Civil Rights Commission regional sessions as school officials and black parents began to gear up for the submission of plans for the coming fall. Participants in the meetings recall that the deficiencies of Seeley's OE operation came sharply into focus during the regional sessions. At the time, the federal education officials seemed unable to meet the expectations of local school officials, of representatives of black communities and organizations, or of the regional OE officials in attendance—none of whom had much information about OE's desegregation requirements before attending the sessions. The meetings took on the flavor of a road show, with the same mixture of Washington-based officials traveling from place to place. In addition to Commission staff members and various federal agency civil rights officials, a number of representatives of national organizations with civil rights concerns joined the entourage to make contacts with their local counterparts. Little, if anything, was done to follow up the regional meetings.

In preparing the national and regional meetings, the Civil Rights Commission put together a listing of organizations concerned about the civil rights issue, including descriptions of organizations, addresses, phone numbers, and contact persons. That listing became the basis for a formal Civil Rights Directory issued and periodically updated by the Commission; the listing was the first attempt by any federal agency (with operating responsibilities or not) to define a potential civil rights constituency. Although the HEW affiliates had this work done for them by another "friendly" federal agency, neither the constituency listing nor the contacts developed in the national and regional meetings was systematically followed through. When federal publications were issued describing HEW programs in civil rights (written in a manner helpful to local citizens), these publications were developed and released by the Civil Rights Commission.

Although one might agree that the officials charged with the nondiscrimination policies had limited opportunities to develop a constituency for their programs, it seems clear that these opportunities were minimized rather than maximized. Staff with contacts were made to feel inhibited about utilizing their relationships. Opened doors leading to closer and more intensive relationships were ignored. Institutionalized association with the outside advocates of school desegregation—especially those with contacts at a community level—was kept at a sometimes friendly but nonetheless cool distance.

Although the civil rights groups were given something approximating second-class treatment, OE officials were not allowed to deal with the constituency of the Big Six in the same off-hand manner. The chief state school officials in the 17 Southern and border states were called to Washington immediately after the Civil Rights Bill was signed and given Lyndon Johnson's best selling spiel. Although neither Keppel nor Seeley was particularly comfortable nor desirous of courting the state school officers, survival dictated a series of meetings with state people and some attention to the questions they raised. Queries about the civil rights issue were forwarded to the Commissioner and his civil rights chief through the regular OE staff as well as through Congressional inquiries responsive to state people. Initially these communiques were basically questions of fact; as the procedure for determining requirements became more convoluted, the information demands and questions from operating staff within OE and Capitol Hill took on an increasingly antagonistic posture.

Whether they liked it or not, the civil rights staff was forced to deal with school desegregation as a question with *state* aspects. The chief state school officers and their allies pulled all the stops in their attempt to circumvent the development of a direct relationship between the feds and local districts. Although strongly opposed to the establishment of OE regional offices, the state superintendents used their basically perfunctory meetings with the regional officials representing the Commissioner to raise questions about the desegregation policy and, from that, to involve the regional level of the OE bureaucracy in their cause. Regular dealings with OE program officials provided still another opportunity for state school chiefs to question the procedure by which the civil rights policy was being implemented. Although OE's civil rights staff continued to deal directly with local school districts, the tentacles of the state superintendents were long enough to gather information about the specific details of the feds' operations. It was not uncommon for OE to receive communications from state school officials questioning the activity of the federal agency in relation to local districts.

Although the extent of the power of state education agencies in desegregation attempts was a relevant question throughout the enforcement activities, the state/local question was never tackled frontally by the OE or HEW civil rights strategists. During the OEEO operations, there was a strong tendency within the federal education agency to keep the civil rights issue separated from other educational problems. The ESEA information meetings, for example, ducked the school desegregation question, focusing on the opportunities with the new legislation for school districts to receive needed financial support, rather than on the restrictions that would accompany the acceptance of these federal funds. When the enforcement authority was located in the HEW Secretary's office, the opportunity to mesh the civil rights issue with the regular concerns of federal education administrators was even more limited because of the structural separation between the two sets of activities.

The failure to develop an effective voice for the new constituency backed OE officials into the political corner controlled by the spokespersons for the Big Six. Keppel attempted to redefine the definition of OE's "customers." He sought to change the definition from an organizational construct (where the OE program did not penetrate into the American education system beyond the organizations already established to "take care of" education) to a relationship in which the federal education agency had opportunities for contact and influence with students, teachers, and the local community of the school. Without representatives of this localized point of view organized to put pressures on the organizational types, Keppel and his successor had limited success in operationalizing a new view of OE's customer market.[10]

Although the absence of an articulate constituency was felt in civil rights matters, it also affected other attempts for the non-state approach by the Kennedy-Johnson Administration's education leaders to "shake up the system." Keppel's attempt to reorganize the OE apparatus to administer the ESEA programs more effectively was subverted by a combination of capricious circumstances (Lyndon Johnson's little-known hatred of Loomis) and political plotting and perseverance by advocates of Big Six interests. Almost primitive considerations of political survival necessitated that the top administrators depend on the middle-level permanent civil servants—the very group that had the closest ties with the Big Six. In a period of stress, when it was necessary to take measures that would serve to consolidate the agency (as a method of recuperating from the turmoil that the Loomis/Mylecraine era imposed on the traditionalists), the top officials within OE were less likely to emphasize a policy—civil rights—that was known to require drastic changes in the behavior of the permanent civil servants. To one degree or another, the strains imposed by attempted change in the "normal" OE pattern of operations took a toll on the civil rights enforcement efforts. Each of these strains—the relationship of OE to the states; the method by which OE would deal with large cities; the internal organization of the Office, including the questions of regionalization and of reorganization by functional areas; and the procedure by which the federal education office would relate to the total HEW program—had some civil rights implications. But those who attempted to facilitate these changes went to battle without backup troops. The allies who could be mobilized were attentive only to blatant civil rights issues at the point they entered the legislative fracas. Although the initial skirmishes between the advocates of change and the defenders of the *status quo* involved some brilliant encounters, the new tactics were short lived. The staying power of the old guard was demonstrated and, with few exceptions, the traditional pattern of federal/state education relationships advocated by representatives of the Big Six was maintained.

12
•
THE MAKINGS
OF A CONSTITUENCY

The failure of either the OE or the HEW civil rights staff to develop a new constituency of support did not occur in a vacuum. The limited attempts by the bureaucrats to move toward new customers were reciprocated by an equally tenuous response from the organized groups within the public potentially attentive to the HEW Title VI enforcement program in education. With the marked exception of the American Friends Service Committee (AFSC) and the NAACP Legal Defense and Educational Fund co-sponsored Task Force on School Desegregation, the administrative activities involving school desegregation were effectively unmonitored by supporters of the policies.

The Leadership Conference

Theoretically, at least, a legislative lobbying group such as the Leadership Conference on Civil Rights would have been expected to perform some role in administrative lobbying on Title VI. Although the coalition had given minimal attention to the potential of Title VI before the legislation passed Congress, it did attempt to organize itself to monitor the administrative activity on the issue by creating a Committee on Compliance and

Enforcement. The Committee, chaired by the National Council of Churches' lobbyist, James Hamilton, was given the responsibility of following through on the legislation "to make sure that the laws for which we have worked so hard are not rendered ineffective through weak administration."[1] The Committee was not created until May 1966, however—nearly two years after the legislation was enacted and after a great deal of administrative activity had already been undertaken in the Title VI area.

To some degree, the Leadership Conference's failure to develop a sustained program on Title VI activities indicated its own preoccupation with other matters. Part of that preoccupation involved legislation pending in Congress—particularly the Voting Rights Act of 1965. But much of the failure revolved around the struggles that were taking place within the Leadership Conference itself on the degree of "militancy" the organization would show in a period in which strong demands for action were being made by the younger, less patient groups within the coalition. Several of the organizations in the Leadership Conference were especially sensitive to the accusations voiced by SNCC and CORE. Both the National Urban League and the NAACP had internal struggles occurring within their own organizational politics; "young Turks" within these groups were demanding new, direct action programs. And the AFL-CIO was extremely sensitive at the time to accusations leveled against the building trade unions for continuing patterns of discrimination against blacks in the apprenticeship programs. Indeed, some individuals argued that the AFL-CIO had a conflict of interest in matters involving Title VI. The sensitivities of the representatives of the NAACP and the AFL-CIO were particularly relevant because the two organizations had an effective veto over all the operations of the Leadership Conference.

Although a Committee on Compliance and Enforcement was created by the Leadership Conference, it was not a priority in the organization's activities. Hamilton's appointment as chairman was viewed by some observers as a reflection of the low priority placed on administrative enforcement.[2] The Committee met fairly frequently, but because it had no staff of its own, it had to rely on loaned staff workers. As a result, the group had no sustained capacity to undertake any research efforts or follow-through on enforcement issues.

During the early period of OE operations, when OEEO staff tended to be expansive in their contacts, the Leadership Conference served a technical assistance capacity for the agency. The Conference brought a group of legal experts to Washington from time to time to advise Seeley.

That period—according to one active Leadership participant—"was our finest hour."

The limited abilities of the Leadership Conference to monitor Title VI enforcement clearly indicated the organization's preoccupation with legislative issues. The coalition had been put together for work on Capitol Hill; to the extent that it was effective, it reflected the abilities of the Washington representatives of member organizations to operate in the legislative situation. Most of the participants in the coalition were novices in the administration setting or had limited contacts and experience within the executive branch. The regular meetings of the Leadership Conference involved strategizing rather than establishing general policy, and were attended by organization representatives who had been chosen and rewarded for their know-how on Capitol Hill. As one participant in the coalition observed, "It is not clear that it is realistic to expect that people who are performing lobbying tasks also take care of the administrative stuff." Another remarked that the nature of the two jobs— congressional lobbying and administrative lobbying—was quite different; "work on Capitol Hill is like a sales job—knowing enough about the product to sell it but not as much as one would need to run it. Even the timing of the two jobs involves a different rhythm. Congressional lobbying has a beginning and an end. You deal with distinct victories and defeats. But there are no beginnings or endings in the bureaucracy; you never clearly win or lose. Administrative lobbying is very tedious, involving less sexy, intricate bureaucratic relationships."

Legislative and administrative lobbying require different strategic timetables. An agenda controlled by Congressional imperatives was bound to collide with the demands of administrative issues. Unless an administrative issue had some Congressional ruboff (which might relate to pending legislation), there often would be some legislative reason for minimizing the public attention to a civil rights issue within the bureaucracy.

The failure of the Leadership Conference to sort out a separate set of administrative imperatives was rationalized by the coalition's tendency to see the administrative process as a continuous flow from the legislative activity. To the extent that the executive branch was separated from Congress, the locus of authority and control in the entire executive branch was viewed as a linear progression residing in the White House and, from there, to the offices of Department Secretaries. It was not unusual, for example, for the leading spokesmen for the leadership Conference to believe, as one informed person put it, "that if you can get the top guy in the Department on the telephone, everything will be fine." For a number of years, the Leadership Conference had emphasized the importance of executive leadership in the civil rights area. There was a strong tendency within the constituent groups to believe that, if the top officials within an agency were sympathetic and were "good guys," the bulk of the enforcement problem would be solved. Members of the Leadership Conference could look around Washington and—from Hubert Humphrey down—find their old friends in positions of responsibility. But instead of using these contacts as points of entry for substantive and sustained lobbying, the Leadership Conference representatives rested with the assurance that their friends would do a good job.

In addition to a generalized reluctance to criticize friends, the organizations within the Leadership Conference were also unable to collect the kinds of specific information about enforcement in local communities that would make administrative lobbying effective. As one observer recalled, "The Leadership Conference would periodically march into HEW to make noises and have an audience with Secretary Gardner. They would make broad statements about policy areas but usually had no information to back up their charges." As a result, the meetings were rarely challenging to the bureaucrats because the Leadership Conference representatives swallowed the explanations of the officials whole. Even the bureaucrats were critical of this experience; as one official put it, "They weren't tough enough on us. I remember being disappointed when meetings turned out to be a zero. I wanted them to be better prepared. And I remember feeling that these guys were in need of help."

Although many of the constituent groups within the Leadership Conference were organized with state or local affiliates, the Leadership Conference did not utilize the organizational potential within these groups as a method of developing information about local situations. Several representatives of the Leadership Conference had traveled with the Civil Rights Commission Title VI regional road shows and had used the meetings as opportunities to make contacts with local and state people. But as one of these participants recalled sheepishly, "We never did follow through on these meetings and didn't set up the state mechanisms we had discussed to monitor the enforcement."

The principal vehicle for information about local situations for the Leadership Conference was the NAACP. But the Washington representative of the NAACP served merely as a receptacle for whatever activity was self-generated in the field; he forwarded the complaints dutifully from local chapters or regional staff to the relevant federal agencies. National deference to the NAACP often seemed to be mirrored in local communities. Other parts of the civil rights movement were involved with other issues (lunch counters, buses, employment, voting), but school issues tended to be set aside for the NAACP. If the NAACP Washington representative was not aggressive, other parts of the coalition would be even less so.

The Leadership Conference never emphasized the utilization of the field potential of its affiliate organizations because it was wary of violating the internal prerogatives of the member groups—particularly the closely guarded defense of independence of the constituent organizations. Usually the jealousy related to competition between organizations or sensitivity to the establishment of organizations competing with member groups. For example, it was noted that the Leadership Conference was reluctant to establish an independent staff on enforcement because such a staff would be viewed as competitive with the Washington bureau of the NAACP. And, in other instances, the interests of the member groups acted to minimize the extent of policy criticism by the Leadership Conference about administrative activity. One can only speculate, for example, that the Leadership Conference did not play as involved and critical a role as might have been anticipated in the Chicago situation because the complaint was originally generated by a question about discrimination in trade union apprenticeship programs.

With limited information from the field, the Leadership Conference was required to make evaluations of the enforcement activity that were transferable to the legislative sphere. Thus the issues related to Title VI enforcement that were consistently the concern of the Leadership Conference involved the size of the appropriation for enforcement and the size of the staff assigned to nondiscrimination activity. Although the appropriation fights were significant to civil rights administrators, the money discussions often did not focus on the major substantive issues faced by the concerned bureaucrats.[3] For example, although the participants in the Leadership Conference were aware of the importance of the regionalization issue raised in Congress during Libassi's tenure, their lack of sophistication concerning bureaucratic organization issues did not allow for the degrees of lobbying mobilization that might have been anticipated on other kinds of policy issues.

The Leadership Conference did constitute the largest coalition of organizations concerned—to any degree—with the Title VI enforcement process. There were several other organizations, however, not in the coalition, also working on the issue. These groups did not participate in the formal legislative lobbying because of their tax exempt status, which prohibited political activity. As a result of their non-lobbying orientation, these organizations focused on the administrative setting as a primary target of activities. The non-lobbyists played two kinds of roles vis-à-vis Title VI enforcement: one group developed a behind-the-scenes, technical assistance posture; the other attempted to articulate the interests of local citizens at the point of the impact of the federal programs, using both specific complaints and problem patterns to document their cases.

The Potomac Institute

Staff of the Potomac Institute—a non-profit, foundation-sponsored organization—performed the major behind-the-scenes functions with Title VI issues. The institute, created in 1961 by philanthropist Stephen Currier, attempted to provide an opportunity for conversations between non-governmental advocates of civil rights policies and their "friends" within governmental agencies. Potomac's full-time president, Harold Fleming, former director of the Atlanta-based Southern Regional Council (SRC), had come to Washington in the early period of the Kennedy Administration to direct Potomac's program. Under Fleming's leadership, Potomac—as well as the SRC, a non-profit group organized for regional development, especially in race relations—was concerned about the bureaucratic fate of the civil rights legislation. With other staff of Potomac, Fleming saw a role for a group that would serve a behind-the-scenes, supportive and technical assistance function. Without troops (neither Potomac nor SRC was a membership organization), the strategy relied on the power of ideas and the personal connections of the individuals involved.

According to Fleming, Potomac's approach began with an acceptance of the validity of the problems articulated by the bureaucrats involved and, within that context, attempted to press for the civil rights agenda. The strategy involved a constant pull between the priorities of the administrator and the priorities of the civil rights advocate, requiring constant and conscious thought by the advocate to the possibility of being co-opted. Because of Fleming's contacts, he was often used by both Seeley and Libassi as a sounding board for ideas and strategies.

As useful as the behind-the-scenes approach might be, an inside advocate of a cause must also depend on the public articulation of that issue to legitimize the private action. Because this strategy relies on a translating role (the broker translating and mediating among several viewpoints), the failures of the membership organizations to define the demands limited the usefulness of the Potomac approach. It is difficult for the translator to be the sole advocate of the position critical of the officials. Participants in the activity remember that the activities of the behind-the-scenes individuals (who acted partially as technical assistance advisors and partially as advocates) had limited political impact.

School Desegregation Task Force

Although officials within federal agencies have recalled that the civil rights people based in Washington had "virtually no impact" on the administrative policy level, a single exception was frequently made to the general pattern. As one former official commented, "In my view, Jean Fairfax was more effective in her few visits from New York than anyone in Washington. I remember her coming down with a long list of special complaints—factual and well documented."

At the time of the enactment of the 1964 Act, Jean Fairfax was a field staff person for the American Friends Service Committee (AFSC)—the service organization for the Quakers. Based in the South and working on civil rights issues within a local community setting, Jean Fairfax has recalled that "from the point of someone working in the field, the potential of Title VI did not surface until months after the bill was signed." In this case, the "surfacing" of the impact of the Title VI provision came with the national conference on Title VI sponsored by the Civil Rights Commission—a meeting held in January 1965, six months after the legislation went into effect. The invitation given during that conference to concerned groups to "watchdog" the administrative activity was not viewed as simply a rhetorical request by Ms. Fairfax. A meeting with Commissioner Keppel during the sessions convinced the AFSC representative that it was incumbent on someone or some group to prod the OE civil rights staff if significant action were to be taken to facilitate school desegregation.

The initial contacts with the OE enforcement program pointed to a need to document what was happening to Title VI as it was applied to communities throughout the South. Thus a School Desegregation Task Force was organized, sponsored jointly by the AFSC and the NAACP Legal Defense and Educational Fund—known as the Inc. Fund—to monitor 200 school districts in the South. Monitoring, to the Task Force, not only involved a determination of the impact of the policy but also encompassed a serious public information effort—release of information about the policy, listing of rights of black parents, and, as well, a series of statewide meetings to explain the provisions and set up mechanisms to allow feedback from local settings.

The Task Force was established during the summer of 1965 to provide information about the status of the 200 communities during school openings in the fall. The efforts resulted in a 59-page report on the *Implementation of Title VI of the Civil Rights Act of 1964 in Regard to School Desegregation*, presented to HEW Secretary Gardner in November 1965. The report was released on the opening day of the planning conference of the White House Conference on Civil Rights, and, as one participant recalled, "scared the pants off the administration." According to the report, the Task Force—with 20 people working as volunteers or at subsistence wages—had disseminated 3,000 school desegregation kits and over 85,000 copies of a brochure, "Message to Parents about Desegregating Schools," during the course of the summer months—an information program that shamed the OE officials.

The bulk of the report, however, was written to support recommended changes in the guidelines and procedures that might be adopted for the coming school year. The discussion in the document indicated that the Task Force had done its homework; the presentation mixed a sophistication about administrative and legal issues with an urgency based on community, grass-roots contacts.

Some of the general policy issues discussed in the Task Force report were also included in the SNCC report on school desegregation, issued in September. SNCC, however, was not organized in the South to systematically develop local information; its report reflected some access to internal bureaucratic dealings and mainly dealt with general policy issues. The information on which SNCC based its report stemmed from the early open climate with the OE civil rights staff—an open climate that was short-lived.

The SNCC report cited the time lag between the policy enactment from Congress and the issuance of operational policies, the reliance on paper compliance, poor community relations, and detailed the violations and inadequacies of school officials in enforcing the policy. Because the enforcement staff was relying on paper submitted by school districts (a school district could simply certify itself by signing the 441 assurance form that said no discrimination was occurring or could submit a plan for desegregation), the detailed knowledge by Task Force members of individual district situations initially overwhelmed the OE staff.

The November meeting of the Task Force with Gardner began a series of sessions and communications among representatives of the

AFSC, the Inc. Fund, and HEW people. (In December, Jean Fairfax joined the Inc. Fund staff.) The contacts established during the first summer were continued throughout the administration of the school desegregation policy within OE and then in the HEW Office for Civil Rights. As the structural changes in authority unfolded, the Task Force participants attempted to determine where the power was located, who was making decisions, and, from that information, where to put pressures and bring complaints. Relationships were cultivated or, in some cases, maintained with friends who staffed the state and area desks in the early period and with regional officials—mainly in Atlanta—during the regionalization era. According to a participant, flexibility was necessary to continue to bring effective pressure: "So many changes were made that there was no clear relationship and no certain way of dealing with the officials. Uncertainty and shifting responsibility as well as constant changing of the regulations meant that the situation was very fluctuating and fluid."

Although the locus of the efforts shifted with the internal structural decisions, the strategy of pressure remained somewhat constant. One of the participants characterized the strategy:

> We accumulated complaints to show patterns of problems. We became convinced that the heart of the problem was that HEW had no way of finding out in a sustained, independent way what was going on at the school level. We felt our job was to provide HEW with information from the local level but to package it in a way in which they could see the policy implications of what they were doing. We had to be careful doing that—we didn't want to let the government cop out on its own responsibilities. To the degree that we were able to convince the officials of our seriousness they either took notice and acted or, at least, had to go through the motions of dealing with us.

At least a part of the flexibility maintained by this strategy was allowed because the Inc. Fund (when Jean Fairfax moved to the Inc. Fund it became the policy and organizational base for the activities) is not a membership organization. Unlike the groups within the Leadership Conference who were required to be responsive to their own memberships' demands, the Inc. Fund could develop a strategy and program based on the imperatives of the situation. Although, for example, the Washington representative of the NAACP had to make sure that he forwarded all the complaints that were generated in the field to the proper officials, treating them with equanimity, the Inc. Fund procedure provided opportunities for weighting the complaints, timing them for political effectiveness, and, when necessary, using the information system already developed to find examples of general problems.

But in addition to the differences in approach generated by the membership/non-membership variations, the NAACP and the NAACP Legal Defense and Educational Fund, Inc. had other contrasting aspects.[4] The NAACP membership as well as the staff were not interested in administrative issues. The emphasis on Congressional lobbying reflected the concerns of the leaders of the organization; the result was a situation in which the style of Hill lobbying was rewarded to a degree that diminished the importance of substance. The Inc. Fund—prohibited from an active Congressional role—found the administrative level an important and fruitful center of activity. The failure to focus on administrative issues meant that the NAACP representatives were totally unsophisticated in their understanding of how government agencies work. Accepting the paper structure of control by the top officials in an agency, they did not learn the intricacies of shifting responsibilities within agencies, both between groups in Washington and between officials based in regional offices and in D. C. The Inc. Fund, although equally as unsophisticated at the beginning of the activity, quickly learned the ropes as attention was given to administrative concerns.

Having worked in a hostile climate for so many years, the representatives of the NAACP assumed that individuals who publicly accepted the goals of desegregation would be advocates of these policies when appointed to administrative positions—that is, public friends would also be administrative allies. As a result, the NAACP staff did not focus on the activities of these friends unless a critical and blatant situation developed. The Inc. Fund, by contrast, learned that friends who became administrators could not play simple, clearcut advocacy roles from their official jobs; assumption of new roles changed these individuals. Thus, although not considering the officials to be "opponents," the Inc. Fund staff people learned how to work with the administrators as friendly adversaries. The characterization of the situation as a quasi-adversary process also allowed the Inc. Fund to develop some skepticism about the legal aspects of the administrative activity. After a number of opposed policies were adopted within the administrative setting because of the advice of legal staff (particularly the HEW Office of General Counsel), the Inc. Fund obtained its own attorneys to develop legal arguments in opposition to the legal advice being given within the agency.

A Limited Response

Although the activities of the Task Force indicated that a few people, with a relatively small amount of information, can have a significant impact on the decision process within the administrative enforcement offices, the task of monitoring Title VI as an active constituent required more extended staff and organizational capacities than the AFSC and the Inc. Fund had available. The successes of the Task Force had not gone unnoticed by the participants within the Leadership Conference. The Task Force had begun operations in the spring of 1965; approximately a year later the Leadership Conference Committee on Compliance and Enforcement was formed. Although the skeleton machinery was established to focus on administrative issues, the capacities of the organization to act, according to a student of the efforts, "generally has lain dormant. These groups have had interest, experience, numbers, and knowledge potentially on call, yet with severely restricted time, staff, and money these resources have been untouched and undirected."

One can only speculate whether the Leadership Conference spokesmen were motivated to consider activity in the enforcement area because of competition with the Inc. Fund.[5] As the Johnson Administration continued, however, the coalition became increasingly conscious that it needed "help" in performing a monitoring role. The "help" needed was always perceived as a financial need; money to provide staff and support would be the key to effectiveness. Periodically, attempts were made to solicit funds from foundations for monitoring activity. One participant recalls that a solicitation to the Field Foundation received a resounding "no" from foundation officials; "the word was that if it was the Leadership Conference doing the monitoring, no funds were available."

By the end of the fiscal year in 1968—when many of the administration friends in civil rights jobs had left their positions—manna fell into the laps of the Leadership Conference in the form of a grant from the Office of Economic Opportunity. The OEO funds were to be used to develop a study of Title VI enforcement around the federal agencies. This study, in turn, would be the ammunition that the Leadership Conference thought it needed to convince a foundation that it needed staffing help and had the technical capacity to be an effective monitor.

The project officially involved a contract between OEO and the A. Philip Randolph Institute (the non-profit organization serving as a home for the long-time black labor leader and his colleague, Bayard Rustin) because the Leadership Conference did not have the non-profit status necessary to receive such a grant. Although the contract was signed with the Randolph Institute, the Leadership Conference was making all decisions about the project. The study was considered an official activity of the Compliance Committee; thus the determination to choose a project director was made by Committee Chairman, James Hamilton; by Leadership Conference part-time staff member Marvin Caplan (loaned to the coalition by the Industrial Union Department of the AFL-CIO); and by

Conference Secretary, Arnold Aronson, from the National Jewish Community Relations Advisory Council. The threesome agreed to hire Barney Sellers, former special assistant to the Director of the HEW Office for Civil Rights, as project director.

When Sellers began the project, he was told that the document that would emerge from his efforts should include arguments in two areas. One would indicate the failures of federal officials to enforce Title VI adequately; the second would document the existing inadequacies within the Leadership Conference to monitor the administrative enforcement. Several months and two drafts later, Sellers had a major jolt. A chapter of the report discussing the inadequacies of the civil rights groups became the center of a controversy within the Leadership Conference. Although the report simply made a case for funding for the coalition to maintain additional staff, the representative of the NAACP attending the review session perceived the section of the document as a major criticism of the civil rights organizations—his, in particular. Observers at the session remember that the NAACP representative berated Sellers for more than 20 minutes, climaxing his speech by saying, "I will not tolerate an independent staff working out of this office not under my control." Once the door of criticism was opened, the report was also attacked by staff of the AFL-CIO, sensitive to a reference in the document concerning the relationship between the building trade unions and discriminatory practices of the U. S. Department of Labor.

Sellers' report was more than 300 pages in draft form, detailing through extensive interviews and analyses of documents the extent and nature of the subversion of the Title VI policy across the federal government.[6] After the attacks by the NAACP and AFL-CIO representatives, the report was pared down to a 48-page, innocuously written document that was hardly the stuff to convince a foundation of the value of supporting future Leadership Conference projects.

The fate of the OEO-funded project indicated that the Leadership Conference's abilities to follow through on monitoring the Title VI enforcement involved more than scarce financial resources. In what may be viewed as a pathological situation, the Leadership Conference was unable to bring itself to focus on the issues that blocked monitoring. Whether power plays and need for deference (as with the NAACP) or refusal to recognize situations of potential conflict of interest (the AFL-CIO), the obstacles to such a recognition appeared to have been insurmountable. The Leadership Conference chose to continue to survive by using its known and "tested" legislative abilities;[7] apparently there was not enough incentive for it to "learn" about Title VI enforcement.

Conclusions

The Title VI policy in education reached the administrative level with minimal direction from its legislative constituency. As the policy took administrative form, requiring quite drastic changes in thousands of school districts across the country, one could expect that the requirements would generate opposition. That opposition would come from school districts and would be reflected in conflict within the administrative agencies involved as well as through Congressional pressure. If conflict was generated, administrators needed some way of protecting themselves against the political reactions that could be anticipated.

Opposition to the civil rights demands also focused on the requirements as a part of a larger change in the federal role in education. OE was reaching toward a new focus in its "customer" market: reaching beyond the state school officials to the local school board, superintendents, teachers, parents, and students themselves. By calling on a new customer group, OE had to contend with the influence and power of the traditional education interest groups. This influence and power were not only externally expressed but were also part of the standard operating procedures for the agency.

Although the realities of political survival seem to dictate the development of a constituency supporting the general thrust of OE's new approach, the agency took the opposite approach. Instead, the OE leaders tried to establish an administrative operation that could exist without supporters. By using this strategy, the officials thought they could put themselves above the inevitable battle between Southern school officials and civil rights groups. The methods of contact that were devised within the agency to deal with outside groups were meant to keep potential supporters at a distance. The agency attempted to protect its authority with a veil of secrecy and failed to inform possible customers of the scope and meaning of its responsibilities. Some of the customers— particularly community-level individuals who sought assistance—were not sophisticated in bureaucratic dealings. The response they received from OE seemed to be yet another chapter in a long, drawn-out story of put-downs and run-arounds.

The organizations already on the Washington scene with some experience in civil rights matters were preoccupied with the legislative world in Congress. The Leadership Conference on Civil Rights appeared to be unable to "learn" from its experiences with the administrative activity and never could mobilize itself to develop a staff and political capacity to deal with the bureaucratic level. The influential groups in the

Conference had little interest in pushing the umbrella organization to follow through on administrative lobbying, although some of the groups were skilled at lobbying inside the bureaucracy for other issues. Whether because of a conflict of interest or because of internal political squabbles, the major lobbying groups would not give enforcement questions equal status with legislative questions.

It is not surprising that the strategy used by Title VI OE staff met problems. Whether or not these officials wanted to play the game of interest group politics, that game was being played around them. The opponents of change in the pattern of relationships established by the federal education agency were formidable. As such, they could make their case in Congress and in day-to-day operations of the agency, calling on long-time friends to be their advocates. Despite OE's Title VI strategy, an implicit constituency of opponents was operating and affecting its program. OE Title VI activities needed friends.

OE's avoidance strategy also affected its substantive ability to perform its job. As long as the agency relied on paper compliance (whether through assurance forms or through the submission of desegregation plans), it had no way of knowing whether the paper submission accurately described conditions in a community. In some cases, federal action was counterproductive to activities for desegregation undertaken by local black groups,[8] but without information sources, the feds were unable to know if this might be occurring. Although staff limitations made it difficult for OE to follow up on complaints, one might argue that it would have been better for the agency to know something about the perceived problems than to operate without any knowledge of them.

Despite OE's reluctance to encourage supporters or to respond to friendly adversaries, the Task Force on School Desegregation of the AFSC and the Inc. Fund was able to make some impact. That small effort indicated that an active constituency could have some impact on the administrative enforcement program. Given the time and funds spent, the impact was significant. But the Task Force was not able to have the same kind of effect on policy that would have been generated by the activity of large membership organizations with on-going operations in the field and a national reputation.

The absence of a politically-connected constituency for the administrative enforcement of Title VI in school matters locked in the local education administrators. They were controlled by the powers that were already influential within the established OE bureaucracy—the advocates of state control. Because it is never possible to separate implementation from legislation, the administrators were forced to appear on Capitol Hill, hat in hand, to defend their activities. The major advocate of the desegregation policies in the legislative forum, the Leadership Conference, had not focused on the administrative intricacies. Thus they were not always the most helpful allies in legislative battles when these battles centered around administrative issues. The officials were forced to stand alone before Congressional adversaries, forced to be the sole advocates for the desegregation policies.

V
CONCLUSIONS

13
•
UNCERTAINTY, CONFLICT, AND INTERDEPENDENCY

This study has assumed that every administrator approaches his or her job with an underlying conceptualization of the job to be done and some view—often intuitive and rarely articulated—of what constitutes success. The study has also assumed that this underlying perspective assists the decision-maker in determining the appropriateness of administrative tools, shapes a model of internal organization decision-making, and provides the basis for relationships with individuals and groups outside the agency.

Although a specific definition of policy success has attributes that are idiosyncratic to both the individual administrator and the particular policy setting, conceptions of administrative success appear to cluster around two poles. In one view, success can be measured in terms of the attainment of specific goals of a particular administrative program during a given time period. But for others, success must be measured over a longer time frame—a sustained dimension that values administrative survival.

To a significant degree, these divergent perspectives reflect the agendas of two varieties of administrators. A political appointee, coming to a job for a short period, projects a short-term time frame on an evaluation of success. A policy life span, to that administrator, is rarely longer than a four-year presidential term, and success is defined by Congressional appearances and press treatment. For a career civil servant, however, success transcends any particular administration. Presidents and department secretaries come and go, but the career civil servant must continue to depend on Congressional favor and extra-bureaucratic support for survival.

In the popular political view, the administrator who is concerned about achieving change in existing bureaucratic practices has usually been identified with the short-term time frame and the viewpoint associated with it. Conversely, the permanent civil servant tends to be viewed as the defender of the *status quo*. As the preceeding analysis of Title VI policy within the Office of Education and HEW indicates, however, the ahistorical perspective of some political appointees may also have adverse effects on short-term survival and the attainment of specific goals within particular policy areas.

A decision world with clear boundaries, precise definition of tasks, and tight control of a policy setting clearly makes sense in some policy areas. In other cases, however—such as that involving Title VI implementation in federal education programs—administrative leadership does not appear to be demonstrated by steps that lead to closure, precision, and tight control. Rather, the activities generated by such a conceptualization led the decision-makers into a political inferno, where the entire range of the administrators' action was challenged.

Each of the decision clusters analyzed in this study—decisions about the law, decisions related to internal structural determinations, and decisions involving consumers or constituents—reveals an incongruity between the administrative world as seen by the top decision-makers and the reality they faced as they attempted to implement the policy with which they were charged. Time after time, attempts to enforce Title VI policy in federal education activities met one form or another of resistance. Although resistance to policy change is not synonymous with defeat for the entire policy, in this case the resistance to enforcement efforts could not be absorbed into the implementation strategy. Officials charged with enforcement of nondiscrimination requirements in federal education programs were not able to achieve the explicit goals of the civil rights policies and, at the same time, to deal with the reality of organization structure, administrative tools, and political relationships defining the bureaucratic world in which they were located.

Decisions about Structure

The policy determinations made by the administrators of Title VI in federal education programs indicated a disparity between imperatives viewed as necessary for the attainment of the goals of the enforcement program and imperatives that the on-going system demanded for organizational survival. In this case, organizational survival seemed to require the acceptance of two kinds of structural reality: (1) the requirements of HEW as a department, and (2) the specific reality of federal education programs within OE.

To be located within HEW meant that any program had to accept a number of constraints generated by the structural home. Although often viewed as a single, unified department, HEW was historically a collection of autonomous agencies, bureaus, and offices. The autonomy of these units was maintained by professional identifications outside the bureaucracy and by political relationships cultivated with interest groups and interests on Capitol Hill. With the historical reality of autonomous units, the powers of the HEW Secretary over the old, established agencies were minimal. When the Secretary wanted to expand power and influence within the department, the most usual procedure was to create new units to administer new functions. But for Title VI, the expansion of power and influence by the centralized HEW operation had to be conceived and administered without significantly disrupting the operations of the old units.

Heaped upon the struggle between the office of the Secretary and the operating agencies was another historical battle for power between the functions of the federal department located in Washington and the functions that were dispersed in the field. No HEW Secretary had been able to strike a workable balance between the functions of these two organizational cores. The contest between the field and Washington was enmeshed within the battle between the agencies and the Secretary; both groups attempted to control the locus that would set the bounds for decentralization. If the agency was viewed as the pivot, the determination for decentralization would rest upon functional decentralization as the first order and, following that, a geographic determination of the location of field offices. If, however, one viewed the Secretary's office (representing a unified HEW) as the pivotal center, then geographical decentralization might become the first order of business, followed by some decision about a functional division of labor. Although the immensity of the nation and the diversity of its population demanded an acknowledgment of the need for some sort of field apparatus, HEW Secretaries and agency chiefs—regardless of political party—had been unable to devise a method for dealing with that need.

On top of the structural constraints established by HEW, the U. S. Office of Education also sent out a series of messages about organizational reality. Any action or policy set forth by OE had to acknowledge the ideology of local control of education and the historical role of state education agencies. One did not directly or openly challenge this belief without some anticipation that the educational establishment would react to that action. Although the role of the Office of Education had been gradually expanding during the period from the passage of the National Defense Education Act up to the time of the enactment of the ESEA, OE policy-makers had attempted to exert a federal role in education without appearing to do so. The problem for federal education officials was one of getting assistance to state and local school systems through procedures that brought services closer at hand to the states and localities without evoking accusations of federal control. Federal education officials were wary of organizing their activities in ways that provoked antagonism from the education establishment. Any strong independent operation emanating from Washington was vulnerable to criticism as leading to complete federal control of American education. But decentralized offices, with representatives of the U. S. Commissioner of Education operating as mini-Commissioners, were also opposed by powerful education interest groups. These groups feared that a multiplicity of decision centers would diminish their influence over federal education activities.

If a Commissioner were willing to go along with business as usual, allowing the activities of the Office of Education to be determined by autonomous bureaus within the Office (bureaus with intimate relationships with the education interest groups), decisions about organization structure were rather insignificant. If, however, a Commissioner wanted to exert an independent controlling force over the activities of the operating agencies and bureaus, then structural decisions—particularly determinations about centralization and decentralization—were of major import.

These structural constraints within HEW and OE were operative and thus presented a problem to anyone who attempted to make changes within the traditional pattern of federal education policy administration. No matter what policy was at hand, the reality of perceived power relationships and their expression in organizational terms had to be dealt with. It was rare for any reorganization plan within OE to be viewed as a simple exercise in efficiency. It was almost inevitable that a reorganization plan would be associated with a push for new power arrangements within the federal education activities. Even those efforts that were defended on straightforward management grounds—such as the push for more "rational" decision-making attempted by Deputy Commissioner Henry Loomis—were extremely vulnerable to pressures and opposition stemming from past relationships with the education establishment, Congress, the White House, and the Secretary's office.

The Title VI policy, as it was thrust forth on the federal education programs, could not avoid a frontal collision with the ongoing structural patterns within HEW and OE. Because it was a policy that affected all the programs within the office, the enforcement activities could not be separately organized simply as an independent operation. Although an independent office would allow the enforcers to take their place alongside other programs (operating as one of a number of specialized activities), the civil rights issue could not be isolated from the other programs and given protective coloration to do business in an autonomous fashion. Enforcement of Title VI depended on all elements within the educational system. The location of enforcement activities within OE and HEW was an important consideration as activities were conceptualized to relate to other operations involving federal education policies. If Title VI were viewed as a comprehensive conditioning policy, then those charged with implementation in OE had to worry about how their activities related to the state education officials, to local educators, to representatives of national education organizations, to the bureau chiefs within OE, to the regional people in OE, and to the various aspects of the HEW apparatus.

Although the Title VI policy implementers defined their task as one that involved comprehensive, encompassing activities, their formulation of the enforcement operation betrayed an inability to relate structure to the broad nature of the task at hand. Although their rhetoric acknowledged the decision interdependencies between Title VI activities and the actions of ongoing programs, the *organization* of the civil rights operations did not bespeak interdependenices. Rather, the civil rights organization was structured and operated as a technical, self-sufficient unit that depended solely upon professional and competent staff members to do the job. The complex system of federal, state, and local relationships in American education was virtually ignored as the Title VI policies were operationally defined on their own terms, standardized, and limited to a regional application.

When the civil rights enforcement structure was moved in 1966 from the Office of Education to the Office for Civil Rights within the Secretary's office, the HEW enforcement staff confronted problems very similar to those experienced by the OE officials. The OE decision-makers had to deal with the reality of resistance by bureaus within the Office to a policy imposed upon them by the Commissioner. HEW staff were faced with resistance by agency and office heads to a policy pronouncement emanating from the Office of the Secretary. In each case, the proponents of the civil rights policy faced not only opposition to their efforts based on the merits of their policy, but also a reaction to the policy as change *qua* change—a power reaction to a power play.

Throughout the period studied, officials charged with enforcement of Title VI in federal education leaned toward a definition of organizational success that was defensible as a neat, efficient operation. Civil rights activities were pushed toward a self-contained status, emphasizing routinized work, precisely defined goals, and explicit tasks. This urge never really took fullblown shape because it was clearly incompatible with the attainment of Title VI's ultimate goal—the elimination of discriminatory patterns in the method of allocating federal education dollars. That is, the reality of HEW organizational politics and the ideology of American education were such that messy organizational functioning was inevitable—whether or not the decision-makers anticipated it and devised a neat organizational form.

Most decision-makers conceive of their authority as an all-or-nothing resource. On one hand, an individual in power is thought to have the authority or capacity to do whatever he or she wants to do. On the other, a top position is considered little more than frosting on a cake, and an administrator filling that role is essentially powerless to change existing practices. Few decision areas so clearly exemplify the either/or view as do policies involving organizational structure. The urge for centralized authority is very often interchangeable with an urge for control. Conversely, the push for decentralization frequently stands as an acknowledgment of the inability or non-desirability of a change in administrative organization. It is extremely rare for change to be associated with decentralization in the administration of federal programs.

The conceptualization of Title VI enforcement activities clearly illustrates the tendency for officials to view centralized decision-making as the method of achieving change. Within the Office of Education, decentralization to the field or to the operating agencies was seen as a capitulation to patterns of states' rights, which, in turn, meant non-enforcement of civil rights policies. Within the HEW Office for Civil Rights, policy decentralization to the agencies meant a loss of control—and that control was viewed as essential to the administration of Title VI. Although the

HEW-based operation sometimes used the language of decentralized decision-making, the decision-makers were protective of their perceived ability to determine policy as they alone saw fit.

Because decentralization involves the dispersion of both geographical and functional decision-making, the series of determinations made by Title VI policy-makers in OE and HEW were often difficult to separate in the usual manner of classifying centralized and decentralized activities. When HEW attempted to push the OE civil rights staff to organize in terms of geographic field divisions (the most common conceptualization of decentralization is geographic), they were using their *centralized functional authority* to call for *geographic decentralization*. Opposition to moves in that direction came in two ways: from those who opposed the assertion of any sort of power by the implementors (and thus reacted to use of centralized functional authority) and from those who opposed administrative decentralization (and thus focused on the geographic decentralization plans).

Although moves for decentralization of either variety can be defended on grounds of flexibility—that is, providing the basis for the federal government to respond to the diversity of 25,000 school districts—in this case no such argument was made and decentralization was attacked and defended as a power play. Opponents of substantive as well as procedural change combined to back the implementors into a corner. Once there, the administrative staffs were forced into a very weak posture; their very authority to act was under fire. Congressional attacks on the autonomy of the administrators sapped their ability to make structural decisions that reflected the political imperatives and made "sense" in terms of the policy to be administered.

Given the organizational reality of HEW and OE and the task of imposing a significant change on many of the 25,000 school districts within the country, implementors of Title VI policy could anticipate an administrative world fraught with uncertainty and conflict. In some ways—especially in its symbolic proportions—administrative policies that reflected both functional and geographic decentralization as some part of a strategy might have indicated a greater understanding of that uncertain administrative world. Acceptance of some level of decentralized decision-making—like an acceptance of the due process requirements in administrative law—might have protected the administrators of Title VI policy in HEW from the opposition generated on procedural grounds. Although the officials charged with enforcement of the nondiscrimination provisions perceived demands for decentralization as a method of eroding their discretionary authority, their long-run discretion might have been better protected through acceptance of a larger measure of decentralization. For in the context of the enforcement activities, decentralization was a structural euphemism for uncertainty and conflict.

Decisions about the Law

As a policy that was defended on constitutional grounds, the Title VI requirement took its language and substance from the legal world. Although law is often a codification of patterns and practices already found in the social, political, or economic mores of a society, in this case the law was an overt tool to achieve social change. Precedent for the policy could not be found in administrative practices. Rather, Title VI policy as an administrative issue was built on what was occurring within the judicial system.

The characterization of Title VI as a constitutionally-mandated question involving rights of citizenship also affected the scope of the policy definition. One is either discriminated against or not. By its very nature, the Title VI question took shape as a comprehensive policy that was difficult to place within an incremental apparatus. The nature of Title VI emphasized and valued a wholistic approach to federal action. Yet this approach flew in the face of the pattern of the federal administrative process. The legal machinery already available within the administrative level was devised to *curb* the power of the federal government to act in a unitary, unilateral, and uniform fashion—the very attributes of action that proponents of Title VI saw as essential to enforcement attempts. The body of tools and knowledge to be found in the administrative legal bag of tricks was thus viewed as particularly inappropriate to those who were concerned about eliminating discrimination in the expenditure of federal dollars. They saw the urge for extended administrative discretion as a positive aspect. To those reared in and responsible for continuing the precedents of administrative law, however, the level and forms of discretion sought by administrative officials appeared to extend uncontrolled powers of the federal government.

In addition to the conflicting attitudes about the extent of administrative discretion desirable in the implementation attempts, there was also a generalized skepticism among the legal advisors around Title VI about the applicability of existing administrative law to the enforcement activities.

The Title VI issue was posed by lawyer and politician alike in a way that made it difficult for anyone involved with implementation efforts to deal with the legitimate question of the extent of federal authority. It was easiest and—they argued—most politically advantageous for implementors to deal with the issue in terms of good and evil. To talk about limitations on federal action or to acknowledge that authority was dispersed through a number of jurisdictions was viewed as a capitulation to the patterns of segregation and discrimination that Title VI had been enacted to eliminate. Consistent and forceful action—stemming from strong, centralized leadership—was considered the only way to combat discriminatory practices. To talk about state and local power was to wave a red flag—merely another way of using the states' rights arguments to maintain segregation.

The lawyers involved with implementation were primarily concerned about the basis for the *substantive* requirements of enforcement activities—the substantive standards that the feds would impose upon state and local officials. Action related to school desegregation within the federal court system provided the basis for these substantive requirements. But before long, because of the twisted and involved method used to codify existing court action into administrative requirements, enforcement officials were also unhappy with the curb on their substantive autonomy. Both the question of inclusion of Northern school systems and the struggle over the freedom-of-choice issue made the federal civil rights officials less than content with their pattern of substantive deference to the courts. In effect, the administrators of Title VI policy found the incremental behavior of the federal court system also incompatible with their perceptions of the job to be done. In large part, the political challenges to the legal autonomy of the administrators resulted from the way the administrators and their legal counselors tended to adopt noncredible positions—requirements that were unenforceable, that did not relate in fact to the goal of the efforts, and that sent out other messages of noncredibility. The assumed scenario of reaction to the requirements was rarely played out.

Legal decisions taken to implement Title VI bypassed basic due process requirements. Neither the beneficiaries of the Title VI programs nor the groups asked to change their practices were provided the procedural opportunities to comment systematically on policies or, once policy was made, to express opposition to it. The diversity of the groups affected by the policy was ignored; instead, administrators attempted to control their enforcement procedures by promulgating guidelines that were overly explicit and subsequently too rigid to be enforceable.

The good/evil dichotomy that shaped the ideology of the administrators combined with the officials' general unfamiliarity with administrative legal practices to produce a set of rules and regulations that did not appear "fair" to either supporters or opponents of Title VI. Participation of affected parties—the most accepted method of limiting the extent of power of the federal agency—was effectively inconsequential, either ignored altogether or, when participation was required by law, structured in such a way and at such a time in the decision process as to be meaningless.

As can be expected when administrators neglect to balance their desire for control with "fairness," Congress was quick to attack the rules of Title VI enforcement as arbitrary and capricious. The overt opponents of civil rights policies joined forces with those who were opposed to the style and scope of the administrative action used in the enforcement activites. Beginning with the Chicago fiasco, the discretionary authority of the implementors was openly challenged. From that point on, attacks on Title VI were fair political game in Congress, through the White House, and on the state and local political fronts. The administrators charged with Title VI policy within HEW no longer were trusted and the very legality of proceedings was openly questioned.

Decisions about Constituency

The previous discussions concerning the decision clusters surrounding legal and structural questions have indicated a disparity between the assumptions held by the implementing officials and the bureaucratic world in which the officials were required to act. The bureaucrats charged with enforcing Title VI in federal education programs were unable to devise their activities, choose their enforcing tools, and structure their staff operations to survive in a tense political setting. Both the legal and the structural decisions made by officials were fashioned in such a way as to encourage opposition to the implementing procedures on procedural grounds.

It is clear that opposition to the enforcing efforts went beyond simple opposition to the civil rights content of the issue. Rather, opponents of the policy opposed a variety of decisions and procedures that were used during the process of implementation and that changed the accepted and existing pattern and style of bureaucratic operations. For these reasons, civil rights officials in OE and HEW could have been expected to need—and hence cultivate—a network of supporting relationships that could have protected the civil rights activities from the seemingly myriad corners of opposition.

Following passage of the 1964 Civil Rights Act, it would appear that administrators were in a position to develop such a supportive network, utilizing the legislative lobbying groups as the basis for a new administrative constituency. But the nature of that potential civil rights constituency—its inability to conceptualize the differences between the administrative process and the legislative, its insistence on viewing decision-making in simplistic terms, its own internal battles, and the failure of beneficiaries of the programs most affected by Title VI to be represented in the coalition—meant that the initiative for change had to come from the bureaucratic setting.

Within that setting, the decisions about constituency followed a pattern similar to decisions about the law and organization structure. Title VI officials within HEW did not use their initial discretionary authority wisely. Although the early stages of the enforcement efforts could be viewed as an essentially formless and fluid situation, the implementors failed to capitalize on that fluidity. Rather, the officials used a strategy of avoidance and failed to see the inevitable competition between the Title VI agenda and that of the existing education establishment. Enforcement procedures were devised that isolated the bureaucrats from their potential supporters. No new network of relationships was cultivated with proponents of the Title VI activities. Neither the staffing patterns used nor the enforcement procedures adopted effectively reached out beyond the bureaucracy to the few organizations that were able to comprehend the dimensions of a role within the administrative process.

Closed decision-making—that is, decision-making that did not reach beyond the organization's borders for input or for information dispersal—was viewed by the officials as the most effective way of protecting their autonomy and authority. But closed decision-making was not possible in a policy area involving federal education programs. Until ESEA, the federal government had played a subordinate role to the states; even with ESEA it was not clear how aggressive the Office of Education could be in determining how federal education monies would actually be spent in the schoolroom. Deference to state control of education was a well-institutionalized policy within OE, with a labyrinth of staffing patterns and procedures established to make sure that the interests of the *status quo* prevailed. This interlacing of relationships with the representatives of the existing education establishment was a reality in OE. Thus, in terms of involvement of a constituency in decision-making, the Title VI implementors were again bucking a procedural as well as a substantive pattern of operation. Substantively, Title VI policy attempted to bypass the states and deal directly with local school districts to require school desegregation. Procedurally, the implementors were attempting to contain decision-making within the organization, whereas the entire pattern of federal education programs involved participation (in one way or another) of a selected group of education organizations outside the federal family.

Title VI Enforcement: Some "Natural" Attributes

Throughout the recapitulation of the problems involved in Title VI enforcement policy in law, structure, and constituency, a single theme has been emphasized: the disparity in the administration of this issue between the world conceptualized by the policy-makers and the world they faced on a day-to-day basis. That world can be described as one containing three attributes: uncertainty, conflict, and a recognition of new customers.

Uncertainty

The reality of a policy-maker concerned about enforcing Title VI in education could be described as a world containing two varieties of uncertainty: the uncertainty created by a flexible enforcement methodology and the uncertainty created by the interrelationship between the civil rights issue and other education issues.

The flexibility issue involves two givens: an acknowledgment that school desegregation is a slippery and difficult-to-measure product, and an assumption that desegregation involves many symbolic questions related to equity and distribution of power. Symbolic issues such as busing are clearly viewed as a reality by both supporters and opponents of desegregation but are often hard to understand away from their contextual home. If one acknowledges that desegregation is both slippery and symbolic, it would be rational for the policy-maker to move toward a flexible enforcement machinery possessing at least two attributes: (a) rules applicable to diverse situations but written in a way that communicates minimum performance or process criteria; and (b) an administrative structure for enforcement that facilitates policy inputs throughout the system. The latter attribute might emphasize participation of affected parties as well as participation from officials up and down the agency structure. Flexible rules and dispersed decision-making emphasize uncertainty by spreading authority throughout the system.

The second variety of uncertainty involving Title VI and education was created by the interrelationship between the civil rights issue and other education programs. Title VI might be described as a comprehensive conditioning policy dependent on the ongoing activity of an incremental system. If no federal monies are to be spent, then Title VI is meaningless. The interrelationship between the operating programs (especially after ESEA) and the Title VI policy meant that a policy-maker charged with civil rights activities was in a no-win situation if he or she chose a consistent authority base for enforcement. If civil rights activities were located in a single separate office—e.g., the Equal Educational Opportunities office or the Office for Civil Rights—and if they relied solely on technical capacities, then there was limited impact on the day-to-day activities of the individuals who actually decided how the federal monies were to be spent. If, instead, civil rights enforcement activities were delegated to the operating program staff members (the people who made the "real" decisions about money), then civil rights imperatives would be lost in the shuffle. Perhaps a knowledgeable administrator might establish a procedure that covered both bases: set up enforcement activities in an office of civil rights and yet assume that operating program staff would be in charge of much of the enforcement. Such an administrator would attempt to live with the uncertainty created by this messy situation and calculate action on the basis of a higher propensity to risk.

The interrelationship between the civil rights issue and ongoing programs also meant that the basis for political support for or opposition to enforcement was not always clear. As is usually the case in politics, someone might go to Capitol Hill as a supporter of the civil rights policies for reasons that had little direct relationship to the desegregation issue. Conversely, civil rights activities might elicit opposition from other quarters because of their impact on other educational or administrative matters.

Conflict

The second attribute focuses on conflict. With a good measure of accuracy, one might predict that any issue that attempts to redistribute power, authority, or resources usually engenders a sense of loss in at least one sector, and usually at least one sector does not give up easily. Whether or not one agrees that this sort of change *must* involve loss, the school desegregation issue provoked a situation in which there was perceived loss everywhere. Inside the bureaucracy, conflict was fanned in debate on the merits of the desegregation issue as well as on the level of organizational politics. The desegregation policy demanded that federal education officials change their practices—practices that had been comfortably played out and rewarded for years. Conflict occurred when officials within the education bureaucracy were asked to change specific policy practices. Conflict was also predictable on the level of organizational politics. A new policy usually brings with it a new structure of authority of one sort or another. The presence of any new structure creates a situation of bureaucratic organizational competition. If the new policy staff is not to prevail and lower the leverage and power of established staff, the established groups must do battle to make sure their interests win out.

Similar although more public forms of conflict were found outside the bureaucracy at the state and local levels. School desegregation was opposed in every form imaginable—from overt political resistance in both the North and South, to more subtle forms of opposition. There can be little doubt that school desegregation was and continues to be an extremely volatile issue within American society.

The political effect of both internal-bureaucratic and local resistance to the policy was unnerving. Both federal bureaucrats and local educators had close relationships with members of Congress, and both were expert in the use of these political connections. An official charged with enforcing school desegregation policies could assume that opponents of the policies would be able to contact powerful members of Congress, who, in turn, would use their oversight authority to make life difficult for the official or at least throw obstacles in the way of enforcement.

Customers

The presence of conflict at each level of the enforcement procedure meant that the enforcement activities were implicitly political. Whether the conflict took place within the bureaucracy, in the states, in local school districts, or in Congress, school desegregation policy engendered political battles. Bureaucrats rarely win open political battles by themselves. They need support from outside quarters: interest or constituency groups advocating the position of the bureaucrat. Without such support and once the policy has reached the open political stage, it is hardly rational for the official to take action that seems suicidal. The relationship between officials and their customers is a reciprocal arrangement. The inaction of an official may be directly related to a fear of loss of outside support.

What does this all mean in the case of school desegregation?

One of the effects of Title VI—theoretically, at least—was to franchise an entire category of people who previously had been denied a place at the table when the educational benefits were being distributed. These new customers somehow had to be identified and accorded some status on the local level to facilitate opportunities for their participation in the development of educational policy. In other words, a right within Title VI was a right to be a fully-franchised customer. These new customers—acting as new constituents—could be a protective device for the official, supporting the bureaucrat in Congressional squabbles and playing an advocacy role within the bureaucracy and in federal, local, and state debates. The voice of the new customer would help to counter the claims of existing interest groups who—for whatever reasons—opposed the activity of the officials responsible for Title VI functions.

These three characteristics of Title VI—tendencies to uncertainty and to conflict, and a reliance on the development of new customers—combine to send out some clues to the decision-maker. These clues might first be described in their negative aspects; that is, what Title VI policy in education was *not*:

—It is not an issue that can be easily handed to a bureaucracy that operates in a literal, linear pyramidal fashion or be placed in a single, centralized locus for administration;

—It is not an issue that relies solely on the technical, specialized capacities of administrators;

—It is not an issue that can be provided a self-contained status, independent of an outside environment;

—It is not an issue that can be described as consistent or unchanging over time; and

—It is not an issue that is easily measurable and conducive to distant and formal control devices.

The disparity between the world described by these clues and the decision-makers' view of their job can be summarized as follows:

Attributes of Title VI	*Title VI Enforcement Decisions*
Not an issue easily handed to a pyramidal organization with specialized, functional organization.	Legal procedures developed assuming organizational control at top; due process not taken seriously.
	Structures created that assumed linear, pyramidal operation.
	Constituents assumed their job was completed once they contacted top officials of the organization.

Not an issue that relied on technical, specialized administrative capacities	Lawyers conceptualized problem as a technical, legal issue; saw themselves as possessing sufficient technical capacity to get job done.
	Individuals hired in lower- and middle-level jobs tended to be particularly insensitive to political aspects of issue within bureaucracy. Definition of technical not congruent with demands of education technicians.
	Constituent "friends" scattered in bureaucracy were assumed to represent interests. They assumed traditional intergroup skills were needed to carry on job.
Not an issue that operated in a self-contained status, independent of outside environment.	Legal procedures had the effect of closing out participation, emphasizing inwardness of enforcement. Hearings and other due process forms unutilized for participation purposes.
	Structure and operating procedures in both OE and HEW had isolating tendencies. Issue defined as one to be handled alone by a certain kind of expert. Relationships with other education officials avoided.
	Passivity of potential constituent groups allowed closed decision-making to go essentially uncriticized.
Not an issue described as consistent or unchanging.	Guidelines promulgated tended to treat the issue as consistent, stable, and predictable.

Inflexible operating apparatus created on grounds that flexibility of enforcement procedures would lead to capitulation to discriminatory patterns.

Non-process view of enforcement by potential constituents. No sense of Title VI issue as redistributional. Tendency to define issue in absolute, nonchanging terms.

Not an issue easily measurable and conducive to distant control devices.

Formula for determining compliance relied on numbers supplied in paper reports.

Washington-based operations minimized organization's ability to know what was happening in local communities. No way for federal officials to play facilitating role.

Failure of constituent groups to mobilize local and regional apparatus meant that federal compliance reports were sole source of information.

14
•
NOTES FOR
FUTURE POLICY

The story that has been told in the preceding pages must also be examined in a broader context. The drama of Title VI implementation in education was played in the theatre of federal activity during the 1960's. During that period, as Sundquist and Davis have put it, "Through a series of dramatic enactments, the Congress asserted the national interest and authority in a wide range of governmental functions that until then had been the province, exclusively or predominantly, of state and local governments."[1]

Two issues emerged from the new and dramatic legislation that provide a backdrop to the Title VI discussion: (1) efforts at coordination between programs, and (2) an examination of the posture assumed by the federal government in its role as a change agent.

In the policy vocabulary of the 1960's, the question of coordination between and among federal programs was most often associated with federal efforts to encourage community development. Concern about coordinating various federal efforts was expressed early in the decade through the President's Committee on Juvenile Delinquency; was heard in community development efforts within OEO and the model cities program; and was voiced in rural development programs like those devised by the Appalachian Regional Commission. Although advocacy for coordination of federal programs came from a number of quarters, one strong expression of the need came from individuals involved in policy implementation, who argued that the irrationalities of federal programs effectively killed attempts at implementation at the local or grass roots level. For the programs, although conceived and administered separately—sometimes in conflict—dealt with different aspects of the same social and political fabric of a community.

The programs might be viewed as messy and nonaesthetic from the Washington perspective; in the locality, however, they were much more than that. Competing and conflicting messages, sent out by a plethora of federal departments, agencies, and bureaus, effectively incapacitated a local jurisdiction's ability to move. Heaped upon that situation, a locality often found itself further constrained by conflicting requirements from state, local, and even private endeavors. Local interdependencies were effectively ignored by federal policies.

As the situation developed in the 1960's, its hydra-headed character seemed to many to be a gross flouting of traditional principles of good public administration and of theories of equity advanced by the social democratic tradition. Both public administration and equity concerns led many to argue along with Sundquist and Davis that "What remains for the federal government is to reconcile its competing strategies and settle upon a unified approach to perfecting the design of the community-level machinery, getting it established, and then supporting its coordinating efforts."[2] The strategy that flowed from a concern with coordination pointed to the creation of centralized power cores, operating out of the Executive Office of the President, to push the divergent departments, agencies, and bureaus into line.

Those who cried "neatness" had little doubt that, once their authority was consolidated, they had the tools and strategies to use to achieve the desired change. The bag of tricks assumed to work included financial assistance, the use of federal regulations, and technical assistance strategies. Jerome Murphy has noted that these conventional options available to the federal government assumed that the states (or other jurisdictions) would be treated basically alike.[3] In his analysis of Title V of the Elementary and Secondary Education Act (the section of ESEA that provided grants to states to strengthen state departments of education), Murphy found that the conventional options available to the federal government had limited utility when applied to the varied and complex political environments that surrounded each state department of education. Although Murphy did not argue that the traditional options be thrown out entirely, he found that too much was expected from them.

Murphy's analysis of Title V stands as another in a growing body of literature that reexamines the posture assumed by the federal government in its role as a change agent. As Alice Rivlin has noted, there is "a new realism about the capacity of a central government to manage social action programs effectively . . . [and a] change of attitude that occurred during the 1960s among those who helped design federal social action programs and tried to make them work."[4] Rivlin notes that, during the 1960's, she, among others, thought that the effectiveness of a program "could be increased by tighter management from Washington . . . transmitted to the local level through federal guidelines and regulations and technical assistance."[5]

> This view now seems to me naive and unrealistic. The country is too big and too diverse, and social action is too complicated. There are over 25,000 school districts, and their needs, problems, and capacities differ drastically. Universal rules are likely to do more harm than good.[6]

Rivlin cites Robert Levine, who has written:

> By and large, those programs which have stressed detailed planning and detailed administration have either not worked, or have worked only on a scale which was very small compared to the size of the problem. . . . The detailed administrative approach does not work for clear enough reasons— which start with the impossibility of writing detailed rules to fit every case, and end with the lack of highly trained people to administer every case, assuming even that an administrative solution is possible.[7]

Although neither Rivlin nor Levine argues for federal retrenchment, they suggest that new administrative technologies have yet to be devised to achieve the goals of federal change.

The Case of Title VI

As discussed in this study, the Title VI implementation efforts involving education might be viewed as further evidence of the limitations of the existing administrative technology. Ironically, however, advocates of the enforcement program have not focused on the civil rights effort as a part of a general class of administrative problems in the 1960's; rather, they continue to argue for more of the same: more centralization, tighter guidelines, less participation, and uniform administration.[8]

Yet the complex system of political relationships that Murphy has described around Title V of ESEA is simple when compared to the relationships surrounding the Title VI implementation effort. Complexity in Title VI was defined by a number of relationships:

—Education and civil rights efforts were operationally inseparable.
—The policy was formulated as a national policy yet was acknowledged to include regional, state, and local variations.
—Congress would continue to hover over the policy as it was administered.
—Presidential politics were never far away.
—The policy had to be administered within existing federal agencies with defined relationships from the past.
—The policy had to be administered in existing educational systems in states and localities that were also in varying stages and processes of change and flux.

Each set of relationships, taken separately, would suggest an administrative posture that acknowledged complexity and uncertainty. But when heaped together, they are simply mindboggling. As such, prediction of specific results and controlled response is nearly a futile act.

Although we acknowledge fluidity and complexity in the decision-making process during policy formulation, a comparable conceptualization has not been devised for the policy implementation stage. We continue to seek marble cake administration. We search for stabilized relationships in implementation that allow policy implementors to predict *whom* they will talk with even though they do not know *what* they will say.[9] This search is a far cry from the attempt to devise an administrative program that meets the requirements of a Weberian bureaucratic form or that is comparable to a business enterprise.

If we begin from the concept of interdependency, then the goal of an effort similar to Title VI implementation in education is to provoke change everywhere. If local, state, and federal relationships prop up the system that is to be changed, then all must be somehow touched by the change efforts. If such a change is to take place within a democratic pluralist state, no system of change may be established through a single action or a tightly devised series of actions. The effort is thus both unpredictable and risky.

If the implementors of Title VI are at all typical, then it seems fairly clear that officials have great difficulty in dealing with attributes that are both risky and unpredictable. The culture of the federal bureaucracy makes it difficult for anyone in that setting to live with nonpredictable consequences or knowingly to take actions that are risky. These difficulties appear to be particularly real for career officials within the agencies involved in this study.

What is risky and predictable for one official is not always viewed that way for another person, however. This study has attempted to illustrate one such aspect of this confusion. Officials both in OE and within other parts of HEW created a dynamic that initiated (or at least exacerbated) risk situations and also set up forces that easily wriggled out of control.

But although it is relatively easy to criticize the decision-making around Title VI implementation in education, it is much more difficult to establish even hypothetical alternatives for action. The past, however, does provide us with some clues. Although viewed as peripheral to the thrust of the main decision-making process, there are three clusters of actions in the Title VI implementation process that suggest paths for future exploration. For purposes of shorthand, the activities will be characterized through the individuals who advocated them: Herbert Kane, "Pete" Page, and Jean Fairfax. Although each was concerned with a different aspect of Title VI implementation, each viewed the implementation as a process of change rather than as a series of static requirements that could be established by the feds to be imposed on state and local educational systems.

The Kane Approach

Herbert Kane was the sole member of either the OE or the OCR staff who had experience with labor-management negotiations. That background appeared to have provided him with the basis for establishing an operating style and using techniques within the Office of Education that were unusual and unique. Assuming that the goal of the effort was a process of change, rather than the act of simply writing compliance plans, Kane's strategy was to coopt state and local officials, whenever possible, to involve them in the process of change. Included in that process were a state education agency, local school superintendents who were hired as federal consultants, and federal staff members. The method used was a face-to-face negotiating mode; a number of opportunities were provided for both the feds (the regular officials as well as the superintendents as deputized feds) and the local school officials challenged by the desegregation requirements to save face.

Although it is hard to know whether the results of the Kane road shows (meetings held across the state) actually yielded more compliance, some of the state officials who were involved in the process remain convinced that it was an effective way for the federal government to operate. Cooptation is a two-way process; the feds received help, but the state and local people felt that they also had an opportunity to make their case. As one former superintendent hired as a federal consultant put it, "I loved being a fed; I got an insight into the role of the superintendent that I never had before." And although that superintendent perceived himself to be operating as a federal official during those negotiations, the local superintendent across the table (who was attempting to negotiate a satisfactory plan) knew that he would continue to deal with this individual as his colleague even after the negotiations were over.

The Kane approach uncovers two possible directions for future policy development. First, compliance must be locally defined. That local definition is needed not only because conditions are different from place to place but, in addition, because the process of negotiating a unique plan for the community has the effect of binding the parties involved in the negotiation to have a stake in its outcome. Second, federal officials alone cannot provide the stimulus for negotiations. No matter what they say, federal officials carry with them the imprint of the villain, and provoke some level of resistance simply because of their presence. Cooptation procedures—using and cultivating allies from state and local levels—give the feds increased credibility and help to devise momentum for compliance.

The Page Approach

"Pete" Page, as Regional Director of the HEW Atlanta office, also was a unique case. He believed that native Southerners were to be found who could and would enforce the desegregation requirements. He believed that regional offices provided an opportunity for the development of an effective administrative posture and, thus, regional offices should be given real authority to make decisions. And he believed that permanent civil servants and federal officials involved in administering other programs could be made to respond to civil rights requirements.

Page used his position as Regional Director as the podium from which to speak out as an advocate of civil rights policies. Although it may have been more effective as a quiescent symbol than anything else, Page's Southern accent gave his outpourings a different tone; the Yankees may have invaded, but they did it through the mouth of a Southerner. Page also argued that there was no way that civil rights policy would be enforced unless it was programatically entwined with other programs; he viewed the decentralized structure of the regional office as one that could cultivate this enforcement procedure more effectively than could individuals operating from Washington.

The Page approach also uncovers two possible directions for future policy. It suggests that attention should be given to regional (or other) variations in policy implementation and, wherever possible, individuals associated with those variations should be placed in positions of advocacy. Federal directives for change are difficult enough for many communities to swallow as substantive requirements; they are even more difficult to accept when they come from strangers or outsiders. Friends may be found or cultivated with different accents or packaged in different shapes from the Washington staff.

The second direction revealed by the Page approach is crucial: it clearly indicates that regional offices could play an effective role in federal policy change if they are allowed to do so. Operating through the regional office structure, a policy implementor could have the ability to deal with state officials on a regular, personal basis. It would allow the federal policy-maker to more easily identify local people at both ends of the policy spectrum of compliance and noncompliance. If regional program people were given authority to disperse funds (within established policy limits), then a conditioning federal policy such as Title VI could be more closely tied to the dispersal efforts and related to the specific programs devised.

Regional offices also provide the potential for a policy-maker to establish an information system that is developed as intelligence beyond paper submissions. Regional officials could become a part of the informal network that produces evaluative information that would be useful for review procedures. That information could be fed both up and down the system—to states and localities as well as to Washington. Although Page was not allowed to develop the Atlanta operation fully, his work gives an indication that regional offices have a much greater potential than was acknowledged in the Title VI implementation effort.

The Fairfax Approach

The activities undertaken by Jean Fairfax provide the final set of clues. The organization of the School Desegregation Task Force, sponsored jointly by the American Friends Service Committee and the NAACP Legal Defense and Educational Fund, produced the only systematic grass roots information about compliance with the federal requirements. The information developed by local groups in 200 school districts in the South had a dual effect. It provided black parents and other concerned citizens in those communities with details about the federal policy and encouraged them to undertake activity within that community to pressure for compliance. It also provided a national group with information about compliance activities in a significant number of localities. That information could have been used by federal officials (if they had wished to do so) and, at the same time, released to the general public to inform interested individuals within the country of the effects of the policy implementation at the grass roots.

Jean Fairfax was able to combine community organization techniques with administrative lobbying procedures. The combination sends out additional clues for future policy development. It indicates that lobbying efforts in Washington must be tied to information sources from the field. Otherwise, as some individuals indicated was the case, meetings between advocate and official turn into a mutual trading of ignorance. The Task Force activities also indicated that compliance activities in policy areas as intricate and complex as education have to be linked with serious public information efforts. If new rights are to be seriously established for citizens, those citizens must know about them in as great detail as is possible. Instead of viewing these individuals are outsiders, federal officials must acknowledge that their demands and federal policies are intertwined: without aware citizens in the communities and states, federal policy directives are worth little more than the paper on which they are written. If federal officials acknowledge their dependence on citizen awareness, then the concept of a constituency takes on new meaning. That is, constituents are not a group to be called upon simply for support when federal officials need help. Rather, the constituents are intrinsic to the program operations; without them, the program fails.

What Might Have Worked

The clues that have been indicated by the Kane-Page-Fairfax experiences are tied together by two concepts discussed at various points in this study. Both concepts indicate that the forms of bureaucratic behavior that might have worked violate traditional views of effective public administration— that is, clear delineation of bureau and office authority; roles perfectly and separately defined; and units of the organization precisely connected, reliable, and compatible.[10] The first concept indicates that the change that should be desired by the federal officials is a *process* of change. The second concept indicates that the policy change process is one of *interdependencies*. The clues lead to some specific suggestions.

The Question of Strategy

Title VI implementation activities bounced around, from, among, between, and through the strategic approaches of voluntarism, warfare, confusion, bluffing, and avoidance. Rarely did the implementing officials use the strategy most appropriate to the effort—that is, the bargaining mode. Bargaining is one of the few techniques for decision-making that assumes a number of attributes that were found within the Title VI policy. It assumes that conflict—at some level—exists between legitimate parties to the policy. But perhaps most importantly, the bargaining mode allows a decision-maker to deal with uncertainty by providing the opportunity to modify and redefine various aspects of the policy under consideration and to change specific demands within that policy.

Bargaining, as inferred from the limited Kane experience, would include a number of factors:

1. all parties with a legitimate voice in the negotiations would be involved;
2. the policy would be devised at the level at which it would be applied and tailored for the particular needs of that level;
3. efforts would be made to make sure that advocates of the policy be involved in the negotiations;
4. the limits of the negotiations would be clearly set in federal guidelines. Those limits might be formulated in a number of ways; for example, they might establish what was prohibited but not what was possible; or they might establish general categories of questions that the locality had to answer.

Involvement of State and Local Officials

When a policy requires changes in the behavior and administrative patterns of state and local officials, federal staff must begin their operations based on the assumption that the compliance of those officials is needed for sucessful implementation. Thus state and local officials (or others where appropriate) should be involved in the policy implementation whenever possible. Involvement, however, does not mean that the responsibility for implementation is handed over to them, *carte blanche*. Rather, these state and local officials are given a legitimate role in negotiations or policy development and provided the opportunity to be heard.

The current policy debate over revenue sharing indicates that it is extremely difficult to strike a balance between federal/national imperatives and legitimate state and local interests. The Title VI policy experience stands as an example of one end of the pole—that is, an attempt to define federal policy nationally and uniformly. Although the returns are not yet completely in, however, it appears that the general and special revenue sharing approach is also flawed. It fails because of limitations at the other end of the pole—an absence of administrative machinery to express federal/national interests.

Involvement of Clients

When compliance with a federal policy directive requires a change in the behavior of citizens in a community, federal officials must assume that it is their responsibility to support that behavior change. (It seems rather ironic that a policy such as Title VI was devoid of even superficial participatory devices during an era in which techniques for participation became almost faddish.) On the local level, for policies comparable to Title VI, local community people historically disfranchised need some method of becoming a part of local decision-making. Federal policy must be directed toward franchisement of these citizens and require that they be involved in the development of the local compliance plan. A certification procedure might be developed that gives local groups the formal right to be a party to those negotiations. Such a procedure might be supported by a federal requirement that no plan developed through a negotiating process would be acceptable unless the local group signs off on it. Through such a requirement, organizations such as that formed by Jean Fairfax would be encouraged to develop.

On the national level, federal officials should attempt to develop a national advisory group that would include citizens affected by the policy implementation. Such a group would not only help the federal agency as a supporter, but would also provide the federal agency with a more informed attentive public. That public would make the compliance effort more viable.

Use of the Federal Agency Structure

If a policy requires changed behavior on the part of other federal officials, those officials must be informed about the policy and, whenever possible, involved in its development. Again, such involvement does not mean that the responsibility for the policy is delegated completely to those officials. A separate staff with specific responsibility for that policy could be established, but that staff would operate in consultation with all other officials involved in the success of implementation. Shared authority and messy organization lines are inevitable.

Regional offices should be used as an essential part of an implementation strategy. A separate regional office staff might be established as a microcosm of the Washington staff; but that staff would work closely with other regional people affected by the policy requirements. Such staff would report both to Washington and to the top regional official. Regional staff should use their geographical proximity to work with state and local officials. A regional advisory group, replicating a national body, might be established that included state and local officials as well as citizens affected by the policy.

Staffing decisions should be made with some sensitivity to regional, professional, and other variations in style of the individuals of whom changed behavior is expected. Sensitivity to these issues is indicated not only in regular staffing decisions but also in single-shot, crash efforts. For example, it may be more effective to use 200 school officials or teachers for special summer employment than to hire 200 law students.

Dealing with Congress

It is probably unrealistic to believe that a policy as volatile as the Title VI effort may be implemented without significant Congressional reaction and pressure. Although this may not be true for all policies (and some may be receptive to legislative finessing), it is difficult to avoid Congressional flak for such policies as this one. As a result, it may be more effective for federal officials to play it straight with Congress—that is, to make it clear what they are planning to do and, whenever possible, to resist the inevitable legislative pressures (such as pressure to act rapidly). It is interesting to speculate on what would have happened had HEW and OE officials told Congress that they needed a year to gear up for Title I of ESEA; or that they needed additional legislation to clarify some of the problems that emerged during the early stages of Title VI implementation; or that they needed funds for adequate staffing. Although they might have taken some risk if Congress said no, an early request by the officials might have been supported by the still intact Congressional majority that had ratified the original legislation.

*   *   *

The Title VI issue has been presented as an example of a policy area that took administrative form without a clear blueprint for enforcement emerging through the legislative process. To some, the problems in enforcement simply indicate that the issue's time had not yet come and that the difficulties that ensued were a result of inadequate politicization prior to the issue's arrival as an administrative question. This, however, begs the question. If the administrative level is to be used as a vehicle for change in American society, there appear to be fewer and fewer areas in which a policy can be clearly established outside the administrative process and then handed to a machine-like bureaucracy to carry out.

This study has been undertaken with the assumption that in another time the federal bureaucracy may be once again asked to play a role for change with an issue where conflict is a reality and where the interrelationships between that issue and other policy areas mean that fluidity and uncertainty characterize the administrative task. Perhaps—like the Title VI administrators and like most of us—that future administrator will attempt to create a world of stability and certainty as a method of coping with the assigned task. But should that policy be anything like Title VI, it is clear that such a world will exist only in the administrator's mind.

NOTES

Chapter 1

[1]Jeffrey L. Pressman and Aaron B. Wildavsky, *Implementation* (Berkeley: University of California Press, 1973), p. 143.

[2]Although the Civil Rights Act applies to discrimination because of race, religion, or national origin (thus including Puerto Ricans, Chicanos, Native Americans, and others) and, in the case of employment, discrimination because of sex, both the political and administrative discussion about the prohibitions centered around problems and opportunities for blacks. Thus this study—set in the period from 1964 to 1968—will concentrate on enforcement attempts to facilitate new opportunities for black citizens.

[3]The 1115-page Civil Rights Commission study, *Federal Civil Rights Enforcement* (Washington, D. C.: U. S. Government Printing Office, 1970), found that Title VI activities were "disappointing" and "inadequate."

[4]U. S. Commission on Civil Rights, *Southern School Desegregation* (Washington, D.C.: U. S. Government Printing Office, 1967), p. 80.

[5]This debate certainly surrounded the publication of Christopher Jencks, *et al.*, *Inequality* (New York: Basic Books, 1972).

[6]U.S.C.C.R., *Southern School Desegregation*, p. 5.

[7]U. S. Commission on Civil Rights, *Federal Enforcement of School Desegregation: A Report* (Washington, D. C.: U. S. Government Printing Office, 1969), p. 8.

214

[8]*Ibid.*, p. 2, Appendix.

[9]The Potomac Institute, *Administrative Repeal of Civil Rights Law: A Case Study* (Washington, D. C.: The Potomac Institute, 1972).

[10]See Robert Crain, *The Politics of School Desegregation* (New York: Anchor Books, 1969), Part III.

[11]The Potomac Institute, *Administrative Repeal of Civil Rights Law*, pp. 29-30.

[12]See Gary Orfield, *The Reconstruction of Southern Education: The Schools and the 1964 Civil Rights Act* (New York: Wiley Interscience, 1969); the Potomac Institute publication, *supra*, note 9; and reports of the U. S. Commission on Civil Rights, *supra*, note 3, note 4, note 7.

[13]U.S.C.C.R., *Southern School Desegregation*, p. 3.

[14]U.S.C.C.R., *Federal Enforcement of School Desegregation*, p. 3.

[15]*Ibid.*, p. 14.

[16]See Orfield, *Reconstruction of Southern Education*, Chapter 4, pp. 151-207.

Chapter 2

[1]See, for example, Orfield, *Reconstruction of Southern Education*.

[2]For an exception in the literature, see James W. Fesler, *Area and Administration* (University: The University of Alabama Press, 1949).

Chapter 3

[1]HEW, Office of Education, "Developing and Defining the Role and the Relationship of the Office of Education, Regional Representative, Office of the Commissioner," June 23, 1960.

[2]*Ibid.*, p. 1.

[3]*Ibid.*

[4]*Ibid.*, p. 2.

[5]*Ibid.*, p. 11.

[6]Memo from John F. Hughes, Executive Officer, OE, to Sterling M. McMurrin, "Operating Problems of Current Significance," February 7, 1961.

[7]*Ibid.*, p. 2.

[8]*Ibid.*, p. 3.

[9]*Ibid.*, p. 6.

[10]Memo to James W. Moore, Director, Program Planning Branch, from Jack Ciaccio, Program Planning Specialist, November 1, 1963.

[11]This may be a bias shared by others at the Harvard Graduate School of Education. When Harold Howe replaced Keppel as Commissioner in 1965, he is said to have been shocked that OE had a regional system and that one of those offices was located in Boston.

[12]Memo to Keppel from Herman L. Offner, March 6, 1963.

[13]Memo to Wayne O. Reed, Deputy Commissioner, from Keppel, March 14, 1963.

[14]Monthly reports to the Commissioner from Herman Offner, especially during January, March, May, and June 1964, contain this information.

[15]There was no mention of civil rights in the field reports for October, November, and December 1964.

[16]The literature on decentralization tends to view centralization as the logical method of dealing with new authority. See, for example, David B. Truman, *Administrative Decentralization* (Chicago: University of Chicago Press, 1940); and Francis E. Rourke, *Intergovernmental Relations in Employment Security* (Minneapolis: University of Minnesota Press, 1952).

Chapter 4

[1]See discussion of centralizing tendencies and program planning and budgeting (PPB) in Louis C. Gawthorp, *Bureaucratic Behavior in the Executive Branch* (New York: Free Press, 1969), p. 234.

[2]Cresap, McCormick, and Paget, "Plan of Organization Management Staff Activities," transmitted to Mrs. Olveta Culp Hobby, December 23, 1954, Department of Health, Education, and Welfare, p. D-1.

[3]*Ibid.*, p. D-4.

[4]Memo from Secretary of HEW to Agency Heads, July 29, 1966.

[5]*Ibid.*

[6]Telegram from Page to HEW Secretary Gardner.

[7]Page's speeches included talks on "Status of School Desegregation in Six Southern States of DHEW," "Federal Grants and Civil Rights," and "DHEW Regional Plan for Implementation of Title VI in Health and Welfare Services."

[8]Page lost his job when the administration changed and his political enemies had new support in the Department and in the White House.

Chapter 5

[1]Orfield, *Reconstruction of Southern Education*, p. 27.

[2]*Ibid.*, p. 29.

[3]Prince Edward County closed its schools completely rather than begin desegregation. The Administration, in response, set up integrated private schools until the Supreme Court ordered reopening of the public schools. See Orfield, *Reconstruction of Southern Education*, pp. 217-218.

[4]*Ibid.*, p. 50.

[5]*Ibid.*, p. 59.

[6]*Ibid.*, p. 78.

[7]This information was particularly significant because the activities were taking place during a period when extensive school consolidation was occurring. In 1949, for example, the figure of 109,000 school districts was given; the figure that was finally used by OE in the mid-1960's was a plus or minus 25,000.

[8]One could argue that the "beautiful moment" interpretation is the logical conclusion flowing from Orfield's book.

[9]Orfield, *Reconstruction of Southern Education*, p. 280.

Chapter 6

[1]Memo from James M. Quigley, Assistant Secretary, to the Secretary, December 21, 1964.

[2]Memo from Francis Keppel, Commissioner of Education, to the Secretary, Re Organization for civil rights activities, July 7, 1964.

[3]*Ibid.*

[4]Memo from David S. Seeley, Director, EEOP, through John F. Hughes, Executive Officer, OE, to Commissioner Keppel, May 4, 1965.

[5]Memorandum from James F. Kelly to HEW Executive Staff, November 16, 1965.

[6]Memo to James F. Kelly, Acting Assistant Secretary for Administration, from Henry Loomis, Deputy Commissioner of Education, November 18, 1965.

[7]*Ibid.*

[8]Memo from Keppel to the Secretary, December 1, 1965.

[9]Memo, F. Peter Libassi, Director, Federal-Programs Division, U.S.C.C.R., to Burke Marshall, Consultant to the Vice President, March 31, 1965.

[10]Memo, Ruby G. Martin to Libassi, January 20, 1966.

[11]From an unpublished history of the Office for Civil Rights, by Elaine Heffernan, former assistant to Peter Libassi, Chapter V, p. 27.

[12]Memorandum from Harold Howe II to the Secretary, Re Your Memorandum of March 3 Regarding Decentralization of Civil Rights Activities, March 8, 1966.

[13]Office of Education, "Equal Educational Opportunities Program," Analysis transmitted from F. Peter Libassi to Harold Howe II, March 22, 1966, p. 3.

[14]*Ibid.*, p. 5.

[15]Heffernan's unpublished history of OCR, Chapter V, p. 27.

[16]*Congressional Record*, May 4, 1966, p. 9332, unbound.

[17]Report on Organization of the Office of Equal Education Opportunities, forwarded to Howe from Reed, July 17, 1966. (Reorganization within OE had made Seeley an Assistant Commissioner and elevated the EEOP to program status—hence OEEO.)

[18]*Ibid.*, p. 1, Recommendations.

[19]*Ibid.*

[20]Press release, HEW, OE, September 9, 1966.

[21]Reed memo, p. 3, Recommendations.

[22]*Ibid.*

[23]Memo to David Seeley from Howe, September 22, 1966.

[24]Memo, Howe to Members of the Executive Group, OE, October 10, 1966.

[25]*Ibid.*

[26]Draft document, written by Stephen Trachtenberg, included in the Howe memo, October 10, 1966, p. 1.

[27]Memo to Seeley and Nash from Libassi, October 11, 1966.

[28]Memo from Seeley to Libassi, October 26, 1966.

[29]Memo, Ruby Martin to Libassi, November 7, 1966.

[30]Memorandum, John Corson and James Kelly to the Secretary, December 9, 1966.

[31]Memo, Libassi to the Secretary, December 15, 1966.

[32]Memo, Seeley to Sullivan, Re Problems of Decentralization of EEOP, February 6, 1967.

[33]*Ibid.*, pp. 2-3.

[34]*Ibid.*, p. 3.

[35]Memo, Seeley to Sullivan, February 6, 1967.

[36]*Ibid.*, p. 1.

[37]*Ibid.*, p. 2.

[38]*Ibid.*, p. 4.

[39]Memo, Seeley to Howe, March 6, 1967, p. 2.

[40]*Ibid.*, p. 3.

[41]Memo, Paul Rilling, Atlanta Regional Civil Rights Director, to Ruby Martin, Director, OCR, October 16, 1967.

Chapter 8

[1]Frederick M. Wirt, *Politics of Southern Equality: Law and Social Change in a Mississippi County* (Chicago: Aldine Publishing Company, 1970), p. 183.

[2]See the Code of Federal Register, Title 45, Public Welfare, 80 and 81.

[3]Heffernan's unpublished history of OCR, Chapter II, p. 2.

[4]See remarks of Senator Hubert Humphrey, 110 *Congressional Record* 6544-6547 (1964).

[5]Orfield, *Reconstruction of Southern Education*, p. 78.

[6]Memo, G. W. Foster, Jr., to David Seeley, January 25, 1965.

[7]48 *Saturday Review of Literature* 60 (March 20, 1965).

[8]See memo from Ruby Martin to William Taylor, U. S. Commission on Civil Rights, March 31, 1965, reporting conversations with Southern school officials.

[9]Memo from Celebrezze to Douglass Cater, March 23, 1965.

[10]Comment: Title VI of the Civil Rights Act of 1964—implementation and impact, 36 *The George Washington Law Review* 914 (1968) (hereafter called G. W. Comment).

[11]Memo from Seeley to Keppel, November 5, 1965.

[12]*Federal Register*, Volume 31, No. 69, April 9, 1966, Title 45 Public Welfare, Chapter 1, Part 181.

[13]Heffernan's unpublished history of OCR, Chapter VI, p. 28.

[14]Included in a letter to Senator J. William Fulbright from Harold Howe II, May 24, 1966, p. 5.

[15]Memo issued May 20, 1966, by the Office of Education, HEW.

[16]Heffernan's unpublished history of OCR, Chapter X, p. 66.

[17]Quoted in *ibid.*, pp. 66-69.

Chapter 9

[1]James M. Landis, *The Administrative Process* (New Haven: Yale University Press, 1938), pp. 28-36.

[2]Karl Llewellyn, "The Bramble Bush," in Carl A. Auerbach, *et al.*, *The Legal Process* (Scranton: Chandler Publishing Company, 1965), pp. 13-14.

[3]372 F. 2d 836 (Fifth Circuit, 1966) aff'd en banc, 380 F. 2d 385, cert, denied, 389 U. S. 840 (1967).

[4]372 F. 2d at 859-860.

[5]James R. Dunn, Title VI, the guidelines and school desegregation in the South, 53 *Virginia Law Review* 57.

[6]Landis, *The Administrative Process*, pp. 144-145.

[7]Memo from David Seeley to John Doar, July 14, 1965.

[8]270 F. Supp. 859 (M. D. Ala. 1967).

[9]See G. W. Comment, p. 850.

[10]*Clark v. Board of Education*, 374 F. 2d 569, 570-571 (Eighth Circuit, 1967); accord, *Bowman v. County School Board*, 382 F. 2d 328 (Fourth Circuit, 1967); *Jefferson County*, 372 F. 2d at 848.

[11]240 F. Supp. 709 (W. D. La. 1965) aff'd, 370 F. 2d 847 (Fifth Circuit, 1966).

[12]Section 603, P. L. 88-352.

[13]H. L. A. Hart, *The Concept of Law* (Oxford: The Clarendon Press, 1961), p. 127.

[14]G. W. Comment, p. 856.

[15]*Ibid.*, p. 852.

[16]A brief filed in the U. S. District Court for D. C. by NAACP attorneys (*Adams v. Richardson*) states that, from the period between 1964 and the fall of 1970, aid was terminated to 200 school districts—the results of approximately 600 administrative proceedings.

[17]The difficulty in using the cutoff sanction has been recently experienced by another group. Women have found that the federal government, especially HEW, is reluctant to terminate funds from a university even if sex discrimination has been demonstrated. In those cases where aid has been cut off or deferred, the sanction has been less than effective.

[18]Orfield, *Reconstruction of Southern Education*, pp. 297-299.

[19]Landis, *The Administrative Process*, p. 92.

[20]Memo from Keppel to Alanson W. Willcox, February 20, 1964.

[21]Memo from Quigley to Celebrezze, July 25, 1965.

[22]See Orfield, *Reconstruction of Southern Education*, p. 151.

[23]Memo from Libassi to Wilbur Cohen, Undersecretary of HEW, January 26, 1966.

[24]G. W. Comment, p. 921.

[25]*Federal Register*, Volume 33, No. 58, March 23, 1968.

[26]U. S. federal administrative systems tend to use individuals who have received legal training as general civil servants; legal training is viewed as a firm grounding for anyone thrust into the federal bureaucratic world.

[27]For example, Memo from Ruby Martin to Derrick Bell re Sumpter County, Georgia, hearing, September 15, 1966.

[28]G. W. Comment, p. 865.

[29]*Ibid.*

Chapter 10

[1]These are based on Lon Fuller's "eight distinct routes to disaster" for a legal system. Lon L. Fuller, *The Morality of Law* (New Haven: Yale University Press, 1969), p. 39.

[2]That staff member, Herbert Kane, set up an operation in 1965 in Texas, where ten of the top superintendents within the state were deputized to negotiate compliance plans together with Washington officials. The three-week operation was a traveling road show held in five separate locations around the state. In each place, a team of federal and state officials set up shop in a large room and called local school officials to meet with them. The process was an efficient one; it allowed the feds to make a dent in reviewing plans from the 1250 school districts within the state, convinced many school officials that the feds meant business, and allowed Kane's staff to identify problem districts with dispatch.

Chapter 11

[1]Stephen K. Bailey described the efforts as "some of the most intensive lobbying efforts in modern legislative history." Stephen K. Bailey, *The New Congress* (New York: St. Martins Press, 1966), p. 80.

[2]David B. Truman, *The Governmental Process*, Second Edition (New York: Alfred A. Knopf, 1971), p. 441.

[3]*Ibid.*

[4]SNCC, Report on Southern School Desegregation, released on September 30, 1965.

[5]See *Public Advisory Committees*, issued by the U. S. Department of Health, Education, and Welfare, Office of Education.

[6]Most of the groups are created by statute, but it is interesting to note that a quasi-formal advisory committee was established to advise OE staff on Title IV programs.

[7]Memo from Keppel to Cohen, April 9, 1965.

[8]Memo from Keppel to Sam Halperin, September 10, 1965.

[9]Letter, Seeley to John Lewis, June 11, 1964.

[10]During the course of interviews for this study, I asked each individual interviewed to define "constituency." The traditionalists within OE had little difficulty answering that question, noting that first state and then local education agencies constituted their constituency. The officials who were less traditional, however, had some difficulty with the question. Some, after hesitation, talked about the school children of America—"Kids are my constituency," one noted.

Several knowledgeable individuals, however, realized what I was getting at and answered to the effect that, although the children of the nation were their constituency, they had to deal with the children through the existing organizational apparatus in states and cities.

Chapter 12

[1]Memo, Leadership Conference on Civil Rights, May 11, 1966.

[2]This was disputed by one participant in the Leadership Conference, who said that any appointment to that chairmanship would be criticized. Hamilton, according to this observer, was named in response to critics' allegations that the leadership of the group was never spread beyond the NAACP or the unions. He noted, "We were damned if we appointed a union or NAACP person and damned if we didn't."

[3]Budgets are often no clue to civil rights enforcement intensity; the 1975 budget called for the largest staff ever in civil rights enforcement; many believe that the expenditure for enforcement is inversely related to its intensity.

[4]The Inc. Fund was originally established by the NAACP to operate as the tax exempt wing of the organization, with an emphasis on litigation. During the years, however, the policy differences between the two organizations became greater and the two had few interrelationships. Indeed, a rarely stated but generally accepted competitive situation exists between the two groups.

[5]Although the Leadership Conference had "cleansed" itself of the activists by 1966, by the end of 1967 plans were beginning to be laid for Martin Luther King's Poor People's Campaign in Washington. The Campaign eventually resulted—as a byproduct—in the establishment of the Washington Research Project, supported by foundation funds and focused in the same direction as was the Task Force.

[6]Several years after Sellers' try, the U. S. Commission on Civil Rights released a much-praised document surveying Title VI enforcement that in effect reworked Sellers' earlier efforts. U.S.C.C.R., *Federal Civil Rights Enforcement, supra,* Chapter 1, note 3.

[7]Recently, the Leadership Conference has been less than successful in its congressional lobbying role; failures to stop legislation on school busing indicated its inabilities to change strategy even in the legislative sphere.

[8]See Orfield, *Reconstruction of Southern Education,* p. 240.

Chapter 14

[1]James L. Sundquist and David W. Davis, *Making Federalism Work* (Washington, D.C.: The Brookings Institution, 1969), p. 1.

[2]*Ibid.,* p. 244.

[3]Jerome T. Murphy, *State Education Agencies and Discretionary Funds* (Lexington, Mass.: D. C. Heath and Company, 1974), p. 131.

[4]Alice M. Rivlin, *Systematic Thinking for Social Action* (Washington, D. C.: The Brookings Institution, 1971), p. 123.

[5]*Ibid.*, p. 124.

[6]*Ibid.*

[7]*Ibid.*, citing Robert A. Levine, Rethinking our social strategies, 10 *Public Interest* 88-92 (1968).

[8]See, for example, the arguments advanced in the NAACP brief against HEW, published as The Potomac Institute, *Administrative Repeal of Civil Rights Law*; in addition, see the recommendations included in U.S.C.C.R., *Federal Civil Rights Enforcement*.

[9]Although they did not know *what* they would say to Southern school officials, to other OE staff members, to White House staff, or to members of Congress, HEW's civil rights officials did know that they would have to talk to these officials.

[10]For a discussion of the limitations of this traditional view, see Martin Landau, Redundancy, rationality, and the problem of duplication and overlap, 29 *Public Administration Review* 346-358 (1969).

SELECTED BIBLIOGRAPHY

Administrative Conference of the United States. *Report, Committee on Agency Organization and Procedure*. Washington, D.C., November 17, 1971.

Administrative Regulation: A Symposium. 26 *Law and Contemporary Problems* (Spring 1961).

Altshuler, Alan A. (Ed.). *The Politics of the Federal Bureaucracy*. New York: Dodd, Mead and Co., 1968.

Auerbach, Carl A.; Garrison, Lloyd K.; Hurst, Willard; and Mermin, Samuel. *The Legal Process*. Scranton: Chandler Publishing Company, 1965.

Bailey, Stephen K. *The New Congress*. New York: St Martins Press, 1966.

Bailey, Stephen K.; and Mosher, Edith K. *ESEA: The Office of Education Administers a Law*. Syracuse: Syracuse University Press, 1968.

Bennis, Warren G. *American Bureaucracy*. Chicago: Aldine Publishing Co., 1970.

Bennis, Warren G.; Benne, Kenneth D.; and Chin, Robert. *The Planning of Change*, Second Edition. New York: Holt, Rinehart and Winston, Inc., 1969.

Bennis, Warren G.; and Slater, Philip. *The Temporary Society*. New York: Harper Colophon Books, 1969.

Berman, Harold J.; and Greiner, William R. *The Nature and Functions of Law*. New York: The Foundation Press, 1966.

Blau, Peter M. *Bureaucracy in Modern Society*. New York: Random House, 1968.

223

Blumrosen, Alfred W. Antidiscrimination laws in action in New Jersey: a law sociology study. 19 *Rutgers Law Review* 189-287 (1965).
Boulding, Kenneth E. *The Image*. Ann Arbor: University of Michigan Press, 1961.
Braybrooke, David; and Lindblom, Charles E. *A Strategy of Decision*. New York: Free Press, 1963.

Congressional Quarterly. *Federal Role in Education*, Second Edition. Washington, D.C.: Congressional Quarterly Service, 1967.
Crain, Robert L. *The Politics of School Desegregation*. Garden City: Doubleday Anchor Books, 1969.
Crozier, Michel. *The Bureaucratic Phenomenon*. Chicago: University of Chicago Press, 1967.

Davis, Kenneth Culp. *Administrative Law, Cases-Text-Problems*. St. Paul: West Publishing Co., 1965.
Davis, Kenneth Culp. *Discretionary Justice*. Baton Rouge: Louisiana State University Press, 1969.
Dimock, Marshall E. The role of discretion in modern administration, in John M. Gaus, Leonard D. White, and Marshall E. Dimock (Eds.), *The Frontiers of Public Administration*. Chicago: University of Chicago Press, 1936.

Edelman, Murray. Governmental organization and public policy. 12 *Public Administration Review* 276-283 (1952).
Edelman, Murray. *Politics as Symbolic Action*. Chicago: Markham Publishing Company, 1971.
Edelman, Murray. *The Symbolic Uses of Politics*. Urbana: University of Illinois Press, 1967.
Eidenberg, Eugene; and Morey, Roy D. *An Act of Congress: The Legislative Process and the Making of Education Policy*. New York: W. W. Norton and Co., 1969.
Elazar, Daniel J. *American Federalism—A View from the States*, Second Edition. New York: Thomas Y. Crowell Company, 1972.

Fesler, James W. Approaches to the understanding of decentralization. 27 *The Journal of Politics* 536-566 (1965).
Fesler, James W. *Area and Administration*. University: University of Alabama Press, 1949.
Fesler, James W. Field organization. In Fritz Morstein Marx, *Elements of public Administration*. Englewood Cliffs: Prentice-Hall Inc., 1959.
Fuller, Lon L. *The Morality of Law*, Revised Edition. New Haven: Yale University Press, 1969.

Galbraith, John Kenneth. *The New Industrial State*. New York: New American Library, 1967.

Gawthorp, Louis C. *Bureaucratic Behavior in the Executive Branch*. New York: Free Press, 1969.

George Washington Law Review. Comment: Title VI of the Civil Rights Act of 1964—implementation and impact. 36 *The George Washington Law Review* 824-1022 (1968).

Glaser, Barney G.; and Strauss, Anselm L. *The Discovery of Grounded Theory*. Chicago: Aldine Publishing Co., 1967.

Gore, William J. Administrative decisionmaking in federal field offices. 16 *Public Administration Review* 281-291 (1956).

Harmon, Michael Mont. Administrative policy formulation and the public interest. 29 *Public Administration Review* 483-491 (1969).

Hart, H. L. A. *The Concept of Law*. Oxford: Clarendon Press, 1961.

Heffernan, Elaine. History of the Office of Civil Rights, Department of Health, Education, and Welfare, unpublished manuscript.

Holden, Matthew, Jr. "Imperialism" in bureaucracy. 60 *American Political Science Review* 943-951 (1966).

Iannielle, Lynne. *Milestones along the March: 12 Historic U. S. Civil Rights Documents from World War II to Selma*. London: Pall Mall Press, 1965.

Jaffe, Louis L.; and Nathanson, Nathaniel L. *Administrative Law: Cases and Materials*, Second Edition. Boston: Little, Brown and Co., 1961.

Jencks, Christopher, *et al. Inequality*. New York: Basic Books, 1972.

Kaufman, Herbert. *Administrative Feedback*. Washington, D.C.: The Brookings Institution, 1973.

Kaufman, Herbert. *The Forest Ranger*. Baltimore: The Johns Hopkins University Press, 1967.

Kaufman, Herbert. *The Limits of Organizational Change*. University: The University of Alabama Press, 1971.

Landau, Martin. Redundancy, rationality, and the problem of duplication and overlap. 29 *Public Administration Review* 346-358 (1969).

Landis, James M. *The Administrative Process*. New Haven: Yale University Press, 1938.

Lowi, Theodore, J. *The End of Liberalism*. New York: W. W. Norton and Co., 1969.

Miles, Rufus E., Jr. *The Department of HEW*. New York: Praeger Publishers, 1974.

Murphy, Jerome T. *State Education Agencies and Discretionary Funds*. Lexington, Mass.: D. C. Heath and Company, 1974.

Murphy, Jerome. Title I of ESEA: The politics of implementing federal education reform. 41 *Harvard Educational Review* 35-63 (1971).

Neustadt, Richard E. *Presidential Power*. New York: Mentor, 1964.
Newman, Frank C. The process of prescribing "due process." 29 *California Law Review* 215-239 (1961).
Nonet, Philippe. *Administrative Justice: Advocacy and Change in Government Agencies*. New York: Russell Sage Foundation, 1969.

Orfield, Gary. *The Reconstruction of Southern Education: The Schools and the 1964 Civil Rights Act*. New York: Wiley Interscience, 1969.
Ostrom, Vincent. *The Intellectual Crisis in American Public Administration*. University: The University of Alabama Press, 1973.

Potomac Institute. *Administrative Repeal of Civil Rights Law: A Case Study*. Washington, D.C.: Potomac Institute, 1972.
A. Philip Randolph Institute. *The Reluctant Guardians: A Survey of the Enforcement of Federal Civil Rights Laws*, prepared for the Office of Economic Opportunity, December 1969.

Redford, Emmette S. *Administration of National Economic Control*. New York: The Macmillan Co., 1952.
Rheinstein, Max (Ed.). *Max Weber on Law in Economy and Society*. New York: Simon and Schuster, 1967.
Rivlin, Alice M. *Systematic Thinking for Social Action*. Washington, D.C.: The Brookings Institution, 1971.
Rourke, Francis E. *Bureaucracy, Politics and Public Policy*. Boston: Little, Brown and Co., 1969.
Rourke, Francis E. *Bureaucratic Power in National Politics*, Second Edition. Boston: Little, Brown and Co., 1972.
Rourke, Francis E. *Intergovernmental Relations in Employment Security*. Minneapolis: University of Minnesota Press, 1952.

Seidman, Harold. *Politics, Position and Power*. New York: Oxford University Press, 1970.
Sellers, Barney. *The Politics and Policies of Civil Rights Enforcement: A Survey of Federal Enforcement, 1964-69*. M.A. Thesis, Maxwell Graduate School, Syracuse University, 1972.
Selznick, Philip. *Law, Society and Industrial Justice*. New York: Russell Sage Foundation, 1969.
Selznick, Philip. *TVA and the Grass Roots*. New York: Harper Torchbooks, 1966.
Shapiro, David L. The choice of rulemaking or adjudication in the development of administrative policy. 78 *Harvard Law Review* 921-972 (1965).
Shapiro, Martin. *The Supreme Court and Administrative Agencies*. New York: Free Press, 1968.
Simon, Herbert A. *Administrative Behavior*, Second Edition. New York: Free Press, 1957.

Simon, Herbert A.; Smithburg, Donald W.; and Thompson, Victor A. *Public Administration*. New York: Alfred A. Knopf, 1950.

Smith, Lincoln. Lawyers as regulatory commissioners. 23 *The George Washington Law Review* 375-428 (1955).

Sundquist, James L. *Politics and Policy*. Washington, D.C.: The Brookings Institution, 1968.

Sundquist, James L.; and Davis, David W. *Making Federalism Work*. Washington, D.C.: The Brookings Institution, 1969.

tenBroek, Jacobus; and the Editors of California Law Review. *The Law of the Poor*. San Francisco: Chandler Publishing Co., 1966.

Thompson, James D. *Organizations in Action*. New York: McGraw-Hill Book Co., 1967.

Thompson, Victor A. *Modern Organization*. New York: Alfred A. Knopf, 1960.

Thompson, Victor A. *The Regulatory Process in OPA Rationing*. New York: Columbia University Press, 1950.

Truman, David B. *Administrative Decentralization*. Chicago: University of Chicago Press, 1940.

Truman, David B. *The Governmental Process*, Second Edition. New York: Alfred A. Knopf, 1971.

U. S. Commission on Civil Rights. *Federal Civil Rights Enforcement*. Washington, D.C.: U. S. Government Printing Office, 1970.

U. S. Commission on Civil Rights. *Federal Enforcement of School Desegregation*. Washington, D.C.: U. S. Government Printing Office, 1969.

U. S. Commission on Civil Rights. *Southern School Desegregation: 1966-67*. Washington, D.C.: U. S. Government Printing Office, 1967.

Waldhorn, Steven Arthur. Legal Intervention and Citizen Participation as Strategies for Change in Public Serving Bureaucracies. Paper presented at the American Political Science Association annual meeting, New York, September 4, 1969.

Wilensky, Harold L. *Organizational Intelligence*. New York: Basic Books, 1967.

Willcox, Alanson W. The lawyer in the administration of non regulatory programs. 13 *Public Administration Review* 12-16 (1953).

Wirt, Frederick M. *Politics of Southern Equality: Law and Social Change in a Mississippi County*. Chicago: Aldine Publishing Company, 1970.

Witherspoon, Joseph Parker. *Administrative Implementation of Civil Rights*. Austin: University of Texas Press, 1968.

APPENDIX

CIVIL RIGHTS ACT OF 1964*

Title VI—Nondiscrimination in Federally Assisted Programs

Section 601. No person in the United States shall, on the ground of race, color, or national origin, be excluded from participation in, be denied the benefits of, or be subjected to discrimination under any program or activity receiving Federal financial assistance.

Section 602. Each Federal Department and agency which is empowered to extend Federal financial assistance to any program or activity, by way of grant, loan, or contract other than a contract of insurance or guaranty, is authorized and directed to effectuate the provisions of section 601 with respect to such program or activity by issuing rules, regulations, or orders of general applicability which shall be consistent with achievement of the objectives of the statute authorizing the financial assistance in connection with which the action is taken. No such rule, regulation, or order shall become effective unless and until approved by the President. Compliance with any requirement adopted pursuant to this section may be effected (1) by the termination of or refusal to grant or to continue

*42 U.S.C. 2000d-2000d-4; Enacted July 2, 1964, P. L. 88-352, Title VI, 78 Stat. 252.

assistance under such program or activity to any recipient as to whom there has been an express finding on the record, after opportunity for hearing, of a failure to comply with such requirement, but such termination or refusal shall be limited to the particular political entity, or part thereof, or other recipient as to whom such a finding has been made and shall be limited in its effect to the particular program, or part thereof, in which such noncompliance has been found, or (2) by any other means authorized by law: *Provided, however,* That no such action shall be taken until the department or agency concerned has advised the appropriate person or persons of the failure to comply with the requirement and has determined that compliance cannot be secured by voluntary means. In the case of any action terminating, or refusing to grant or continue, assistance because of failure to comply with a requirement imposed pursuant to this section, the head of the Federal department or agency shall file with the committees of the House and Senate having legislative jurisdiction over the program or activity involved a full written report of the circumstances and the grounds for such action. No such action shall become effective until thirty days have elapsed after the filing of such report.

Section 603. Any department or agency action taken pursuant to section 602 shall be subject to such judicial review as may otherwise be provided by law for similar action taken by such department or agency on other ground. In the case of action, not otherwise subject to judicial review, terminating or refusing to grant or to continue financial assistance upon a finding of failure to comply with any requirement imposed pursuant to section 602, any person aggrieved (including any State or political subdivision thereof and any agency of either) may obtain judicial review of such action in accordance with section 10 of the Administrative Procedure Act, and such action shall not be deemed committed to unreviewable agency discretion within the meaning of that section.

Section 604. Nothing contained in this title shall be construed to authorize action under this title by any department or agency with respect to any employment practice of any employer, employment agency, or labor organization except where a primary objective of the Federal financial assistance is to provide employment.

Section 605. Nothing in this title shall add to or detract from any existing authority with respect to any program or activity under which Federal assistance is extended by way of a contract of insurance or guaranty.

INDEX

231